HIGGLERS *in* KINGSTON

HIGGLERS *in* KINGSTON

Women's Informal Work in Jamaica

WINNIFRED BROWN-GLAUDE

VANDERBILT UNIVERSITY PRESS
Nashville, Tennessee

© 2011 by Vanderbilt University Press
Nashville, Tennessee 37235
All rights reserved
First printing 2011
First paperback printing 2020

An abridged version of Chapter 6, titled "Spreading Like a Dis/ease? Afro-Jamaican Higglers and the Dynamics of Race/Color, Class, and Gender," appears in *Lived Experiences of Public Consumption: Encounters with Value in Marketplaces on Five Continents,* ed. Daniel Cook (New York: Palgrave Macmillan, 2008). Reproduced with permission of Palgrave Macmillan.

Library of Congress Cataloging-in-Publication Data

Brown-Glaude, Winnifred R., 1966–
Higglers in Kingston : women's informal work
in Jamaica / Winnifred Brown-Glaude.
p. cm.
Includes bibliographical references and index.
ISBN 978-0-8265-1765-4 (cloth edition)
ISBN 978-0-8265-1766-1 (paperback edition)
1. Street vendors—Jamaica—Kingston. 2. Women merchants—Jamaica—Kingston. 3. Social status—Jamaica—Kingston. 4. Small business—Jamaica—Kingston. 5. Informal sector (Economics)—Jamaica—Kingston. 6. Women's studies—Jamaica—Kingston. I. Title.
HF5459.J25B76 2011
331.4—dc22
2010042223

In loving memory of
Virginette Wilhelmina Brown
(May 3, 1909–December 21, 2005)

Walk good, Miss Coolie!

Contents

	Acknowledgments	ix
	INTRODUCTION Assessing the "Whole of Informality"	1
1	Intersectionality and the Politics of Embodiment	21
2	Higglering: A Woman's Domain?	39
3	"Bait of Satan"? Representations of Sunday/Negro Markets and Higglering from Slavery to Independence	65
4	"Natural Rebels" or Just Plain Nuisances? Representations of Higglers from Slavery to Independence	91
5	Higgler, ICI, Businesswoman: What's in a Name?	119
6	Dirty and Dis/eased: Bodies, Public Space, and Afro-Jamaican Higglers	141
	CONCLUSION Understanding the Nuances of Informality	165
	APPENDIX *List of Higglers Interviewed* *Notes* *Bibliography* *Index*	175 177 191 211

Acknowledgments

From the time I was a little girl growing up in Jamaica, higglers have had a special place in my heart. On Christmas mornings, I always looked forward to going to the Christmas market, where the streets of downtown Kingston would be lined with higglers selling a wide variety of toys. I remember walking along the streets holding my father's hand and making the difficult choice of which toy I wanted. In the mind of a six-year-old, these women were not only special, they were magical, because they had intimate connections with Santa Claus. But even then, I knew that not everyone saw these women as special; there were times they were described negatively. These descriptions were confusing to me. I mean, how could these women, my Santa's helpers, be so bad?

Although it can be difficult to pinpoint the exact genesis of a scholarly project, higglers have been on my mind for quite some time. My interest in them, however, would have remained a loose set of questions if it were not for the wise counsel and prodigious guidance of a very special host of people. Howard Winant has been both a patient and supportive advisor and a friend. I am truly thankful for his support and willingness to accommodate me in my difficult choice to complete my graduate work while living with my family in Maine. The life of a graduate student is always difficult, in my case compounded by my choice to keep my family together. I owe a tremendous debt of gratitude to Sherri Grasmuck, Kevin Delaney, Paget Henry, and Howard Winant for working with me by phone, e-mail, and regular mail to make this project a reality. Thank you all for asking difficult questions and pushing me to think about these women's experiences in new ways. Most of all, this project would not be possible without the voices of the market women and ICIs (informal commercial importers) at the Papine Market, and the Constant Spring and People's Arcades. I truly appreciate you sharing your time with me and showing me how to "make a way out of no way."

The Woodrow Wilson National Fellowship in Women's Studies and the Temple University Research Grant provided research funding for this project. The Rutgers University Presidential Post-Doctoral Fellowship, the Rutgers University Institute for Research on Women Faculty Seminar, the Ford Foundation's Emerging Voices in Caribbean Women Studies Faculty Summer Research Grant, and the Princeton Research Fellowship in Sociology all provided financial and intellectual support. I thank all my colleagues in these seminars for reading versions of my chapters and providing invaluable suggestions.

So many people have contributed to the development of this project. I offer my sincere thanks to Patricia Mohammed and Mitch Duneier for reading and commenting on earlier drafts of the book. I also thank Patricia Mohammed for helping me locate some of the images. I am thankful to the countless librarians, museum curators, and scholars whose assistance and suggestions were invaluable. I am grateful for the support of my editor, Eli Bortz, at Vanderbilt University Press. I especially want to thank the two anonymous readers, whose insightful comments have helped strengthen the book tremendously. I thank them for their insights and take full responsibility for the errors and failures of this book.

My sister friends have sustained me throughout this journey. Thank you, Patricia Saunders (University of Miami), for helping me consider, in the very early stages of writing, the importance of space. More importantly, thank you for the many times you have talked me off the ledge. Michelle Rowley (University of Maryland), thank you for pushing me to think about Caribbean feminism and the particular experiences of Caribbean women. I look forward to reading your book. Rhonda Frederick (Boston College), thank you for your support and faith in me. You are such a beautiful person and brilliant scholar. Simone James Alexander (Seton Hall University), thank you for helping me negotiate this balancing act of family and career. You are a wonderful friend and role model.

My family has been my rock throughout this process. I am blessed to have the constant love and encouragement of my loving parents, Doreen and Wilfred Brown, as well as of my brothers and sister. I am also thankful to my family in Jamaica, who supported me throughout my fieldwork. I especially thank my relatives Joyce and Neville Rhone for opening up their home and supporting me throughout some difficult moments in the field. I am also thankful to Jean Rhone for introducing me to the market women in Papine. I thank my uncle, Donald (Bill) Brown, for always making himself available to me when I needed him. But most of all, I am thankful for the countless evenings I sat on the verandah in Kingston recounting my days in the field with my grandmother, Miss Coolie, as we called her. She is in a better place now, and those precious moments will always be in my heart.

My journey through this project, however, would not have been possible without the unconditional love and support of my life partner—Eddie Glaude. Thank you for your incredible patience throughout this long process, and for reading and commenting on so many versions of this book. I especially thank you for your unwavering confidence in my intellect even in those moments when I had my doubts. And finally, I must offer a special thanks to my son, Langston. You have grown with me throughout this process. I look at you and I cannot believe how far we both have come. It is because of you that each moment of my day is worth living. Thank you for making Mommy want to be a better person.

HIGGLERS IN KINGSTON

INTRODUCTION

Assessing the "Whole of Informality"

In a small rural village in the foothills of the Blue Mountains, Miss Virginette, an Afro-Jamaican market woman, awakens before dawn.[1] It is Saturday morning, market day. She gets dressed, takes a moment to drink some tea, then begins to gather her baskets for the long trip ahead of her. She needs to catch the 5:00 a.m. bus to the city of Kingston. She must hurry. She calls out to her son, who will carry her baskets to the bus stop at the bottom of the hill. As they step out into her front yard, Miss Virginette smells the dampness of the red earth beneath her feet. This smell brings back memories of countless mornings she accompanied her mother and grandmother on this very journey as a child.

When the bus arrives, fifteen minutes behind schedule, Miss Virginette quickly finds a seat as her son packs her baskets onto the back of the bus. Once he sees that his mother is properly seated, her son says his goodbyes and returns home. The bus trip is long and extremely uncomfortable—even dangerous—but Miss Virginette knows she must make this trip in order to support her family.[2] When she finally arrives at the Papine Market in Kingston, Miss Virginette secures her money in the deep pockets of her apron, gathers her baskets, and with the help of a young boy carries them to her stall in the marketplace.

Meanwhile, Miss Carida, an Afro-Jamaican informal commercial importer (ICI), steps out of her husband's car in front of the Constant Spring Arcade, also in Kingston, and unloads some boxes from the trunk. It has been a week since she's been away overseas and she is still experiencing jet lag from the eighteen-hour flight from China. As she and her husband carry some boxes to her stall, Miss Carida still can't believe her good fortune. Her favorite store in Quanzhou was having a blow-out sale, which allowed her to purchase twice as many pairs of school shoes as she had anticipated. She knows they will sell easily, as the new school year is quickly approaching and parents will soon be searching for shoes for their children. The thought of the profits she expects to make brings a smile to her face. They will allow her to pay her daughter's school fees on time this year.

Miss Virginette and Miss Carida are Afro-Jamaican female microentrepreneurs, known as "higglers," in the Jamaican urban informal economy.[3] "Higgler" is a term commonly used by Jamaicans to identify a particular kind of street vendor—a so-called lower-class black woman who sells a range of items on the streets or in government-appointed market areas and arcades (covered passageways with stalls on either side where vendors display their wares). This group of informal entrepreneurs can roughly be divided into two broad categories: traditional and modern.[4] Traditional higglers include, but are not limited to, market women. They specialize in the sale of locally grown produce and have been an integral part of the Jamaican informal economy since slavery (Durant-Gonzalez 1983, 1985; Katzin 1959, 1960; Mintz 1954, 1987; Simmonds 1987).

The modern higgler includes "informal commercial importers" (ICIs). These women entered into the informal economy in the mid-1970s and are transnational traders specializing in the sale of manufactured items (e.g., clothing, furniture, appliances, etc.) they import from areas such as New York, Miami, other islands in the Caribbean, and, most recently, China.[5] This group of informal entrepreneurs acquired the title informal commercial importers in 1982 from Jamaica's Revenue Board, which not only assigned them the title but also imposed upon them various fees, import licenses, and import duties (Harrison 1988; LeFranc 1989; Ulysse 2007). Today, the businesses of market women and ICIs are marginally regulated by the government. For the most part, however, these businesses are largely informal.

The steady growth of microenterprises by women like Miss Virginette and Miss Carida illustrates that the informal economy is here to stay. Indeed, despite predictions of their inevitable disappearance as modern economies evolved, informal economies have not only survived in the modern era but also expanded, providing the majority of employment to the poor, especially poor women, in developing countries. In recent years there has been renewed interest among feminist scholars and practitioners in the informal economy, as large numbers of poor women turn to this segment for work. A key objective among these scholars is to demonstrate that men and women experience their work in the informal economy differently and to expose some of the hidden obstacles to women's advancement.

One outcome of this renewed interest has been an expansion of the concept of the informal economy to include "the whole of informality as it is manifested in industrialized, transition and developing economies and the real world dynamics in labour markets today, particularly the employment arrangements of the working poor" (Chen 2007, 1). This expanded concept not only provides a deeper understanding of employment arrangements and a wide array of labor practices, but also emphasizes how gender impacts those arrangements and practices (Chen 2003, 2007; Espinal and Grasmuck 1997; Grasmuck and Espinal 2000; Tinker 1987, 1995).

To truly capture the whole of informality, however, we must understand that gender is racialized and classed; it is not some hopelessly abstract category. Indeed, conceptualizing gender, race, and class as separate and isolated fields of inquiry provides only a partial picture of women's work experiences in the informal economy. Afro-Jamaican higglers serve as my point of entry into the thicket of the debates about gender and microenterprise development. The lived experiences of these microentrepreneurs demonstrate clearly how race, class, and gender interlock and intersect. Indeed, Afro-Jamaican higglers have much to teach us about race, gender, and informal labor.

In this book I examine the lived experiences of two groups of Afro-Jamaican higglers—market women and informal commercial importers (ICIs)—paying special attention to their public images, self identifications, and interactions with the state and local communities. I argue that public representations of higglers and their bodies expose the co-construction of race, class, and gender, and that these representations affect higglers' work experiences in the informal economy and help reproduce a presumed social and spatial order. Stories about lower-class black womanhood are written on higglers' bodies by the wider society, which often sees higglers as vulgar, unfeminine, and contaminating. Indeed, public discourses about higglers help legitimize the ways in which the state attempts to discipline them. But I also maintain that higglers and their bodies are not passive. They act in ways that reproduce and contest multiple hierarchies of power as they eke out a living in an ever-constricting economy. Attention then to the production of complex meanings about higglers and their "doings" reveals the combined effects of race, class, and gender in the lived experiences of higglers in the informal economy.

I contend that Afro-Jamaican higglers are not simply microentrepreneurs seeking an economic existence in the informal economy, but rather their presences and economic practices in the informal economy expose and simultaneously disrupt established social, economic, and spatial orders shaped by ideologies of race, class, and gender—orders that have been firmly entrenched in Jamaican society since the colonial era. Indeed, representations of Afro-Jamaican higglers and public reactions to their presence in the informal economy reinforce Nirmal Puwar's assertion that "some bodies are deemed as having the right to belong, while others are marked out as trespassers, who are, in accordance with how both spaces and bodies are imagined (politically, historically and conceptually), circumscribed as being 'out of place'" (2004, 8). I would add that the ways in which bodies and spaces are imagined *economically* also factor into the evaluations of certain groups as being "out of place." That is, they help determine which bodies rightly belong in *public* economic spaces.

The very presence of Afro-Jamaican higglers poses this question of belonging as these informal entrepreneurs battle for space in the city to sell their wares. Indeed, poor black female street vendors in public spaces often spark public discussions around their legitimacy as entrepreneurs working in public economic spaces. We particularly hear this in public outcries that accuse Afro-Jamaican higglers as being "out of order," which in Jamaican parlance implies that one is "out of place." But representations of higglers as out of order are not simply economic matters; they are also social and spatial ones: these representations raise the question of whether these bodies—poor black women—rightfully belong in public economic spaces as independent entrepreneurs, positions historically deemed the natural domain of white and brown middle- and upper-class men. Such representations, as I will show, reveal the presumed violation of social, economic, and spatial boundaries of inclusion and exclusion that are not only gendered but also racialized and classed.

Race, Gender, and Informal Work

How is informal labor experienced on a local level, not only regionally but also individually, that is, by individual actors whose bodies are not simply gendered but also racialized and classed? What can these localized experiences teach us about how informal labor is conceptualized and experienced, and how power operates in the larger economy? How do individual actors interpret, negotiate, and contest localized power structures in the informal economy? The guiding assumption of this study is that to understand the experiences of female microentrepreneurs in general and Afro-Jamaican higglers in particular, we need to address each of these questions and take into account the ways in which these individuals live in complex societies that are stratified by race, class, and gender. Neglecting some factors that influence their lives in favor of others leaves us with only a partial picture of their experiences. So, as I engage in an effort to disclose the "whole of informality," Afro-Jamaican higglers provide an interesting example of the subtle and not so subtle ways in which race, class, and gender configurations are infused into public economic spaces and help shape how labor and bodies are conceptualized, managed, and lived.

I examine the work and the lived experiences of Afro-Jamaican higglers through a theoretical lens that I call "embodied intersectionality." In this view, Afro-Jamaican female microentrepreneurs are embodied subjects working in public spaces. These subjects are embedded in multiple, intersecting hierarchies of power that shape their lived experiences. I argue that public representations of higglers and their bodies expose the co-constructions of race/color, class, and gender, and that these representations affect higglers' work experiences in the informal economy. They also help reproduce a presumed social and spatial order that limits the possibilities available to women engaged in this work.

Higglers' bodies are marked as ideological sites—spaces where a variety of discourses about race/color, class, and gender converge. Stories about black working-class/poor womanhood are written on higglers' bodies by the wider society's describing them as vulgar, unfeminine, illegitimate, as contaminating and undeserving. Indeed, public discourses around higglers help legitimize the ways the state attempts to discipline them in order to maintain social and economic order in city spaces. However, higglers' bodies are not simply sites upon which discourses of race/color, gender, and class are mapped; they also act—re/producing and contesting those discursive frameworks within which they are located. We see this, for instance, in their identity formations and performances.[6] We also see this in the ways in which higglers navigate public space, where their working bodies, consciously and unconsciously, help shape and challenge social, economic, and spatial boundaries through their very movements across city spaces.

My purpose here is not simply to make Afro-Jamaican women informal workers visible. Instead, I intervene in the literature on female microenterprise development by offering a different kind of interpretive frame to analyze women's lived experiences in the informal economy: an interpretive frame that is anchored in gender, race/color, and class oppression. Through this frame I examine ways in which mutually reinforcing categories structure social and economic spaces, and how they are lived through black women's bodies.

I do not underestimate the value of the literature on female microenterprise development. Indeed, persistent calls to scholars to pay close attention to the reality of gender inequality and its impact on the lives of poor women makes this scholarship extremely important. More attention, however, must be paid to how gender is racialized and classed in order to capture the complex challenges faced by third-world women/women of color—challenges that are not related just to their gender.[7] As Joan Acker warns: "Most studies on the production of class, gender, and racial inequalities in organizations have focused on one or another of these categories, rarely attempting to study them as complex, mutually reinforcing or contradicting processes. But focusing on one category almost inevitably obscures and oversimplifies other interpenetrating realities" (2006, 442). My approach in this book moves us closer to a paradigm that examines multiple factors influencing the complexity of women's experiences in informal economies.

Afro-Jamaican higglers are part of a large trend throughout the Caribbean and the developing world: women making a living in the informal economy. The *marchantas* (merchant women) in the Dominican Republic, for instance, are similar to traditional higglers—market women—in that they specialize in the sale of local produce. These women usually reside in the countryside and travel to the city to sell their produce on the streets or in designated marketplaces. The *ti machan* (Creole for "little market women" or "little merchants") are familiar sights on the streets of Haiti and are often referred to as the "soul of the Haitian economy" (Powers 2006, 3). The *rebidantes* of Cape Verde (Creole for "those who are able to overcome obstacles and create new life opportunities") are very similar to Jamaica's modern higglers—informal commercial importers—in that these female microentrepreneurs engage in transnational trade, traveling to West African countries, Europe, Portugal, the United States, and Brazil to purchase consumer goods that are then sold in the Cape Verdean informal economy (Marques, Santos, and Araujo 2001; Portes, Guarnizo, and Haller 2002). This pattern shows that as the global economy evolves and local formal economies contract, thereby limiting employment and financial options, poor women develop creative ways to eke out a living. Microenterprises like higglering are not created by women merely for survival; they also provide a means by which women can establish their autonomy and secure a future for their families.

What is particularly interesting about higglering is its general perception among Jamaicans as a low-status, illegitimate, or illegal occupation. In fact, higglers have been publicly regarded as deviant in Jamaican society. The few scholars who have studied Jamaican higglers and their informal work offer a vivid picture of the informal economic practices of higglering and how this work sustains women, their families, and their customers, but there has been no detailed examination of the ways in which intersecting social relations of race, class, and gender shape cultural meanings around Afro-Jamaican higglers' bodies and labor.[8] These cultural meanings are important. They serve as the backdrop to the lived experiences of Afro-Jamaican women in the informal economy. Public representations of higglers not only provide us with clues about what this kind of informal work means to the broader society, but also reveal how city space is imagined and the location of this group of informal entrepreneurs within that imaginary. For that reason, I examine the cultural meanings around this informal work, and I use the term "higgler" throughout this book not to reproduce the negative stigmas associated with this work, but to bring attention to those stigmas (as they are often glossed over in the literature) and to show how race, class, and gender are working together to inform them.[9]

Doing Fieldwork in Jamaica

One hot sunny day in June 2001, my uncle Bill and I were on our way to an interview with a higgler in downtown Kingston. Driving along a major strip, we found ourselves in the middle of a gun battle between rival factions, which forced us to search desperately for an alternate route. As we drove through bushes to get to a different, and safer, street we could hear gunfire and police sirens in the background and see in our rearview mirror people running in all directions. After reaching our location, we parked in a narrow lane only to be approached by three strangers who were suspicious of our presence. My uncle, a veteran of the dangers of Jamaican politics, raised his foot onto the bumper of his truck as if to tie his shoelace, only to reveal, purposively I am sure, a handgun strapped to his ankle—sending a not so subtle message to leave us alone. It apparently worked.

When I began my fieldwork I anticipated some wariness on the part of the higglers in the recruitment process. As in any research project that relies on interviews, gaining access to a community of subjects usually involves a series of what often appear to be insurmountable hurdles. A major hurdle is gaining the trust of the community that a researcher is trying to penetrate; often, there are techniques one can employ to overcome mistrust. I did not anticipate, however, that the typical obstacles in the field would be complicated even further by external circumstances over which I had no control.

The political climate in Jamaica was volatile in 2001, a general election year. Prime Minister P. J. Patterson, the leader of the People's National Party (PNP) at the time, had announced the start of his election campaign but not the election date, a choice that had much to do with the violent history of Jamaican politics dating back to the 1940s. The political violence that emerged in the 1940s intensified in the 1960s with the recruitment of the party gunman, as the two major political parties, the PNP and the Jamaica Labor Party (JLP), established ties with criminal elements in their respective urban electoral districts in downtown west Kingston. Gunmen in these districts were used as enforcers to ward off challenges from the opposing party and to enforce the principle of captive constituencies (Gray 1991). Intimidation, among other strategies, ensured political loyalty in these areas.

As general elections approached and as parties vied for control, an upsurge of political gang warfare reared its ugly and violent head. Over recent years, many believed that if the election dates were not announced, then the degree of political violence would be minimal. In 1980, however, the refusal by candidates to announce the date of the general election resulted in nine months of violence. Jamaicans throughout the country were concerned that this pattern would be repeated in 2001, because the campaigns of both parties had already sparked violence in downtown west Kingston.[10]

Although no one had been able to give a precise reason for the upsurge of violence, Edward Seaga, the leader of the JLP at this time, was convinced that it was politically motivated. Seaga blamed the PNP and the police force for instigating violence between factions in the JLP-dominated Denham Town and the PNP stronghold in Hannah Town (both in downtown west Kingston). P. J. Patterson, however, vehemently denied this. Meanwhile, the political gun battles in these areas had caused the flight of many families from their homes, the closure of area schools, and the injury and deaths of many residents, including children. On July 7, 2001, gunmen and security forces clashed in this troubled area, leaving four people dead and twenty-seven injured. For the next three days, the entire city of Kingston was locked down by public protests and roadblocks as Kingston residents and those from surrounding areas demonstrated their anger and frustration toward the violence in west Kingston and the behavior of the police force.[11]

The political violence in downtown Kingston forced me to revise my research plans. Initially, I had selected four sites to recruit and interview higglers for my study: Papine Market, Coronation Market, Constant Spring Arcade, and People's Arcade. The Papine and Coronation Markets specialize in locally grown produce and are sites where traditional higglers—market women—work. The Constant Spring and People's Arcades both specialize in foreign imports and are sites where ICIs work. The Papine Market and the Constant Spring Arcade are located in uptown Kingston. The Coronation Market and the People's Arcade are both located downtown. The political violence in downtown west Kingston eventually forced me to abort one of my field sites, Coronation Market, located in the heart of this volatile area.

The political violence continued to affect my study in other ways. Although the ICIs at the People's Arcade worked on the east side of downtown Kingston, a significant number of these women lived on the west side in the troubled areas. Because of the violence, many were unable to leave their homes or send their children to school. For weeks, then, some women failed to show up to work, and those who did were understandably preoccupied with the violence in their neighborhoods. Recruitment in this arcade was difficult—even with the assistance of Mr. Eric Clement, the founder and past president (now deceased) of the United Vendors Association, an organization that offers support for higglers working in the downtown Kingston area. Only a few women from this site agreed to be interviewed.

The political violence also affected the market women at the Papine Market in uptown Kingston. I recall a moment when I walked into the Papine Market, heard a commotion, and saw a group of higglers gathered. I walked over to see what was happening. In the center of the group was a higgler fully animated as she told a story in the grand tradition of African griots. She had the full attention of her audience as she relayed the story of her experience that morning at the Coronation Market in downtown Kingston: "I was in de middle of a sale when me hear boom! boom! boom! Gunshots a fire!! So mi jus drap me tings dem, pick up me purse and run! Everybaddy was running! Mi jump over one woman's basket, me slide through a gate, and the next ting me see a minibus, me neva even did know weh it a go, me jus jump pan de bus like a ninja, and de bus tek off outa de." The women all laughed as they imagined their friend hopping onto a moving vehicle as she fled the market. Their laughter, however, quickly turned into a sober silence, which was eventually broken when the storyteller declared in a somber tone: "Bwoy, tings a get rough in Jamaica [Boy, things are getting rough in Jamaica]."

The ICIs at the People's Arcade lived and worked in fear. But the violence also affected the market women at the Papine Market. Many worked in both Coronation and Papine Markets or purchased goods from Coronation Market, generally more affordable, to sell uptown. Because of the political violence, the businesses of the market women at

Papine were hampered by their fear of entering Coronation Market; if they went, they purchased only a limited number of goods so they could leave the area safely and as quickly as possible. This left many market women at Papine to seek other, more expensive suppliers, forcing them to raise their prices, which reduced sales. These issues were of great concern to the market women and made them more reluctant to speak with me. There were many times a market woman told me out of frustration: "Lady, I cyaan [can't] talk 'cause I need a sale right now!"

Another hurdle involved an economy characterized by negative growth, which sparked massive layoffs and high unemployment. These constrictions in the formal economy triggered the swelling of the informal economy and resulted in the presence, as the higglers often declared to me, of "more sellers than buyers." Because of this, high levels of frustration existed among the higglers, who find it more and more difficult for their businesses to survive. Many complained of their inability to earn a living and considered leaving the informal economy altogether. Their frustration and dire need to earn a living made them more reluctant to participate in the study and made recruitment quite difficult.

◆ ◆ ◆

Overall, I interviewed forty-five higglers—twenty-three market women and twenty-two ICIs. I interviewed thirty-eight higglers at their work sites and two by phone, and five higglers (three ICIs and two market women) completed surveys that were replicas of the interview questionnaire. To ensure the confidentiality of the women—an issue of great concern to most, given the informal status of their business—I do not provide their names in the book. In the Appendix, I list each woman by number (#1–#45), identify her as a market woman or an ICI, indicate whether the communication was in person, by phone, or via survey, and note date and place. I identify women quoted in the text by number (e.g., #25).

The stories of these women—combined with archival research; historical analysis of slave higglering; interpretive content analysis of local newspapers; and observations of the markets, arcades, and a local flea market where middle-class women engaged in similar kinds of informal work as higglers—provide a rich picture of the complex ways in which race, class, and gender feed into the practices and experiences of everyday commercial life in the informal economy. Additionally, as Evelyn Nakano Glenn warns, "to understand race and gender we must examine not only how dominant groups and institutions attempt to impose particular meanings but also how subordinate groups contest dominant conceptions and construct alternate meanings" (2002, 17). The stories of these higglers reveal how race, class, and gender are mutually constitutive, as evidenced in the ways in which these women and their work are publicly imagined in light of their interactions with the state and with their local communities. And just as important, these stories demonstrate how marginalized women contest and negotiate local power structures that attempt to exclude them.

Beyond Sisterhood:
The Politics of Embodiment in the Field

We of course should be mindful of the effects of race, class, and gender on the research process. My research experience in Jamaica dispels the notion commonly implied in the very idea of objectivity that the researcher is disembodied in the research process. Indeed, while sociologists try to minimize the effects of their preconceived ideas on the research they undertake, many have come to terms with the fact that our research cannot be completely objective in the traditional sense of this word. We never simply go out and gather social facts (see Durkheim 1982, 50–59). Instead, it is essential that we examine the impact of our presence on the research process and the information gathered. In fact, we must pay close attention to what we bring to the research process, not only conceptually but also physically. Our bodies are visible in the research process and are often read in ways that can enhance or hamper our research endeavors. As we study societies, including our own, which are stratified by race, class, gender, sexuality, caste, and so on, it would be foolish to assume that our own bodies are immune to these systems of inequality. In fact, inattention to our positions within these systems can lead to a reproduction of power relations between the researcher and her subject. Chandra Talpade Mohanty warns, "Beyond sisterhood there are still racism, colonialism, and imperialism" (1991, 68).

My fieldwork in Jamaica revealed that my body became a site upon which localized meanings of race, class, and gender were mapped. I was an outsider to the higglers, although I was born and raised in Jamaica, spoke patois (the Creole language), identified myself as black and working class (like many graduate students), and identified Jamaica as my home. I was perceived as a foreigner, a potential spy, and middle class, and racialized as brown. These interpretations directly impacted my interactions with the women in my study and complicate the construct of the native researcher, which presumes essentialist identities between researcher and subjects. My experiences reveal that embodied similarities of race, class, and gender between researcher and subject do not guarantee the researcher access to the community to be studied. Indeed, localized meanings of race, class, gender, and nation can render the researcher an outsider vis-à-vis the subjects. My experiences are similar to those of other black feminist researchers who have had to reimagine their assumptions of a link between themselves and their subjects (Slocum 2001), but they also illuminate the socially constructed nature of race, class, and gender as fluid and contextual categories of difference.

I began my research by establishing contact with the late Mr. Eric Clement (a.k.a. Ras Historian), who was the founder and president of the United Vendors Association in downtown Kingston, to learn about the association and the experiences of the higglers he worked with, and to seek his assistance in the recruitment process. In our initial phone call, I encountered some suspicion on his part. When asked for an interview, he immediately raised concerns that the Jamaican government—"the Babylon system," as he called it—would use my study to harm the businesses of higglers. He explained that researchers in the past had interviewed him and women in his organization but had not "given back" to his organization or his community. He said an interview would cost me JA$1,000 (US$25 at that time). I agreed to pay.

I interviewed Mr. Clement in his office, a small room, modestly furnished, in the back of his store where he sold T-shirts and other Rastafarian memorabilia. In this interview, Mr. Clement discussed the history of the UVA and its role in assisting higglers and other vendors who were removed from the streets of Kingston. He also described the present state of his organization. He needed office equipment and financial support. At the end of our interview, Mr. Clement mentioned that his organization was also in need of an electric typewriter, which I supplied upon my return to Jamaica.

I spent the first week of research at the Constant Spring Arcade in uptown Kingston walking around and observing the behaviors of the ICIs. I introduced myself to a few of the vendors, described my research, and attempted to recruit them for interviews. In my introductions I spoke patois and identified myself as a Jamaican student living abroad, in the hope that, despite our differences, my Jamaican heritage would be a point of commonality. Two ICIs quickly granted me interviews and offered me a mini-tour of their stalls. Others, however, promptly refused to speak with me, expressing their discomfort with talking to anyone about their business. Many of these said that business was so slow, they simply did not want to talk about it. "Me jus a try mek a sale right now, yaa dahling," was a frequent response.

By the second week, I collected more interviews as a result of a snowball effect, and began to develop a relationship with one older religious woman, Mrs. T., that would prove to be more valuable than I could have imagined. By this time, I had started buying a few personal items from some of the ICIs, and during the transactions, I struck up conversation. My decision to purchase items was not intended to be part of the recruitment process, but I would later learn that this was a mistake.

By the third week, the recruitment process greatly improved with the help and support of Mrs. T., who introduced me to her friends and acquaintances in the arcade. I also had a better view of the wide variety of items ICIs sold, and I was purchasing more frequently from them for my family and myself. One day, after buying a beautiful scarf from an ICI at one end of the arcade, I was walking away when I noticed the women in that area staring at me. I felt uncomfortable, sensing that something was wrong. At that moment an older ICI approached me and in a stern voice asked what I was doing there. I explained that I had just bought a scarf and that I had been in the arcade over the last two weeks because I was a student conducting research. After I had explained my research to her, the ICI appeared to relax, spoke with me for a short while about her business, and promised me an interview at a later time.

I returned to Mrs. T., who had arranged for me to interview another ICI, Mrs. J. When we were introduced, Mrs. J. told me that she worked in the corner of the arcade where I had just purchased the scarf and that she and the other ICIs had been observing me over the last two weeks and were very suspicious. They thought that I was working undercover for the government or the tax office, and had decided not to speak or sell anything else to me. In short, because of their suspicions, the ICIs had decided to shut me out of that area in the arcade. Mrs. J sent the woman who had approached me after buying the scarf to investigate me, and after our conversation, the woman reported back to the group that I was a student. Based on that report, Mrs. J. agreed to the interview that Mrs. T. had organized.

I encountered similar suspicion at the People's Arcade, as well as at the Papine Market. At the People's Arcade, Mr. Clement voiced his concern that the CIA or the Jamaican government would use my study to hurt the ICIs. I found myself several times trying to convince him and other ICIs at this arcade that my work had nothing to do with the CIA or the Jamaican government. Despite these concerns and other difficulties brought on by the political and economic climate of Jamaica, Mr. Clement was able to organize several interviews.

At the beginning of one interview, an ICI declared, after I discussed the goals of the project, that I should not expect her to answer all my questions, especially those about her earnings. Other ICIs from both arcades were reluctant to reveal how much money they earned as well, and I got a sense that a few refused to be interviewed because of this reluctance. I immediately reminded the ICI that I would not audiotape our conversation, that she could refuse to answer any question that made her uncomfortable, and that all the information she revealed was totally confidential. This made her a little more relaxed, but her responses to questions about her earnings were vague.

At the Papine Market I recruited most of my subjects with the help of a family friend, Jean Rhone, who introduced me to the market women and told them I was a student from abroad and a friend of hers. Because of their relationship with and trust of Jean, I interviewed all but one of the market women she introduced me to. One Saturday, while interviewing a market woman on the sidewalk, I noticed a Rastafarian male observing me. I ignored him and completed my interview. I walked away for a moment to collect a questionnaire for an interview with another woman, and as I made my way back to the area, I noticed the Rastafarian male speaking with her. She looked at me and indicated with her eyes that I should wait. When the man left, the woman told me that he was warning her not to speak to me because I was part of the "Babylon system" and would use the information against her. I was concerned because I did not want to lose the interview, but most importantly I did not want to jeopardize the trust between Jean and the market women. Luckily, the woman and others around her, including Jean, laughed at the man. Jean made it clear to the market women that she would never betray them. I then conducted the interview.

These moments taught me important lessons about the need to pay attention to (1) the power differences, real or alleged, between researcher and subjects; (2) the impact of a researcher on the research process; and (3) the ways in which subjects exercise their own power. My presence at the three sites raised suspicions among the ICIs and possibly among some market women who perceived me as a government agent or someone with the power to ruin their businesses. In their view, I was a member of a powerful institution who could harm them. At the Papine Market my relationship with Jean Rhone helped ease any concern the market women may have had. Some of the ICIs' responses to our perceived power differences, however, included interrogating my presence in the field, refusing to participate in the study and, in one instance, shutting me out of their work area.

My behavior in the Constant Spring Arcade, especially my decision to buy from the ICIs, was perceived by them as deceitful. Some ICIs believed the only reason I bought items was to get close to them, and they decided to protect themselves by not selling anything to me. My presence in the arcade clearly made several of them suspicious and uncomfortable, and a particular group of ICIs responded by temporarily shutting me out. I then had to prove to the women through Mrs. J. that I was not a government spy out to harm them. I did this by showing Mrs. J. my interviews and having Mrs. T. and another ICI confirm my story. Mrs. J. suggested that if I wanted to buy their goods, it was best to do so after my interviews were completed to avoid misinterpretation. After our interview, Mrs. J. reported to the other women in her group that I was "okay."

This experience serves as a great example of the agency of the ICIs at the Constant Spring arcade. Many of them exercised their power by refusing to participate in the study and to reveal themselves to me. Others, particularly those from Mrs. J's group, exercised their power by shutting me out of their work area and investigating me. At this moment, our roles and power positions were reversed: I became their subject of inquiry. My conversations with the older woman who investigated me and with Mrs. J. were ways in which we negotiated our perceived power differences. Once they were comfortable with the reports from these women, the ICIs allowed me to continue with my research but changed my behavior in the arcade by telling me when it was appropriate for me to shop. To be sure, our interactions complicate how we view the relationship between access and power.

In *The Power of Sentiment: Love, Hierarchy, and the Jamaican Family Elite*, Lisa Douglass describes a relationship between access and power in her discussion of the Jamaican elite. She explains that one of the privileges of the Jamaican elite is privacy, and making themselves physically inaccessible to others accomplishes this: "Access to the elite was difficult because they are privileged by privacy. Unlike Jamaicans of the lower classes, many of whom live in relatively open 'yards' or who spend a lot of time on the street, members of the upper class live very much inside their homes. When they go out, their cars—especially those with air-conditioning and tinted windows—keep them from public sight." Douglass claims that the only true elite "community" or social setting is within a complex of family homes, and one can gain access to this community only through family members and close friends. She contrasts this practice to that of Jamaicans of the lower classes, who live in open yards and who spend a lot of time in open, more accessible streets. Douglass argues that making themselves physically inaccessible is one way in which the Jamaican elite control information about themselves. "Inaccessibility," she asserts, "is a form of power" (1992, 38).

Although I agree with Douglass that inaccessibility is a form of power, I disagree with the implication of her argument that physical access to a group facilitates access to information about that group. For instance, many higglers do live in open yards, and open sidewalks, arcades, and markets are their work environments. Although many ICIs and market women are unable to limit physical access to them, they are still able to control the degree of access to information about them. In my case, many women exercised this power of inaccessibility by either refusing to participate in the interviews or by filtering and at times editing information about themselves. A more complicated relationship exists between physical access and access to information than the connection Douglass notes. Access to one's body does not guarantee access to one's biography.

Place and Body Matters

My experiences in the field confirmed Stacey Lengel's and other feminists' arguments that we need to avoid delusions of sisterhood when we engage in feminist research.[12] It would have been methodologically misleading for me to rely on the similarities between my subjects and me as Afro-Jamaican women as a means by which I could enter their world. In fact, they would not allow it. Instead, my perceived difference as an expatriate or "from farin [foreign or abroad]," along with my class status, which in Jamaica is associated with education, shaped our interactions. All these differences placed me in the position of outsider in relation to these women—a position I was unable to transform fundamentally.

The women saw me as a college-educated, presumably middle-class woman, a member of a group with whom they have had a history of tensions. The historical relationship between the Jamaican middle class and the lower classes to which most higglers and other street vendors belong can best be characterized as antipathetic. According to Obika Gray, this antipathy is evidenced in their encounters in the commercial districts. "The nature of this social contact," Gray argues, "engendered mutual contempt between these two segments of the Kingston population. As we have observed, the Jamaican middle class possessed an exalted sense of its cultural affinity with the upper class and therefore dealt imperiously with the darker, poorer classes below." Gray adds that given this class contempt, middle-class people "demand submissive compliance from the street vendors," who are often viewed as the "riffraff" of society. Street vendors' animosity toward the middle class is often intensified by a sense of cultural injury and alienation that they usually share with others in the lower classes (Gray 1991, 71).

It is quite possible that this history of class tension and my perceived middle-class status made many higglers and the Rastafarian at the Papine Market suspicious of my interest in them. It can also explain why Mr. Clement at first reacted with wariness to my request for an interview with him and his organization. He assumed that, like earlier researchers, I would take advantage of his people and possibly harm them with the information I gathered. He then shifted the power dynamic by demanding I pay him, a way of getting something back from me. I understood his concern and happily paid his fee. What is interesting to me, however, is that when I described this encounter to my relatives, who are part of the Jamaican middle class, their reactions were typical: Mr. Clement's behavior was consistent with the "riffraffs."

My position as an expatriate or North American foreigner also contributed to my outsider status. My position as a foreigner living in the United States shaped perceptions of my class status, as many Jamaicans who move abroad are of middle-class origins. My foreigner status was equated with middle-class status in the minds of my subjects, and placed me outside their predominantly lower-class experience. My foreigner status also disclosed another dimension of power: the power to escape the social conditions in which these women lived. The United States is often perceived as a place where one can acquire a better life, a better education for one's children, and a better future. It is a place of refuge from the economic and social hardships in Jamaica. My foreigner status indicated that I was one of those lucky ones who escaped, as opposed to these higglers who were left behind.[13] In many ways, my experiences as an outsider were similar to those of black feminist anthropologist Lynn Bolles, who states in her study on working-class Jamaican women that in spite of her genuine commitment to the plight of the powerless, her class, education, and national identity served as barriers to both friendship and research (see Slocum 2001, 140).

One question that remains unanswered is the extent to which my race influenced my encounters with the women. Jamaican men many times called me a "browning"—a term for a brown- or fair-skinned woman that carries a class dimension, according to Leone Ross: "As long as the skin gleams a particular brown, you become part of a special group, you attend particular parties, you are treated a particular way on the street, you are expected to go to certain schools, have money, be educated and eventually professional. Because the 'browning' life is not just about skin shade, it is about class" (1993, 7). Ross identifies a correlation between race/color and class in the Jamaican consciousness—the lighter one's skin color, the higher one is believed to fall in the class structure.[14] Many Jamaicans also believe that brownings or fair-skinned people usually hold the ticket to success, and an association often made between lighter skin and social mobility is evident in the high rate of skin bleaching among some members of the lower classes (Brown-Glaude 2007; Cowell 1999).[15]

Although I do not identify myself as a browning, the public perception of me as one of that class (as evidenced in the few times I was called a browning by Jamaican men) may have had an impact on my encounters with the higglers.[16] The market women made no direct reference to my color, but it is not clear if that was because color was a nonissue for them or if their reactions to my perceived class difference masked perceived color differences, since racial/color discourse in Jamaica is often buried in other ways of talking about structural inequality. Jamaicans pride themselves on having no race problem, but the reality of Jamaican society suggests that patterns of racial/color stratification overlap with other patterns of stratification, especially that of class. I am unable, then, to separate the higglers' reactions to my perceived class status and my color, an inability consistent with the ways in which class stratification in Jamaica is greatly overdetermined by race/color (Hall 1977).

Black feminist anthropologist Faye Harrison encountered a similar challenge in her research in Jamaica in the community of Oceanview, where, she argues, "folk perceived me to be almost anything other than my own self-conception, i.e. a Black social scientist with a strong identification with oppressed Black Jamaicans." She explains that in spite of her self-identification, she was racialized in a variety of ways: "While the majority of Oceanview people saw in me a middle-class 'brown' woman, some presumed and insisted that the 'American doctor doing research' was socially—if not genetically—'white'" (quoted in Slocum 2001, 140). Harrison's education, presumed class status, and North American residence contributed to her racialization as brown and white and in effect positioned her as an outsider in relation to her research subjects in Jamaica. Karla Slocum encountered similar experiences in other parts of the Caribbean—Grenada and St. Vincent—where she was marked as an outsider in relation to her research subjects, an identification that drew on local constructions of color, class, and nationality (Slocum 2001).

My experiences, then, confirm that researchers are not disembodied in the research process. Black feminist researchers and others have insisted that our racialized, classed, and gendered bodies factor into our interactions with research subjects and can influence the research process in subtle and not so subtle ways (McClaurin 2001). Recognizing the differences between higglers and myself, along with my outsider status, is an important step in the process of self-reflexivity. The differences between the higglers and me are not necessarily sources of problems, but can be sources of strength. Challenges lie not in the differences between people, but in the ways in which those differences are inscribed within broader structures of power. The task, then, is not to avoid power relations by hiding behind a notion of sisterhood, but to address them, a process that can strengthen relationships among women across differences. Recognizing these differences through self-reflexivity involves my acknowledging those power relations in the hope of subverting them, and thus avoiding the reproduction of this group of women as others.

I do not suggest that I resolved all these methodological concerns in my study. But my experiences have taught me that researchers, intentionally or unintentionally, bring their own cultural baggage with them when they enter the field. This baggage and their mere presence can influence encounters between researcher and subject. Reflecting on my presence in the field and its impact on the research process helps bring into focus these concerns and allows me to interrogate the relations of power between higglers and me—all with the intention of critiquing that relationship, an essential in black feminist research methodology.

Organization of Chapters

Chapter 1 provides the theoretical framework, embodied intersectionality, that I use in this study to examine the lived experiences of higglers in the Jamaican informal economy—specifically, their public images, self-identifications, and interaction with the state and local communities. Chapter 2 complicates the analytical category "women's informal work" by disclosing how intersectional structures of race, class, and gender influence the labor patterns of higglering in Jamaica, that is, the overrepresentation of lower-class black women in this kind of work.

Chapters 3 and 4 provide a sociohistorical analysis of the ways in which the business of higglering (Chapter 3) and higglers (Chapter 4) have been publicly represented in Jamaica from slavery to independence in 1962. Chapter 5 examines how higglers today identify themselves against this backdrop of representations that often demean them.

Chapter 6 examines higglers' interactions with the state and local communities, focusing on attempts by the state and uptown communities to remove higglers from the streets of Kingston. The concluding chapter summarizes the main points of the book and draws some theoretical implications.

◆ ◆ ◆

The market is closing. It is Saturday evening, and dusk is falling fast. After packing up her stall, Miss Virginette (#3) calls on a young boy to help her carry her baskets back to the bus stop. It has been a relatively good day, but generally business is bad. She has seen better. She mutters to herself, "Business slow bad, bad. Nuttin' ah gwan. First time it did sweet [Nothing is going on. When I first started, business was good]." Meanwhile, dance-hall music blares in the background of the Constant Spring Arcade. Miss Carida (#25) pulls down the shutters to her stall and sucks her teeth. She is visibly disappointed and frustrated. "Jamaica de' pon de laas. It rough." [Jamaica is on its last legs. It is rough]).

1

Intersectionality and the Politics of Embodiment

> The great variety of experiences that characterize women's lives in the periphery requires a special effort to conceptualize a paradigm to include all factors having an influence on the complexity of their subordination.
> **LOURDES BENERIA AND MARTHA ROLDAN,**
> *The Crossroads of Class and Gender*

In recent years, policymakers in the international development field have viewed female microenterprises as solutions to sustainable development as the economies of developing nations continue to contract under pressures of keeping pace with an evolving global economy.[1] International development agencies and practitioners applaud the entrepreneurial spirits of poor women as they eke out a living in the informal economy. The assumption is that small-scale enterprising activities will improve not only the living standards of poor women, but also their national economies (de Soto 1989; de Soto and Orsini 1991; Dignard and Havet 1995). Fueled by this optimism, the World Bank has increased credit and training opportunities to female microentrepreneurs in informal economies in developing countries. The hope is that once they are properly nurtured, these microbusinesses will help alleviate poverty (Ehlers and Main 1998; Eversole 2004; Grasmuck and Espinal 2000; Tinker 2000).

Despite this great optimism, however, most female microentrepreneurs have failed to achieve the level of economic success that was predicted, and have continued to live in poverty. Development practitioners often attribute these failures to the purportedly problematic ways in which these microbusinesses are organized. Operating on the assumption that markets are free and value neutral, they assume that once women have the opportunities and tools needed to participate effectively in these markets, their living standards and eventually their economies will improve.

Feminist scholars have challenged these assumptions by illuminating the importance of gender in the development and success of female microenterprises. Many have argued that in their assessment of women's work and success, international development agencies tend to rely on a market-oriented model that fails to consider the impact of social conditions, particularly gender inequality, that structure opportunities for women in distinct ways. These scholars maintain that purely economic and gender-neutral models miss various hidden barriers women encounter as they try to make a living, and leave us instead with a distorted image of women as poor candidates for business endeavors. Most microenterprise credit and training organizations are often guilty of these assumptions and develop programs that further constrain women's microenterprise development instead of enhancing it (Dignard and Havet 1995; Ehlers and Main 1998; Grasmuck and Espinal 2000; Kantor 2005; Mayoux 2001; Milgram 2005; Tinker 2003).

Feminist scholars have also argued that a theoretical lens that examines the impact of gender inequality on the work experiences of women will provide better insights into the successes and failures of female microenterprises. Catherine Van der Wees and Henny Romijn (1995) note, for example, that while female microentrepreneurs face problems similar to those commonly faced by all microentrepreneurs (lack of capital, training, managerial experience, etc.), their problems are exacerbated by subtle barriers involving the underestimation of women's economic roles, gender-role stereotyping, lack of confidence in women's entrepreneurial and managerial skills, and the relegation of women to low-productivity sectors in the informal economy. Greater attention to gender allows scholars to clarify the particular experiences of women in the informal economy and to develop policies that directly address their challenges.

Although I agree with this argument, I am left with the following questions: How do we conceptualize "women" in our analyses of microenterprise development? For example, can we assume that Afro-Jamaican higglers face problems in the informal economy similar to those of women of different racial/color groups?[2] In a society where racial/color categories carry important meanings and shape social relationships, can we assume that these categories fail to apply in the informal economy?[3] How can we conceptualize "women's informal work" in ways that resist treating that work as an abstract category and the informal worker as either disembodied or simply gendered?

My goal in this study, then, is to nuance and perhaps broaden the analytical category of "women's informal work" by examining the sociohistorical contexts in which that work takes place, illuminating multiple, intersecting hierarchies of power and conceptual frameworks that shape the ways in which that work is imagined and experienced. This approach uncovers a wide range of women's experiences in the informal economy that are not shaped simply by gender or class ideologies, but also by race. A clearer understanding of a variety of experiences of women in the informal economy is an important first step toward creating policies that directly address these women's specific needs.

Embodied Intersectionality

My theoretical approach responds, in part, to Lourdes Beneria and Martha Roldan's insistence, decades ago, that when we examine the experiences of third-world women, we must "conceptualize a paradigm to include all factors having an influence on the complexity of their subordination" (1987, 11). Here the concept of embodied intersectionality plays a critical role. This approach assumes that markets, whether formal or informal, are lived experiences that are embodied.[4] Understanding lived experiences helps prevent researchers from thinking about their subject matter in abstraction and instead concretizes those experiences within the social-economic-geographical contexts in which they take place.

Moreover, understanding lived experiences as embodied encourages the researcher to pay closer attention to those bodies and ask, "Who *are* these economic actors?" "What *kinds* of bodies are we talking about?" These questions make central the reality of difference and help us recognize that, as racialized/colored, classed, and gendered bodies, they are positioned within societies in complex ways that impact their place in various economies. Here the theory of intersectionality plays a critical role. Through the lens of intersectionality, one identifies the multi-textured character of our bodies. By this I mean that our bodies are embedded in multiple, intersecting hierarchies of power—especially, but not limited to, race/color, class, and gender—and are lived and read through frames that reflect these dimensions. Our bodies also act in ways that reproduce or contest those multiple hierarchies of power. Bodies, then, are complex, multidimensional sites and subjects of struggle.

Embodied intersectionality also assumes that embodied experiences are spatialized; that is, they are located both physically and conceptually in social space. In the case of higglering, these embodied market experiences are located in a city of a developing nation—a city that has experienced, among many challenges, economic decline, problems associated with urban density, violence, high unemployment, and spatial segregation shaped by race/color and class (Clarke 1975; Clarke and Howard 1999, 2006; Huber and Stephens 1992; Portes, Itzigsohn, and Dore-Cabral 1994; Weiss 2005; Wyss and White 2004). Cities, however, are not simply material landscapes that are fixed in time and space; they are also symbolic spaces—spaces of the imagination. The ways in which cities are imagined have real consequences on how city spaces, and the bodies that navigate them, are organized, managed, and ordered (Bridge and Watson 2001 and 2002; Watson 2000).

My conceptualization of the body draws from the developing field of the sociology of the body, particularly the work of Chris Shilling, who views the body as "an unfinished biological and social phenomenon which is transformed, within certain limits, as a result of its entry into, and participation in, society" (2004, 11).[5] Like Shilling, I view the body as unfinished, in that it changes/transforms physically and socially throughout one's lifetime. So as our physical bodies change due to aging, disability, or dieting, for instance, so do their social meanings, and this can affect social relations. The unfinished characteristic of our bodies is also evident in what bodies *do*. Here, performances are important. Our behaviors are not necessarily socially determined; they change and transform over time and space, especially in light of environments that consistently exact adjustments and adaptations. Our behaviors then can, and often do, reproduce, resist, or transform social meanings and norms. An understanding of bodies as unfinished rejects ideas of them as precultural, static objects and illuminates instead their flexibility or "volatility" (Grosz 1994).

Shilling further describes the body as a "multidimensional medium for the constitution of society"; it is a source of, a location for, and a means by which individuals are emotionally and physically positioned within and oriented toward society (2005, 11). He joins other theorists of the body, including feminist theorists, in rejecting a Cartesian dualist model of the mind/body relationship that subordinates the body as a source of knowledge. Instead, Shilling centers the body in his analysis, illuminating ways in which it, along with the mind, informs social thought. Moreover, the body-society relationship is understood as an emergent, causally consequential phenomenon. Here, bodies and societies are not fixed or static, nor are they identical or reducible to each other; they are distinctive yet dialectically linked. Embodied subjects are understood as agential, as having the capacity to "intervene and make a difference in their environment" (13). In other words, embodied subjects are central in the re/production and transformation of society.

To claim that the body is a source of society is to illuminate the ways in which embodied subjects are active agents. Shilling argue that "what we can take from this idea that the body is a source of society is that the embodied subject is possessed of an intentional capacity for making a difference to the flow of daily life and of socially creative capacities resulting from its sensory and mobile character which are not always directly accessible to individual consciousness" (2005, 10). Bodies, then, are not passive. They play crucial roles in the constitution of social structures and systems. At the same time, embodied subjects exist within broader structures of power that serve to regulate bodies in various ways. In this way, the body is also a *location* for society. Social structures and cultures impose themselves on our bodies and influence, consciously and unconsciously, our behaviors and ideas.

But society does not wholly determine our behaviors and ideas. Embodied subjects have the creative capacity to reproduce, resist, and transform those social structures and cultures. The strength of this capacity depends on the extent to which embodied subjects feel a sense of attachment to, or detachment from, the social and economic arrangements that circumscribe their life choices. The body is a means by which this sense of attachment to or rupture from society occurs. In other words, we experience social structures and cultures through our bodies, and those experiences influence our general orientation to society as well as our responses to it.[6] What is significant here is that our bodies are vehicles of change. As Shilling argues: "Social change does not happen automatically and nor does it occur simply as a result of purely intellectually-motivated actions. Instead, people's experiences of, and responses to, social structures are shaped significantly by their sensory and sensual levels" (2004, 210).

Shilling notes that structuration theorists, social construction theorists, and phenomenologists will recognize elements of their accounts in this analysis of the body, but each of these schools of thought tends to emphasize one aspect of the body—as a source of, a location for, or a means for positioning individuals in their environments. Instead, Shilling insists, and I agree, that "any comprehensive theory of the body needs to take account of *all three* of these processes" (2005, 19, emphasis original), and an assessment of the body as a multidimensional medium attempts to keep these three processes in view at all times.

With the help of Shilling's theory of the body, my examination of Afro-Jamaican higglers' experiences is not limited to ways in which their bodies become sites upon which discourses of race/color, class, and gender are mapped. I also examine ways in which these embodied subjects make "a difference to the flow of daily life" (Shilling 2005, 10), that is, ways in which higglers' bodies re/produce but also transform their physical environment, and push/contest social, economic, and spatial boundaries as they interact with the state and local communities. Additionally, I examine ways in which higglers are socially and spatially positioned within society as lower-class black women, paying special attention to what this positioning discloses about how public spaces are imagined, as well as its effects on higglers' orientations and responses to society. All these factors illuminate a presumed social and spatial order organized around the co-constructions of race/color, class, and gender in Jamaica that has long been a part of its social and political fabric.

An appreciation of social stratification is important to body studies. We must recognize that the "bodies of men and women, white people and black people, able bodied and those characterized by physical disabilities, and adults and children, for example, have long been differently positioned within society" (Shilling 2005, 20). But bodies not only serve as multidimensional media for the constitution of society, but also are themselves multidimensional. They are, in part, products of (and, in fact, produce) multidimensional hierarchies of power; therefore their positions in, and orientations to, society are complex.[7]

Put differently, bodies are multitextured. They are racialized, classed, gendered, and sexualized (and so on) bodies and so occupy multiple positions in any given time and space. Since bodies are embedded in multiple, intersecting relations of power, the orientations and responses of embodied subjects to their experiences may be difficult to assess based on one particular structural position in which those subjects are located. Examples of this complexity are evident in the expansive scholarship by black feminists and other feminists of color in the United States and the Caribbean. Using a theoretical lens of intersectionality, this literature unpacks multidimensional webs of power in which women of color are located. For example, Kimberle Crenshaw's (1991) research on violence against women of color illustrates that abused women of color are burdened by poverty, child-care responsibilities, and lack of job skills—factors largely the consequence of gender and class oppression. These women's burdens are compounded by racially discriminatory employment and housing practices, which limit the ability of many to create alternatives to their abusive relationships. By highlighting multidimensional webs of power in which women of color are located, black feminist scholarship in the United States illustrates that women of color are not positioned and oppressed in society simply as women in relation to men, but that their positions in society reflect the combined effects of racial, gender, and class hierarchies.[8]

Caribbean feminists have raised similar issues in their research on women in the region. Many agree that the combined effects of race/color, class, gender, and so on also shape Caribbean women experiences (Barriteau 2003, 2007; Mohammed 2000; Reddock 2001). These feminists insist, however, that in order to understand *how* race/color, class, and gender affect Caribbean women, we must operationalize these categories within the context of the Caribbean. That is to say, we cannot simply map constructions of race, class, and gender as they are defined and experienced in the U.S. context, for example, onto the experiences of Caribbean women. Although it is true that Caribbean women and men experience racism, those experiences and understandings of race differ given the particular histories of racial formation in the region.

As opposed to a black/white racial dichotomy that generally governs U.S. racial ideologies and relations, racial categories in the Caribbean are generally divided into black/brown/white and correlate with skin color variations, social class, and ethnicity, producing a "hierarchy of shades" (Cliff 1985).[9] This difference has much to do with the specific history of the Caribbean region, where slavery and colonialism have triggered forced and voluntary migrations of Africans, East Indians, Chinese, English, Portuguese, Spanish, and Dutch peoples into the region and the subsequent formation of various mixed-race groups. Because of the rich diversity of the region, constructions of "blackness" are not easily applicable to all people of color as they are in the United States. Distinctions are made among Caribbean people between those who are racialized as black over and against those who are racialized as browns, and life chances are affected in real ways by these distinctions.

A similar pattern of racialization exists in Latin America. As opposed to the binary racial structure found in the United States, a multitiered racial system exists in Latin America, which has a substantial mixed-race population. As in the Caribbean, skin color plays a significant role in Latin American societies that are organized around a "hierarchy of shades." Many scholars marvel at the high rates of miscegenation in Latin America, arguing that this is evidence of a "racial democracy" in the region. However, numerous studies show that structural patterns of racial inequality exist that privilege whiteness and brownness, and devalue blackness (Telles 2004, Wade 1997).

Given these differences in racial structures between the United States and the Caribbean, the imposition of foreign—that is, U.S.—categories and experiences on the Caribbean region can render the specific histories and experiences of Caribbean women invisible. Lizabeth Paravisini-Gebert makes this point forcefully when she states "that as scholars committed to studying Caribbean women we must anchor our work in a profound understanding of the societies we (they) inhabit. The evaluation of a differing reality from the theoretical standpoint of other women's praxis comes dangerously close in many cases to continued colonization" (1997, 4). Indeed, Caribbean women do not fit neatly into established categories in U.S. feminism. As Christine Barrow argues, Caribbean women are not "marginalized in the same way as their third-world counterparts. They could not be accommodated into private/public dichotomies, which confined them to home, domesticity and motherhood, and though constrained by patriarchal ideology and practice they did not suffer the same subordinate status in relations to their menfolk" (Barrow 1998, xi). Caribbean feminist theorizing, then, must be "indigenous" in that, although influenced by feminist theories outside the region, including black (U.S.) feminist theories, primacy must be given to the sociohistorical specificity of the Caribbean (Mohammed 1998).

Yet both black (U.S.) and Caribbean feminists are concerned with issues of difference and with how knowledge about women is produced. A key concern for both is the historical erasure of women of color from Western feminist discourses, and both aim to tell the stories of the challenges and agency of a diverse group of women and to resist the reproduction of hegemonic discourses. In the end, both black (U.S.) and Caribbean feminist theorists destabilize false unitary conceptual categories within feminist discourses, most notably, the concept "woman." Intersectionality is one theoretical intervention that destabilizes this false unity.

Intersectionality examines the combined effects of race, class, and gender on women's experiences.[10] Patricia Hill Collins argues that a conceptual stance of intersectionality allows us to focus on the fundamental issue of the social relations of domination, where race, class, and gender constitute axes of oppression that characterize black women's experiences within a general matrix of domination. She cautions us to not view race, class, and gender as having singular effects on black women's experiences but instead to focus on their simultaneous effects. Moreover, race, class, and gender are not to be understood as additives, which are reflected in concepts such as "double and triple jeopardy"; instead, we need to emphasize their articulations or intersections (1990). As Floya Anthias explains, "one subordination does not work on those that already exist. The form of subordination is a *product* of their connections. These cannot be mechanistically understood. It is the intersection of subordinations that is important and they cannot be treated as different layers of oppression" (1991, 38, emphasis original). A framework of intersectionality attempts to keep structural connections of race, class, gender, and so on in view at all times as it examines the particular ways in which different configurations of these categories affect various groups of people in different ways (Andersen and Hill Collins 1998).

Categories of race, class, and gender are of course unstable, flexible, and highly contested. Their meanings and formations in societies change over time and space, making these categories historical and contextual (indeed, the concerns of Caribbean feminists illuminate the need to consider the contextual nature of these categories).[11] Categories of race, class, and gender not only shape social structures and cultures, they are also mapped onto bodies and transform human beings into racialized, classed, and gendered subjects. Categories of race, class, and gender, then, are embodied, and their instability and flexibility depends in part on what bodies do. As embodied subjects engage their social world and experience social structures and cultures, the meanings behind categories of race, class, and gender, and the social relations that are influenced by them are re/produced, contested, and transformed.

My use of embodied intersectionality places the body-society relationship at the center of analysis and illuminates the contextual, structural/cultural, and embodied characteristics of race, class, and gender. This framework acknowledges that structural and cultural processes of race, class, and gender are lived through our bodies in contextually specific ways. As we interact with others in our everyday lives, our racialized, classed, and gendered bodies are given meaning, and those meanings are re/produced and contested through our bodies and what they do.

Embodied intersectionality considers structural intersectionality, that is, how diverse structures of race, class, and gender intersect and together are implicated in shaping the experiences of embodied subjects. It does not reduce one structure, such as race, to another, such as class. Instead, embodied intersectionality treats race, class, and gender as distinctive yet intricately connected structures of inequality. At the same time, embodied intersectionality acknowledges that structures of race, class, and gender are also embodied. It assumes that bodies are inseparable from societies and cultures, and argues that our bodies are embedded in multiple, intersecting structures of race, class, and gender, which contribute to their multitextured quality.

To argue that our bodies are multitextured is to acknowledge, then, that distinctive structures collapse within the body, and so we cannot understand gender independently from race and class in our analysis of embodied subjects and their lived experiences. It is essential, instead, to understand the ways in which race, class, and gender are mutually constitutive. That is, one's gender identification, self-identity, and performances are shaped to some degree by one's race and class (and vice versa). So a woman may not see herself simply as feminine. A particular conception of femininity that is racialized and classed may be at work in her identity formation.

We see this, for example, in the distinction made in Jamaica between a Jamaican "lady" and a Jamaican "woman": a lady is commonly understood to be a member of the brown elite, a woman as black and lower class (Douglass 1992; Ulysse 1999, 2007). A Jamaican lady's brownness and middle- or upper-class status influence her perception of femininity and can also influence her performance, especially in public spaces, where a middle-class sense of respectability may, and often does, preclude a lady from breastfeeding her child in public or from speaking patois (the Creole language).[12] As she conforms to these middle-class norms of respectability, a Jamaican lady reproduces her image and identity as a lady and reinforces social hierarchies of race/color, class, and gender. The multi-textured quality of our bodies, then, is the result of multiple hierarchies of race/color, class, and gender in which they are embedded. Categories of race/color, class, and gender interlock in our bodies, shaping our identities in distinct ways.

My understanding of multitextured bodies takes seriously Elizabeth Grosz's description of bodies as "always irreducibly sexually specific, necessarily interlocked with racial, cultural, and class particularities. This interlocking, though, cannot occur by way of intersection (the gridlike model presumed by structural analysis, in which the axes of class, race, and sex are conceived as autonomous structures which then require external connections with the other structures) but by way of mutual constitution" (1994, 20). Here Grosz identifies specific ways in which each of these categories is lived through our bodies—they interlock; they are mutually constitutive. In her view, the framework of intersection cannot capture this nuance because it treats race, class, and gender as discrete categories. Grosz's framework of interlocking captures the idea that race, class, and gender distinctions are collapsed in our bodies, and categories of race, class, and gender inform or shape each other in our identity formation.

Although I agree with Grosz's point, I want to be careful in my analysis not to lose sight of specific ways in which social inequality is structured in society. Race, class, and gender operate as distinct yet intersecting structures of inequality with their own histories and manifestations, and I want to take care not to reduce these structures and the ways they operate in various contexts *only* to bodies. Instead, I want to suggest using the two frameworks—intersecting and interlocking—analytically to examine the body-society relationship. Race, class, and gender operate in distinctive ways in our bodies and society, yet bodies and societies are dialectically linked. I want to keep at arm's length any kind of troublesome reductionism. My concept of embodied intersectionality uses both analytical frames—intersecting and interlocking—to make a distinction between the ways in which race, class, and gender operate outside the body on a structural level and the ways they are lived through our bodies. This concept acknowledges the distinctive relations of race, class, and gender on the levels of structures and bodies, and keeps the body-society relationship in view at all times.[13]

To acknowledge the simultaneous impact of race, class, and gender on our bodies is not to argue that each has equal impact on our experiences and identities at all times, an assumption of a stability that these categories simply do not have. Such an assumption would also ignore the influence of history and social context on the shifting meanings and importance of these categories. As Iris Berger notes regarding South Africa: "Accepting a model of complex interrelationships among different aspects of personal and collective identity does not mean that the weight given to each element in the chemical imbalance necessarily is equal at all times; ... there are historical situations in which an authoritarian state has made a particular aspect of identity the main determinant of individual lives and consciousness. Such situations do not destroy the importance of connections" (1992, 285).

We must avoid a cookie-cutter model of intersectionality that imposes an analysis of race, class, and gender as equally operating variables on the experiences under investigation. My view of embodied intersectionality acknowledges that there are contexts in which one's gender, for instance, may have a greater influence on shaping identities and social relations than does race or class. This does not mean, however, that race and class are invisible. Indeed, race and class often shape how that gender is perceived and lived.

If we return to the example of a Jamaican lady, for instance, we find that her decision not to breastfeed in public or to speak patois may be influenced by her conception of femininity—ladies simply don't do that sort of thing. However, a closer examination of this conception of femininity reveals that class and color are also shaping this enactment of gender. Color and class operate in the background, so to speak, yet are very effective and productive. One may never know the exact degree to which each of these variables influences a particular set of experiences, but it is important to remember that interactions among structures and categories of race, class, and gender vary as embodied subjects, with their mobile agential bodies, engage with their social world.[14] Indeed, this is what Iris Berger means by the "messy complexity of reality" (1992, 286).

The Case of Afro-Jamaican Higglers

Jamaican higglers provide an interesting example of the importance of examining the combined effects of race/color, class, and gender on the public representations and lived experiences of female microentrepreneurs. Three points, in particular, stand out. First, these women are predominantly black or Afro-Jamaican and members of the so-called lower class. Their relegation to the informal economy and to this particular type of informal work is in large part the result of a racialized/colored, classed, and gendered division of labor that has been firmly entrenched in the Jamaican economy since the era of slavery. Second, higglering has been publicly imagined historically as women's domain. Even though over the last few decades more men have been participating in this type of informal work as formal employment options shrink, public discussions reveal that higglering continues to be imagined as a largely feminine occupation. Yet higglering has historically been the domain of a particular kind of woman—one who is black and lower class—and this history has implications for how the legitimacy of this work is assessed.

Third, Jamaicans commonly understand higglering as a low-status occupation, and historically the Jamaican public imagination has constructed higglers as deviant. Indeed, according to Lisa Douglass, in Jamaica the higgler is perceived as "a comical character, a caricature of a woman" (1992, 36). I contend here that public representations of higglering and higglers as deviant disclose assumptions about public economic spaces as the natural domain of upper-class white and brown men. I also demonstrate the ways in which higglers, through their identity formations, reproduce, negotiate, and contest representations of them as deviant. Here categories of race/color, class, and gender are embodied (interlocked) and exposed in higglers' self-definitions and performances.

As I have suggested, embodied intersectionality emphasizes the lived experiences of women workers and encourages the researcher to pay attention to the bodies of women and to recognize that bodies and places are interlinked. In the case of Jamaican higglers, such a formulation directs us toward examining women's bodies as they work in a city of a developing nation. Cities, however, are not passive, material spaces but also imagined spaces, and this imagining affects social relations (Bridge and Watson 2001).[15] Such an effect is evident in the ways the state attempts to discipline these women and relegate them to the margins of the city (and out of sight).

In the Jamaican popular imagination, the city of Kingston is divided into two spheres: uptown and downtown. These divisions are not solely geographical identifiers but are also indicators of social position. Many Jamaicans associate uptown with the brown or white middle and upper classes, and downtown with the black poor. As a result, one's belonging uptown or downtown usually signifies one's membership in a particular racial/color and class group. That the working bodies of higglers, who are members of the black lower class, traverse uptown city spaces poses an interesting dilemma for uptown city residents who purchase goods from higglers, yet want them and their movements contained. This dilemma contributes, in part, to representations of higglers and their bodies as contaminants and nuisances, especially as these women resist attempts by local authorities to remove them from these privileged spaces.

Higglers also work within local ideologies and hierarchies of power. Although many Jamaicans, especially those from the brown middle classes, would argue that race is a nonissue in Jamaica, a three-tiered racial/color system exists of whites, browns, and blacks. White Jamaicans, who constitute the numerical minority in Jamaica, are the most privileged group, while black Jamaicans, the majority, are the least privileged. The brown middle class currently controls the economy and in 2007 regained political control. The social and spatial positioning of these three groups reveals the continued significance of race and its correlation with social class in Jamaica (Austin-Broos 1994; Douglass 1992; Girvan 1981; D. Gordon 1991; Greene 1993; Hall 1977, 1980; Robotham 2000; Thomas 2004).

This race/color structure thrives despite a long-standing multiracial nationalist ideology developed at the time of Jamaica's independence in 1962, and reflected in the national motto, "Out of many, one people." This ideology portrays Jamaica as a meritocracy and Jamaicans as having moved beyond race (Robotham 2000; Thomas 2004). But, race and color in Jamaica are simultaneously visible and invisible. Such duality constrains public discussions around race; race becomes the silent phantom that shapes Jamaicans' experiences. This silence is changing, however, and the racial ideology is shifting: the multiracial ideology is becoming decentered, and in its place we find an emerging "modern blackness," especially among the urban black poor (Thomas 2004). In spite of these ideological shifts, patterns of residential racial segregation, for example, continue: blacks are concentrated downtown.

To further complicate higglers' experiences, the three-tiered racial/color system correlates with class, placing white Jamaicans at the upper level of the socioeconomic system, browns (and some blacks) at the middle level, and blacks dominant at the lowest level. Because of the general reluctance to talk about race/color, racial status is articulated in class terms; class is a dominant theme among most higglers' descriptions of their experiences, reinforcing the presumed invisibility of race.[16]

Local gender hierarchies compound the challenges higglers have to confront. For instance, local gender norms assign to women the primary responsibilities of taking care of families and households. However, twice as many women as men are unemployed, and more women than men live in poverty. That the number of female-headed households continues to increase despite rising female unemployment does not change traditional gender norms: women are still expected to bear primary responsibility for their households.[17]

Race/color, class, and gender structures organize Afro-Jamaican women's options in the labor market by relegating them to the lowest-paying sex-segregated jobs (e.g., in the education, domestic, and health sectors)—usually the first to be dissolved in the country's debt-servicing efforts. Yet Jamaican women are expected to conform to traditional gender norms in the labor market and in their homes. Where systems of race/color, class, and gender domination converge, then, we find that Afro-Jamaican women are burdened by unemployment, poverty, and household responsibilities, factors that lead large numbers of them into the informal work of higglering.

The Current Social and Economic Context of Higglering

Understanding the experiences of women must begin with an examination of the sociohistorical context in which they operate. In the case of Jamaican higglers, that context includes Jamaica's insertion into the global economy, where the colonial era positioned Jamaica as a disadvantaged player, contributed to the fragmentation of the country's economy into multiple sectors, and left behind complex social structures.

Jamaica is the largest of the English-speaking Caribbean islands. It is roughly 50 miles across from north to south and 150 miles long, with a population of about 2.3 million. The island came under European rule in 1494 when Christopher Columbus invaded St. Ann's Bay on the island's north coast on a fruitless search for gold. Jamaica soon became a rest spot and supply base for ships making their way to more profitable islands in the Caribbean. The Spanish presence proved fatal for the indigenous population, which rapidly declined because of diseases, war, and enslavement. By the time Jamaica came under British rule, the indigenous population had nearly vanished.

For more than three hundred years, from 1655 until independence on August 6, 1962, Jamaica was under British rule. Erna Brodber captures succinctly the British ethos that shaped that time: "A stratified society in which a race not its own was enslaved and driven labor was imposed on it so that wealth was produced, enough to be shared between self and native country, was the political formula that guided European life in Jamaica" (1989, 56). British colonial rulers achieved their general goal—to generate large profits for themselves and England—by producing sugar, the labor accomplished by enslaved Africans and later by indentured servants. Jamaica exported sugar and other raw materials to Britain and imported manufactured consumer and agricultural goods (Davies and Witter 1989). The British gave little thought to the economic development of Jamaica as a nation.

Throughout this period, Jamaica participated in the global economy as a disadvantaged player, since most if not all the wealth produced was used in the development of the British economy at the expense of the island's own economic advance. As a result, Jamaica found itself in a peripheral position in the global economy; its primary function then as now was to service the needs of dominant or core economies.

Over the last few decades, the Jamaican economy has taken a sharp downturn, contracting under the pressure of increasing debt. Today, Jamaica's debt burden is the fourth highest per capita in the world, its debt-to-GDP ratio close to 130 percent (CIA 2010). The destructive effects of structural adjustment policies that have undermined earlier solutions to urbanization and economic development weakened the purchasing power of local wages. Drastically curtailed public services and health and welfare programs have produced incredible hardships for Jamaicans, especially those from the lower classes (see Clarke and Howard 2006; Wyss and White 2004). The government's inability to rebuild its failing public school system has limited the traditional route to upward social mobility for most Jamaicans. Although the effects of these policies have been devastating for Jamaica's poor, the brown middle and upper classes have managed to maintain their privileged positions and have actually expanded in spite of structural adjustment (Clarke and Howard 2006, 109–14).

Of the many outcomes of Jamaica's debt crisis, two stand out: (1) the relatively high percentage of the population living below the poverty line, 14.8 percent (CIA 2010); and (2) the termination of many formal sector jobs, which has led to high unemployment, today roughly 14.5 percent.[18] This situation is particularly difficult for Jamaican women, who experience almost twice the level of unemployment (15.9 percent) of men (8.1 percent). The formal labor force of the total population is 46.6 percent. Among males fourteen years and older, 71.1 percent participate in the labor force; among females fourteen years and older, 55.1 percent participate.[19] These figures do not tell us the degree of participation by individuals in the labor force (e.g., seasonal employment, part time or full time) or participation in the informal economy. What they do suggest, however, is that the economy is seriously burdened by debt and that the people, particularly Jamaican women who experience twice the rate of unemployment of men, are struggling under its weight.

These constraints contribute to the rapidly expanding informal economy and women's involvement in it. Caribbean women's work activities occur at higher rates in the informal economy than in the formal economy, as they must earn or supplement (if there is another income earner in the home) their household incomes. In Jamaica, many women turn to higglering in response to such deteriorating economic conditions, limited formal employment options, and their role as the primary wage earner in their household (Bolles 1996; Durant-Gonzalez 1983; Harrison 1988; Joseph 1980; LeFranc 1989; Mason 1985–1986; Massiah 1986).

The informal economy provides opportunities for Afro-Jamaican women to earn a living in these dire economic circumstances. Many Afro-Jamaican women participate in a long tradition of higglering and have continued to play a dominant role in the internal marketing system of Jamaica today as they have since slavery. Women who participate in this kind of work are predominantly black and belong to the so-called lower classes—a pattern consistent with the gendered and racial division of labor structured in the colonial era.

Recently, however, Jamaican women from the working and middle classes have taken up higglering, primarily in its modern forms, which involve their traveling to countries like the United States to purchase items to be resold in the Jamaican informal economy. As members of the working and middle classes, these higglers are more racially mixed than their traditional counterparts, who are predominantly black. Brown middle-class women who engage in this kind of informal work tend to sell in more respectable areas of Kingston, mainly in their homes, offices, or government-established flea markets that cater to middle-class customers, while their lower-class counterparts sell primarily on the streets or in designated marketplaces and arcades. These brown middle-class women are not publicly imagined as higglers, despite the similarity of their informal work to that of black lower-class higglers.

It is within this social-economic-geographical context that I discuss in this book two groups of Afro-Jamaican higglers—market women and informal commercial importers. I examine both groups of female microentrepreneurs to compare their experiences in the informal economy of Jamaica. Specifically, I look at the extent to which the combined effects of race/color, class, and gender shape these women's public images, self-perceptions, and interactions with the state and local communities, and ways in which the women negotiate such complex realities.

My theoretical framework—embodied intersectionality—understands higglers as embodied subjects working in public spaces, as subjects who are multitextured and embedded in multiple intersecting hierarchies of power and whose actions, shaped as they are by interlocking categories of inequality, not only shape who they take themselves to be but also impact the very context in which they perform that identity. This approach allows us to get a better sense of these women's efforts in the informal economy, their joys and triumphs, and their tears and failures.

2

Higglering

A Woman's Domain?

> Social location matters.
> **IRENE BROWNE AND JOYA MISRA,**
> "The Intersection of Gender and Race in
> the Labor Market"

A first step toward complicating the analytical category "women's informal work" involves a close examination of higglering and its conceptualization as a woman's domain by scholars over the years because of the predominance of women engaged in this informal work—a pattern that can be traced back to West Africa, where African women have long played a central role in internal marketing systems (Beckles 2000a; Durant-Gonzalez 1985; LeFranc 1989; Simmonds 1987).[1] Yet as we will see, higglering in Jamaica is not simply a woman's domain, but the domain of a particular *kind* of woman: a lower-class black woman. Although this may seem a minor point, this is a critical distinction, because it illuminates ways in which local power structures operate in Jamaican society, contributing to the association of certain kinds of women with this type of work. This distinction reveals the combined effects of racial, class, and gender ideologies that inform how this work and its workers are publicly imagined and organized. Social location too matters in the labor market and larger society.

In this chapter I examine structural and ideological factors that contribute to the formation of higglering as a lower-class black woman's domain. Three main sources inform my discussion: direct observations of two markets, two arcades, and a flea market in Kingston; in-depth interviews with forty-five higglers; and an analysis of the literature on slave higglering in Jamaica.

The Business of Higglering

As the Jamaican economy continues to contract under unprecedented levels of debt and restructuring, its citizens—particularly women—bear the brunt of its effects, including higher levels of poverty and unemployment. Poverty, unemployment, and established gender norms that require women to be responsible for taking care of their households are a few of the factors that lead many women into the informal economy and the business of higglering.[2]

Most of the sellers in the markets and arcades I observed in Kingston were women, consistent with earlier research on higglers and confirmation of popular representations of higglering as a woman's domain. Upon closer examination, however, I noticed that black women in particular engaged in higglering. Notably absent were women from other ethnic and racial/color groups, such as Chinese, Lebanese, brown or white women (see Figures 1 and 2).

British economist Melvin R. Edwards made similar observations decades ago in his study on Jamaican higglers and raised the following questions: "How is it, we must ask, that Chinese and Indians who migrated to Jamaica, Guyana, Surinam and Trinidad in large numbers

FIGURE 1. Market scene in downtown Kingston.
(Copyright Boris Kester/ *www.traveladventures.org*.)

between 1880 and 1920, have not emerged as significantly in this area of enterprise? Or how is it that the Jews and Arabs who came as refugees to the region from the Middle East at the end of both world wars, have not been noticed in this category?" (1980, 16). Edwards's questions are significant, given that in Jamaica trading has long been an accepted and effective means of upward social and economic mobility for ethnic minorities. The history of Lebanese immigrants, for example, is rich with stories of their ancestors' engagement in petty trading as the genesis of their upward social and economic mobility in Jamaican society. Why, then, are they not represented in the business of higglering?

Edwards suggests that, in addition to economic variables, factors such as immigrants' knowledge of available opportunities in the region, the tendency of Caribbean nations to bestow on immigrant groups better opportunities for economic advancement than long-term residents, stubborn retention of family customs, and traditional entrepreneurial orientations among immigrants may contribute to their upward social and economic mobility. Although I agree with Edwards that these factors are indeed at work, the successes of ethnic immigrants in the Caribbean are not only the characteristics found in their communities or their relationships with host countries; they are also shaped, in large part, by local

FIGURE 2. Woman selling fruits and vegetables on the sidewalk in downtown Kingston. (Copyright Boris Kester/ *www.traveladventures.org*.)

power structures. By this I mean, the absence of various racialized/ethnic groups from certain segments of the labor market today is the result, in part, of a racialized/ethnic (and gendered) division of labor in Jamaica that originated in the nation's plantation societies.

The higglers I interviewed confirmed my observations of the labor patterns in the markets and arcades. When specifically asked to identify the number of Chinese, Lebanese, brown, or white women they've observed higglering, almost all the higglers reported not seeing any.[3] These responses are significant, given that many of these women have been higglering since they accompanied their mothers and grandmothers to markets as children. Their responses suggest that the racialized/ethnic labor patterns I observed at the markets and arcades were not aberrations but embedded in the business of higglering.

When I probed further on this issue, I found the higglers' responses interesting. For instance, in her open-ended response, one market woman stated: "I haven't seen any Chinese women higglering; they are mostly in the shops. I haven't seen any whites either; they are mostly in the clothes business" (#1). This market woman's open-ended response was supported by an informal commercial importer (ICI), who stated: "Chinese people get the breaks, they get the shops" (#25). Other higglers gave similar responses, such as that the Chinese, browns, or whites "sell in stores that's rented," "they own the stores," and "they have their own business enterprises." One market woman explicitly stated that the Chinese do not sell at her work site "because of the location," which in this case was the public market at Papine in uptown Kingston, an area historically occupied by black market women. These higglers identified the spatial location of racial/ethnic groups in the economy: Chinese and Lebanese Jamaicans are overrepresented in the formal economy and are not found higglering.

Chinese Jamaicans are dominant actors in the retail grocery and banking sectors of the formal economy in Jamaica; families and individuals own restaurants, bakeries, and supermarket chains. Their predominance in the retail grocery sector dates to the nineteenth century, when large groups of Chinese immigrants arrived in Jamaica as indentured servants to replace newly emancipated slaves on sugar plantations. After a brief stay on the plantations, these immigrants created an economic niche for themselves in the grocery retail business, setting up shops all across the island. They eventually expanded their businesses into large enterprises, which facilitated their rise into the middle class (Anderson and Lee 2005; Wilson 2004).

Lebanese Jamaicans are currently giants in retail, tourism, horse racing, and the industry and manufacturing sectors of the formal economy. Their predominance in commercial activities can be traced to the late nineteenth and early twentieth centuries, when they arrived from the Middle East as refugees fleeing religious persecution. Many went into the banana industry, but as it began to decline around the beginning of the twentieth century, they turned to petty trading, peddling goods from door to door. Large numbers of these immigrants eventually were able to advance from peddling to building retail stores (Sherlock and Bennett 1998).

Despite their humble beginnings in Jamaican society and smaller number in relation to the large black population, the two immigrant groups and their descendants have achieved greater upward social and economic mobility than most Afro-Jamaicans. Today, Chinese and Lebanese Jamaicans are disproportionately represented among Jamaica's brown and white economic elite. The ascension of these groups, however, is not solely the result of their economic ventures but also of a confluence of racial and economic factors. When these immigrants arrived in Jamaica, the nation was already organized, as it is now, into a multitiered, triangular racialized class structure with a small white planter elite at the apex, a brown or colored middle sector, and a large black poor sector at the bottom. Shortly after their arrival, these immigrants quickly occupied, or were placed in, an intermediate position in Jamaica's racial structure, above the large black population, a placement that helped reinforce racial polarity between the small white elite and the black poor masses.

For example, Walton Look Lai (2005) investigated images of the Chinese during the nineteenth-century indenture period in the Caribbean and demonstrated that many colonial elites perceived and treated Chinese immigrants as a racial buffer group between whites and blacks, which helped the white minority group create greater social distance between themselves and the majority black and colored population, and helped reinforce white cultural and economic superiority. I would add that the placement of the Chinese in an intermediate position in the colonial racial hierarchy also benefited this group, since their placement, along with their distinctive ethnic culture, helped distance Chinese immigrants socially from the large black population and shielded them from the kinds of racial discrimination and degradation that blacks struggled against. As a racial buffer group, the Chinese had greater access to privileges associated with the brown/colored population than did blacks. As they became more upwardly mobile, many Chinese immigrants assimilated into the colored middle class, reinforcing their social distance from blacks.

Although Chinese immigrants encountered discrimination in Caribbean societies throughout the colonial era, their ability to develop and nurture ethnic enclaves in host countries while maintaining cultural ties with their homeland allowed them to become independent of white-owned businesses and banks, circumventing local (white) economic power structures by borrowing from their own communities at home and abroad. As the Chinese began to generate wealth as a result of their economic ventures, and as their culture became creolized through their intermixing with racial and ethnic groups from the higher classes (especially browns and whites), they became more integrated into the colored/brown middle class. Their ascension into the colonial racialized class system, then, was the result not solely of their economic ventures but also of their racial placement in colonial society.

The ascension of Lebanese immigrants into the colonial hierarchy in the Caribbean is similarly the result of both economic and racial factors. Lebanese immigrants were not part of the indenture system but followed the established Jewish community, becoming merchants and traders, which eventually brought them wealth (Sherlock and Bennett 1998, 334). For example, the Issas, a social and economically powerful family on the island, can trace their origins to the 1890s, when their ancestors owned dry-goods and haberdashery stores. Other Middle Eastern families had ancestors who owned import/export houses (Douglass 1992; Reid 1977). As was true for the Chinese, ethnic and racial distinctions were made between Lebanese immigrants and the larger black population in the colonial racial/color system. Although not part of the white planter elite, Lebanese immigrants occupied the lower segments of white society. Their placement in the racial hierarchy helped reinforce the polarization between whites and the large black masses. The economic successes of these immigrants in petty trading and eventually in the retail and manufacturing sectors further integrated them into the white upper classes.

The transformation of the Jamaican economy in the post–World War II era from agriculture (mainly bananas) to manufacturing further solidified the positions of Chinese and Lebanese immigrants as economic elites.[4] As the agricultural sector declined, the manufacturing sector grew, which in turn stimulated the development of the construction and commercial segments of the economy (Phillips 1977, 6). The decline of agriculture shifted the economic power of the white agro-elite, making way for the ascendance of a new economic elite. This new economic elite consists of minority ethnic groups—Jews, local whites, Lebanese/Syrians, and Chinese—and is mainly dispersed among twenty-one families and their interests groups (Reid 1977, 15).

According to Stanley Reid: "The emergence of the present elite and its ability to maintain an independent economic base and thus secure its hegemony was related to its ownership of land and its control of the distribution trade through import/export agencies and commission houses" (1977, 17). Minority ethnic groups had already played a dominant role in commercial activities as well as import/export trade in the post-emancipation era, and members of prominent Jewish families had owned large acreages since the seventeenth century. When the agricultural sector declined after World War II, large acreages that had grown sugar and bananas became available for those who could purchase them, and minority ethnic groups whose wealth was already growing took advantage of this opportunity.

The new economic elite, including the Chinese and the Lebanese/Syrians, further solidified their privileged position via their influence in the political sphere, exercised on the state level through governmental and executive positions they sought and occupied (Phillips 1977). For instance, in 1956 six of ten members of the Agricultural Development Corporation, including the chair and vice chair, were representatives of these groups, as were five of nine members of the Banana Board who were among the largest operators of banana holdings on the island (Phillips 1977, 9). Through these positions and many others in the government, this group successfully shaped policies in ways that served their best economic interests. "The net effect of these patterns was the exclusion of views of some of the more deprived and powerless sections of the population from the policy-making forums" (ibid.).

The privileged positions of this group was also solidified and protected through social networking and marriage patterns. Endogamy was an effective strategy the group used to secure family wealth, and exclusive clubs served as an informal means of networking and information sharing among its members (Douglass 1992; Reid 1977). Additionally, family members used their privileged positions to strategically place their heirs in important roles in their own corporations as well as in the government. Indeed, kinship ties correlated with and facilitated corporate and political ties. Through these means the minority ethnic group was able to wield significant influence in the economy and the state and to exclude others, especially black Jamaicans, from these centers of economic and political power. In the end, these strategies help concentrate power in the hands of this minority group, excluding the large black population (Reid 1977).

These strategies and patterns of inequality have persisted. Although a younger generation of minority elites is more inclined than the older to marry outside the confines of the twenty-one families, patterns of exclusion continue to reproduce color/class/gender hierarchies (Douglass 1992). The brown economic elite continue to wield significant economic and political power in Jamaica today, despite an expanding black professional class that occupies a larger role in the state. (From 1992 to 2006, Jamaica was under the leadership of its first publicly identified black prime minister.) Yet the black professional class has limited economic power; the economy continues to be dominated by the brown economic elite (Robotham 2000).

To be sure, the privileged positions of Chinese and Lebanese immigrants vis-à-vis black Jamaicans do not negate their ongoing struggle against ethnic tensions, discrimination, and anti-immigration policies at various moments in Caribbean history. My point is that the current position of these ethnic minorities as part of the economic elite, where they have significant economic, social, and political power—and, as one ICI puts it, "get better treatment and get the breaks" (#38)—is not solely the result of their individual initiatives in the economy. It is also structural, tied to a colonial legacy of race/color and class stratification, and the unequal distribution of power and resources in the society.

Slave Higglering

Although Chinese and Lebanese immigrants were able to create niches for themselves in the retail sector of colonial economies, higglering has been the reserve of black Jamaicans, especially black Jamaican women. These labor patterns have structural origins dating to the slave era, when the Jamaican rural economy adopted a plantation model for the production of sugar, with slaves imported first from the Eastern Caribbean and later from Africa as its primary labor force. Jamaican plantations rapidly expanded; by 1789 the approximate ratio of slaves to whites was 11 to 1 (Stinchcombe 1995). Plantation owners and managers had two options for feeding the increasing population of slaves on rural plantations: either have slaves produce as much of their own food as possible, or import all food for slaves, thus raising the cost of maintaining their plantations. Plantation owners chose the first option—a decision that would have lasting effects on the structure of the Jamaican economy.

On the plantations, slaves were given small provision grounds, plots of land deemed unsuitable for sugar planting at some distance and set apart agriculturally from the small patches of land located around the houses of slaves. On these plots, slave subsistence production was largely unsupervised. On designated days, slaves planted food and raised small livestock for their own consumption; they were allowed to sell their surplus goods in the towns on Sundays in designated areas known as "Sunday markets" (Beckles 1989, 1999; Berlin and Morgan 1993; Bush 1990; Mintz 1989).

This arrangement benefited both plantation owners and slaves. Plantation owners saved on the cost of feeding their slaves and were comforted by the thought—or hope—that slaves would be less likely to desert the plantations or to revolt because of their investments in their plots of land.[5] Slaves, on the other hand, enjoyed the benefits of not only producing and selling their own food with minimal supervision, but also earning a small income that they were allowed to keep. With this income slaves could improve their nutrition by supplementing their diet, which generally consisted of highly starched and poorly nutritious foods, with the occasional meat and vegetables. Some slaves also used their income to purchase medicines and thus were able to improve somewhat the quality of their and their families' health through their cultivation and marketing activities (Beckles 1989, 1999, Berlin and Morgan 1993; Mintz 1989).

But perhaps most importantly, slaves benefited from this arrangement because it afforded them the opportunity to create a life and identity for themselves outside the oppressive slave system. Slave marketers enjoyed limited freedom in the Sunday markets, where they traded with town residents and socialized with slaves from other plantations. These markets became important sites where slaves could exercise some agency beyond the gaze of their slaveholders; slaves thus struggled to protect this arrangement. As Hilary Beckles notes: "Marketing symbolized the spirit of independence, and was central to the process of non-violent protest and resistance which characterized day-to-day anti-slavery behavior" (1989, 73).

It is within this economic arrangement that the Jamaican higgler or huckster emerges as a central figure. According to Lorna Simmonds: "by the latter part of the 18th century, the internal marketing system was a well-entrenched part of the Jamaican economy, dominated by rural slave provision producers and urban slave hucksters" (1987, 32). These higglers were primarily slave women who sold a variety of dry goods, provisions, handicrafts, and baked items. They obtained products from slaves on surrounding plantations, some located in remote areas, and brought them to town to sell in the Sunday markets; they were thus a principal means by which slave producers could move their goods from rural provision grounds to urban marketplaces. Some higglers also sold products for their owners, bringing an additional income for slaveholders who lived in the country as well as in the towns (Higman 1995; Welch 2003).

Although missionaries often deplored Sunday markets for violating the laws of the Sabbath, they continued to grow. Several marketplaces were established, maintained, and formalized under the British government, and new laws that acknowledged and protected the rights of slaves to market regulated the kinds of meat they could sell, the weighing of meats, occasions of sale, and market days. Despite these regulations, slaves monopolized the internal marketing system and "one century after the first legal Jamaican market was created, slaves had made a place for themselves in the free economic activity of the country which would never thereafter be challenged" (Mintz 1989, 201).

The independent slave production and marketing systems inadvertently fragmented the plantation economy into formal, semi-informal, and informal segments. The formal segment rested primarily on the plantation system and slave labor, both of which were heavily regulated by plantation owners and the colonial government. Sugar production and export were dominant features of the formal economy and the profits generated remained in the hands of plantation owners, who lived either on the island or abroad. The formal labor force—slaves—was heavily regulated in this segment of the economy: labor was organized on the plantation according to the needs of the owners, and slaves produced what and when they were told to. This formal segment of the plantation economy predominated, yet at the same time patterns of cultivation and marketing developed largely outside the demands of the formal segment, either with the cooperation of plantation owners or, in many cases, without it (Beckles 1989, 1999; Berlin and Morgan 1993; Higman 1984; Mintz 1989).

The unsupervised cultivation and marketing of produce by slaves gave rise to the semi-informal and informal segments of the plantation economy. The slave system of cultivation was largely unsupervised by plantation owners, and the colonial government's regulations were few;

these regulated the weighing of meats, designated spaces where marketing could occur, and allowed slaves to market only on Sundays. Slaves determined the kinds of produce to be sold and set their own prices.[6] Indeed, slaves had complete monopoly over the operations of the Sunday markets (Mintz 1989; Beckles 1999; Bush 1990).

The colonial government created laws that restricted the movement of slaves in society and ensured their obedience to their owners. But these laws did not restrict activities associated with marketing or higglering, as evidenced in the following excerpt from a law enacted in 1807: "No slave, such as only excepted as are going with firewood, grass, fruit provisions, or small stock and other goods, which they may lawfully sell, to market, and returning therefrom, shall here after be suffered or permitted to go out of his or her master or owner's plantation or settlement, or to travel from one town or place to another, unless such slave shall have a ticket from his master, owner, employer or overseer" (quoted in Mintz 1989, 205–6). The law thus officially recognized slave marketing or higglering and allowed slaves some concessions regarding their movements and activities associated with the market.

Despite the official recognition of the slave markets, these economic activities were not held accountable to the government regulations that applied to local (formal) merchants. Slaves were not taxed, they were not forced to acquire licenses to operate their businesses, nor did they have to pay market fees. Requiring such obligations of slaves would be tantamount to officially recognizing them as free agents capable of entering into binding contractual relations. Such a concession would undermine the system of slavery. In an interesting way, then, the enslaved status of slaves freed them from certain government regulations associated with marketing, allowing them access to the internal marketing system different from that afforded formal businesspersons.

The marketing activities of slaves were both semi-informal and informal. They were semi-informal in that the colonial government marginally regulated these activities, yet they were informal in the sense that slave cultivation and price decisions occurred outside government regulatory structures. Additionally, some of the products slaves sold they acquired through informal means. For instance, there have been numerous claims by slaveholders of slaves taking livestock from plantations to sell in the markets without the owner's permission (Beckles 1999).

The Jamaican plantation economy, then, was not monolithic; its segments were intricately connected. Slave markets, as part of the semi-informal and informal segments of the plantation economy, supported modern capitalist accumulation by providing goods and services at low cost to formal workers (slaves) and to plantation owners who regularly shopped in the markets for local food. In fact, slave provision grounds and markets helped sustain the formal labor force, because plantation owners left the responsibility for them to the slaves. The semiformal and informal segments also offered formal urban merchants off-the-books suppliers of items for export. Many urban merchants established a commercial relationship with slave producers who provided them with items such as turmeric, cow's horn, oil nuts, and goatskins for foreign markets. The semi-informal and informal slave economy, then, was an integral part of the British capitalist enterprise.

The Division of Plantation Labor

In addition to fragmenting the slave economy into multiple segments, the plantation system sorted people into a distinct hierarchy. Slavery shaped social relations not only between plantation owners and slaves, and slaves and freemen, but also between men and women, and whites and nonwhites (Bush 1990; Higman 1995). One area where this arrangement applied was on the plantations, where a racial and gendered division of labor was developed for the purpose of disciplining the laboring bodies of slaves to maximize slave productivity. Although it had always existed in the slave system, the disciplining of slave bodies took on great importance after 1807 with the abolition of the slave trade, which drastically reduced the importation of slaves. Between 1807 and emancipation in 1834 and 1838, slaveholders faced the challenge of maximizing output of slave labor with a relatively fixed number of slaves, and this contributed to the intensification of disciplinary measures against slaves (Higman 1995).

The laboring bodies of slaves were disciplined in at least two ways, through physical coercion, and through the organization of social and physical space. Slaveholders devised numerous kinds of physical punishment, including rape, to discipline slaves. Conceptualized as slaveholders' property, the bodies of slaves were whipped, tortured, and exploited at will and molded into a work regimen that suited the capitalist demand of a rationalized system of production. But it is to the second disciplinary mechanism, the organization of space, that I turn our attention.

On the plantations, slave bodies were partitioned and ranked in order to increase slave productivity and to maximize output. According to Barry Higman: "The master saw the allocation of slaves to particular tasks as being determined by their sex, age, color, birthplace, and state of health, so that he was forced to make a compromise between the demand for labour on his property and the characteristics of the available slave population" (1995, 187–88). Skilled artisans and drivers formed the slave elite, and then, in rank order, "domestic servants, the slaves involved in more menial 'ancillary' tasks such as washer women, the field labourers, the children's gangs and the 'unemployable,' sick or superannuated" (Bush 1990, 34).

In addition to division by skill level and age, the slave labor force was stratified by gender and race. Barbara Bush (1985, 1990) explains, for instance, that the elite segment of the slave labor structure consisted primarily of men; enslaved women, for the most part, were restricted to the lower ranks. Elite slaves were predominantly not only male but also colored, since most slaveholders believed that colored slaves "should not be employed in field labour and that they should be given preference in the training of tradesmen, 'the flower of the slave population,'" according to Higman, who adds that "colored slaves were also given preference in the appointment of headmen, except that the 'drivers' of the field slaves were generally black" (1995, 189). Enslaved black women, relegated to the lower levels of the slave labor force, were disproportionately assigned to field work, while most domestic slaves were colored/Creole women.[7]

A clear racialized division of labor among women on Caribbean plantations reserved the most privileged and least labor-intensive occupations for white women, and the least privileged and most labor-intensive occupations for black women. As wives, mothers, and house managers of domestic slaves, white women were discouraged from engaging in economic activities and physical labor on the plantations, their activities confined to the home. In the middle sector were colored women—the product of miscegenation—many of whom were domestic slaves and enjoyed social privileges that their black/African counterparts did not, including domestic work, often perceived as a more prestigious occupation among slaves than the backbreaking labor of field work. Although a disproportionate number of female domestic slaves were colored, their position was often precarious, in that many faced the constant threat of rape and of banishment to the fields as punishment. At the bottom of the labor scale was the mass of black/African women whose productive and reproductive labor served as the engine of the plantation economy. These women were subjected to the most labor-intensive work in the fields alongside enslaved men and were punished by similar methods. They were also the primary food producers and distributors of goods to slave communities (Bush 1990; Massiah 1986).

More colored than black slaves were concentrated in urban areas (Higman 1995; Welch 2003). As Leonard Broom explains in his classic essay on social differentiation in Jamaica, "colored slaves were more often than blacks employed in domestic, urban, and entrepreneurial activities (e.g., as peddlers) where they could acquire the prerequisite skills for further mobility" (1954, 118). More female than male slaves worked in urban centers, to a large extent because of the practice in British colonial towns of female-on-female slavery: most slaveholders in the towns were white (and some colored) women, who generally owned more female than male slaves (Beckles 1998; Welch 2003). The slave labor structure, then, was quite complex. Its fragmentation by race, gender, age, skill, and urban/rural distinctions spatially disbursed bodies into certain segments of the economy and also helped reproduce white domination socially, spatially, and economically.

The multiple distinctions in Caribbean slave societies between and among women were used to justify the exploitation of black women's labor while preserving white privilege. These distinctions were fueled by stereotypes of black women's bodies as physically capable of hard labor and in many ways indistinguishable from black male bodies: "The supposedly strong physical and muscular build of African women provided a perfect rationale for their economic exploitation on slave plantations. The "corporeal equality of the sexes" among black people became a firmly entrenched notion amongst European observers, enduring well into the nineteenth century" (1990, 14–15).

Numerous texts by white men and women in this period describe black women as lacking "feminine" qualities and as having a natural capacity for hard labor. While black women's bodies were viewed as indistinguishable from black men's, they were marked as physically different from white women by, among other things, their supposed "'feminine harshness of feature' and 'robustness of form'" (15).

There were numerous depictions of black women's "aggressive carriage" and "sturdiness" in plantation discourses. Black women were often depicted as "Amazons" who could "drop children at will, work without recuperation, manipulate at ease the physical environment of the sugar estate and be more productive than men." These depictions of black women's bodies were used to naturalize socially created conceptions of difference, marking them as intrinsic and permanent. In the end, field work and other physically taxing, unskilled labor, including higglering, became associated with the "essential nature of blacks" (Beckles 1999, 10).

In contrast, most slaveholders believed that brown/colored women were physically incapable of field work. As Higman explains, the masters "had strong convictions about the capacities for labour of people of color. The greater the infusion of white blood, the weaker the slave was thought to be" (1995, 208). On several plantations, some colored men and women were manumitted and replaced by black slaves because their presumed incapacity to engage in field work made them liabilities to plantation owners (ibid.). Although we can find some colored slaves working alongside black slaves on plantations (Beckles 2000c), because brown women were the children of white planters and enslaved black women, their lighter skins in a society heavily coded by race/color and their spatial location in the rural plantation labor structure as domestics allowed them to differentiate themselves from black field slaves.

The perceptions of black and brown women's bodies not only justified their relegation to field and domestic labor, but also protected white elite women, as we have seen, consigning them to the home. Generally, white women's bodies were viewed as markedly different from those of white men and black and colored women. In accordance with European ideals of womanhood, white women's feminine bodies along with their white blood marked them as unsuitable physically and socially for physical labor, especially field work. This perception was applied to white women of all classes and restricted their activities in the labor market and the economy, which left many economically dependent upon men. An important consequence of this socially created differentiation of white or colored women's bodies and labor from black women's is the tendency to link "images of down-trodden labour directly to black skin" (Beckles 1999, 29).

Distinctions between black and colored women's bodies and those of white women also justified the sexual exploitation by white men of black and colored women. The supposed physical and moral inferiority of black and colored women relegated them to the role of concubine. When compared with white women's bodies, the bodies of black and colored women—inferior and tainted—deemed them unsuitable for marriage; leaving that privilege for women whose white bodies ensured the presumed purity and superiority of the white race (Petley 2005). All these distinctions among women contributed to the organization of Caribbean slave society; according to Lucille Mathurin Mair, "the black woman produced, . . . the brown woman served and the white woman consumed" (quoted in Beckles 1999, xv).

After emancipation, this race/color, class, and gendered division of labor lingered. Many black women continued to work in public marketplaces or in urban areas as domestics (see Chapter 3); Indian women introduced as indentured laborers in the emancipation era replaced or supplemented the black female agricultural labor force; Chinese women moved into small family-owned and -operated grocery and retail shops; colored women dominated the hotel industry and moved into teaching and nursing; and lower-class white women moved into clerical positions in commerce and banking, as well as into retail sales (Massiah 1986). Variations of this labor pattern continued to shape opportunities for upward social mobility for many Jamaicans well into the postindependence era (Girvan 1981; Gordon 1991).

Although many Afro-Jamaicans have achieved significant upward social mobility after Jamaica's independence in 1962, racial and class structures still organize the labor force in varying degrees, especially for black women. Black/Afro-Jamaican women continue to dominate public markets today as they did during the periods of slavery and postemancipation. Brown and white women continue to dominate in formal businesses and, as one market woman puts it, "get the shops." In the formal economy, Jamaican blacks tend to be concentrated in low-paying, low-status jobs (Gordon 1991). This is especially problematic for Afro-Jamaican women, who tend to be relegated to the lowest levels of this sector with the lowest pay—in the teaching and health professions and in midlevel white-collar occupations and low-level service jobs such as private domestic work (Davies and Anderson 1989). These occupations are usually the first to be terminated by the government in its attempt to restructure the failing economy, leaving large numbers of black/Afro-Jamaican women unemployed and pushing the poorest of them into the informal economy.

All this suggests that to understand current labor patterns of black/Afro-Jamaican women, it is essential to note how historically created racial and class structures and cultural ideologies narrow the range of occupations for them in the formal economy, limit their chances of finding and securing adequate employment, and force many into microentrepreneurship.[8] These structural and cultural factors contribute to the overrepresentation of black women in public markets and arcades, as many turn to higglering to support themselves and their families. An examination of the sociohistorical factors around higglering helps clarify how limited the options are for black women in the formal economy, which explains their larger numbers engaged in higglering in comparison to women of other racialized groups.

Brown Women and Higglering

One might assume that the racial makeup of the Jamaican population, with an overwhelming majority—about 90 percent—of African descent, accounts for the overrepresentation of black women higglering. If this were the case, we would see a similar racial distribution of women in other areas where higglering activities occur, such as in the flea market; that is, there would be a disproportionate number of black Jamaican women working at the flea market. My observations, however, did not support this hypothesis.

I observed the Small Business Association of Jamaica Family Market (commonly known as the Lady Musgrave Flea Market, in part because of its location on Lady Musgrave Road), a popular weekly Sunday flea market in New Kingston. Many vendors in this flea market engaged in activities similar to higglering in the arcades where items are purchased abroad and sold. At this site there was roughly an even number of men and women vendors, who primarily sold items acquired from the United States such as apples, grapes, Bounty paper towels, Charmin toilet tissue, cans of olive oil, Ocean Spray cranberry juice, Tide laundry soap, and Downy fabric softener. Others sold stationery, pens, bath crystals, body lotions, and artificial flowers. Many vendors sold their items in bulk at wholesale prices.

What is particularly interesting about the vendors in this market is their racial/ethnic makeup. Almost 40 percent of the sellers were brown (with a significant representation of Chinese women in this group), one was Indian, and the rest were black, as opposed to Coronation and Papine Markets and People's and Constant Spring Arcades where all the vendors were black. Many of the Lady Musgrave Flea Market's brown vendors were small-business owners; at the arcades and Papine Market, the vendors were microentrepreneurs. The small-business owners, of a different class status than microentrepreneurs, could sell high-ticket foreign items in bulk at wholesale prices; the microentrepreneurs at the flea market sold low-ticket clothing and shoes at affordable retail prices. They also sold imitation-designer clothing such as Tommy Hilfiger, Gucci, and FUBU, and dance-hall-style clothing such as batty riders that are principally worn by black urban youth.[9]

The makeup of the vendors in the flea market and arcades illuminated a confluence of class and race/color. The small-business owners I observed selling in bulk were largely Chinese and brown; the microentrepreneurs selling imitation designer clothing were black. The items sold in the flea market represented the cultural tastes of the upper and lower classes, those sold by the brown women appealing primarily to the brown middle and upper classes, those sold by the black women appealing to the black working and lower class.

What was more striking, however, was that despite the fact that their work closely resembled that of the black informal commercial importers (ICIs), the brown sellers at the flea market were not constructed as higglers in the Jamaican public imagination, and thus were shielded from the stigmas associated with this informal economic activity and were able to reproduce racialized class distinctions between themselves and higglers. They created these distinctions through the products they sold, the customers they interacted with, and the physical space of the flea market.

Brown Women and Their Customers

Like the vendors, the customers I observed at the Lady Musgrave Flea Market were racially mixed, with a significant number of Chinese shoppers. They also appeared to belong to the upper and middle classes, their status indicated by the luxury cars they drove (BMWs, SUVs, and Lexuses), the designer clothes they wore, their jewelry and cellular phones, and their speech patterns.[10] One of the customers was a public figure and media personality who was shopping with his family. The middle- and upper-class brown customers did not buy clothing from the black vendors but purchased items such as Charmin tissues, olive oil, and stationery from the brown vendors.[11] This observation is consistent with Douglass's study on the Jamaican elite family, in which she argues that the middle and upper classes shopped for clothing, shoes, and jewelry at the row of plazas above New Kingston and in Liguanea, both located in uptown Kingston, instead of acquiring them from street vendors. Many also shop in New York and Miami (1992, 69).

My observations revealed that color and class distinctions and hierarchies were reproduced among the women at the Lady Musgrave Flea Market, evidenced by the kinds of products these women sold and consequently the customers they attracted. The items, both of which symbolized their membership in particular racial/color and class groups, and their participation in specific cultures. As Douglass argues, although Jamaicans do not talk about race, "they tend to gravitate to others who are like themselves in making friends, establishing business relationships and especially in the processes of constituting family" (1992, 8).

As members of the brown middle class, the brown vendors knew the cultural tastes of their group, which influenced their choices of products to sell. It is no accident, for instance, that the brown women did not sell batty riders, symbols of a lower-class black culture they view as "vulgar" (Cooper 1994); members of the respectable brown middle class do not desire batty riders, nor do brown vendors sell them. The products they do sell precipitated their sustained interactions with customers of similar race/color and class in the flea market and reproduced their own class/color identity and status.[12] This interaction in turn reinforced a racial and class social and spatial boundary between themselves and the black women in the flea market, even though the brown women were engaged in similar informal work at the same site. By reproducing this boundary, those brown middle-class vendors were able to shield themselves from the stigmas associated with their informal work.

I do not argue that the social and spatial boundaries between the brown and black vendors were intentionally produced. They are in large part the result of existing structural arrangements and social relations. The privileged positions of the brown middle-class women gave them access to the cultural preferences of their group as well as the economic means by which they could cater to them. Their class privileges intersected with other privileges that produced dimensions of empowerment for this group and reinforced a hierarchal structure between it and other groups, in this case the black women in the flea market.

Additionally, the physical space of the Lady Musgrave Flea Market catered to upper- and middle-class sensibilities, as opposed to the targeted customers of public markets and arcades. First, the stall fees at the flea market were higher on average than those at the markets and arcades.[13] The more costly stalls prevented large numbers of lower-class women from working there, reserving this space for the economically privileged. The atmosphere of the market also catered to the upper and middle classes. Soca and gospel music played in the background, no yelling or cursing (behaviors usually associated with the lower classes) could be heard, the vendors and customers used standard Jamaican English, the market was very clean, and there was visible security (armed police officers) at this site.[14] I did not observe this type of atmosphere at the arcades or markets, where many higglers often complained to me about the unclean and unsanitary conditions, as well as the lack of security. Dance-hall music often played at the markets and arcades, where I heard loud patois, which was sometimes peppered with cursing.

What is significant here is the physical context in which this kind of higglering was conducted. In the public imagination, black and lower class are often associated with the unclean or dirty, vulgarity, and impropriety, while brown and middle class are often associated with cleanliness and decency, discursive constructions mapped onto the physical sites at which particular kinds of higglering occur. For the brown women who engaged in higglering at the flea market, status was reinforced by the clean, heavily protected, and respectable physical environment. For the black ICIs and market women in my study, the dirty, unprotected, and indecent environment reinforced their status as black and lower class.[15]

Structures of race/color and class, then, influenced the practices of higglering at the flea market, arcades, and public markets: what kinds of women sold there (Chinese and brown women at the flea market versus black women at the arcades and markets); the physical environment in which they sold; what they sold (high ticket versus low-ticket items, batty riders versus olive oil), whom they sold to, and how they sold (in bulk or at retail prices). These structures, then, helped reproduce social and spatial boundaries between middle- and lower-class, brown and black higglers and reinforced the position of lower-class black women at the lowest levels of the stratification system.

Black Women and Their Customers

When I asked the ICIs and market women in my study to describe their customers, both groups of higglers reported serving a mixed clientele with variations in class and gender. It was difficult to get them to talk in detail about the color of their customers, but most higglers reported serving a primarily black working-class and poor clientele.[16] Most of the ICIs who worked in the People's Arcade in downtown Kingston described their customers as primarily black, and all reported their customers as working class and poor (I observed their customers as well). One ICI described the buying patterns of the brown middle class and the black lower class: "Ghetto people buy here everyday; rich people buy uptown!" (#35). An ICI working at the Constant Spring Arcade in uptown Kingston explained that no Chinese or whites come there to shop because "this is black people area" (#24). The market women at Papine, however, reported a greater racial/color mix among their customers. I also observed this.

As with the women at the flea market, the differences in the types of customers served by the ICIs and market women can be attributed to the kinds of products they sell. At Papine, the market women sold fresh produce from neighboring farms, whereas the ICIs sold clothing and shoes (among other things) they imported from abroad. As discussed earlier, members of the brown middle and upper classes are likely to purchase their clothes from the boutiques in uptown plazas, from shopping malls, or from abroad when they travel. They are less likely to purchase clothing from ICIs or other street vendors, because this practice would contradict the image of uptown living.

The brown middle and upper classes, however, are more willing to buy fresh produce from the market women at Papine.[17] Buying fresh fruits and vegetables from market women does not carry the same symbolism for the middle and upper classes as buying clothing at the arcades. That is to say, ground provisions do not carry the same weight of social status as clothing; they are readily available to any Jamaican, irrespective of color and class. Most of the food is associated with the natural resources of Jamaica—the ackee, bananas, callaloo, yams, and coconuts.[18] Consuming these distinctly Jamaican foods is, on some levels, a performance of one's national identity; they are among the ties that bind us as Jamaicans. Clothing, however, is one means of illuminating class and status differences among Jamaicans, and so members of the middle and upper classes are more discriminating in where they purchase them.

The products sold by the ICIs catered to a predominantly black, lower-class, urban culture. When asked what influenced their choices of items to sell, more than half of the ICIs named their customers' needs or "what is in fashion" as primary factors. As was true of the brown women at the flea market, the position of the black lower-class ICIs gives them access to the cultural desires of their specific group and the economic means to fulfill those desires. These women are tuned in to the cultural needs of the clients they serve and choose their products accordingly; many sold clothing that symbolized dance-hall culture, in addition to imitation-designer clothing such as Tommy Hilfiger, Gucci, and FUBU.

It is significant that the ICIs select these brands (although imitations) instead of Abercrombie and Fitch or J. Crew, brands associated with white U.S. youth culture. Their choices have less to do with the availability of these items in the U.S. informal markets than with what these clothes symbolize for their predominantly black urban customers. Hilfiger, Gucci, and FUBU clothing represents black U.S. hip-hop culture. These brands became popular among black Americans when hip-hop artists such as Biggie Smalls, LL Cool J, and Lil' Kim began wearing them. In these artists' view, these clothes symbolize high (social and class) status and by wearing them, one positions him/herself among a black elite. Lower-class black, urban Jamaican youth embrace hip-hop culture. Despite the fact that these young people are unable to afford the original designer clothing the hip-hop artists wear, the ICIs provide a means by which they can construct themselves as part of a transnational black elite group through the designer imitations.

This is also true for dance-hall culture: the ICIs provide black urban poor youth a means by which they can participate in the construction of themselves as part of this black culture. Black women, for instance, wear batty riders to construct or enhance their beauty and sexuality. Their constructions of beauty and sexuality radically depart from brown middle-class and white European constructions; there is a racial dimension. These women are unapologetically black and are often rejected by the brown middle class and whites as ugly, unfeminine, and vulgar. The dance-hall culture, with its particular style and standards of beauty and excellence, celebrates these same women as beautiful and deeply sexual (Bakare-Yusuf 2006; Cooper 1994). Racial, gender, and class structures and identities are re/produced among the black lower classes, and ICIs help facilitate this.

In addition to the products that are sold, the public images of the higglers also influence the kinds of customer the two groups of women attract. Higglering and higglers are publicly viewed as having low status. The perceived aggressive behaviors of the higglers contribute to this perception, especially the ICIs' so-called aggressive behaviors in contrast to the respectful peasant market women's (Macfarlane-Gregory and Ruddock-Kelly 1993; Ulysse 2007). These perceived aggressive behaviors contradict middle-class norms of respectability and gentility, and deter middle- and upper-class shoppers from patronizing the arcades in their effort to minimize social contact and interaction with these unruly women. The image of the respectful peasant market women, especially at the Papine Market, makes them more appealing to the brown middle and upper classes.[19] The customers served by the ICIs and market women contribute to the reproduction of class differences between them. The interactions of the market women at Papine with middle-class and upper-class brown customers reproduce their statuses as peasants. The interactions of the ICIs with working-class and poor black customers contribute to their status as lower class.

What I find fascinating is that these higglers are publicly constructed as deviant, and in these constructions, differences between ICIs and market women are collapsed. They are one in the same. When the ICIs and market women are compared to brown middle-class women at the Lady Musgrave Flea Market, their status is similar. These women have lower social and economic standing than the brown women. Despite the general tendency to treat these groups as the same, a close examination of the ICIs and market women reveals subtle variations between them.

Although both groups serve a predominantly lower-class clientele, more market women than ICIs serve brown middle-class customers.[20] Products like ackee, callaloo, and bananas, as symbols of Jamaica's national culture, are not race- or class-specific items but perceived as raceless and classless.[21]

The products sold by the ICIs, however, cater specifically to the black working-class and poor. They symbolize black urban culture (U.S. and Jamaican) and blackness in general (especially racialized constructions of femininity, masculinity, and sexuality). Members of the brown middle class reject these items in order to culturally distance themselves from a degraded black lower class. The public images of both groups also vary: the market women at Papine are usually represented in the newspapers as respectful peasants, unlike the ICIs, who are usually portrayed as aggressive and vulgar. The construction of market women as respectful peasants subtly reinforces class hierarchies (such descriptions introduce notions of the idyllic and ideas of service).

The class perception of the traditional group as peasants thus carries a different social image among the middle and upper classes than does their perception of the ICIs. As peasants, the traditional higglers appear to be nonthreatening, respectful, and hardworking and are often celebrated in Jamaica as the archetype of Jamaican womanhood: they are symbols of strength, endurance, and courage (Durant-Gonzalez 1985). ICIs are constructed as aggressive, vulgar, and boorish, perceived as threats not only to formal-sector businesses but also to customers, who believe these women would harass and possibly curse at them. The ICIs deviate from middle-class notions of propriety and are often described as having no class.

The discursive constructions of respectful peasants versus aggressive ICIs also draw from predominant racial/color discourses. When mapped onto these two groups of higglers, these discourses portray the ICIs as black, vulgar women who are to be avoided by the brown middle class. In contrast, the market women at Papine are portrayed as nonthreatening and more appealing, and their race/ color is benign—simply the color they happen to be. This construction stands in stark contrast to the market women at Coronation Market in downtown Kingston, whose perceived aggression makes them unappealing to the brown middle class. The physical space of downtown, which is associated in the minds of many Kingstonians with the black poor, helps contribute to the construction of market women at Coronation Market as unruly, for these behaviors are often associated with a presumed culture of poverty. Racial/

color distinctions are operative here in the public imagination as subtle differences between these groups of informal workers.

Structures of race/color and class organize the work patterns of Afro-Jamaican women in several ways. These categories locate a disproportionate number of lower-class black women in the informal sector, particularly in the business of higglering, by limiting options for them in the formal sector. Structures of race/color and class also influence how higglering is practiced in the informal sector, affecting women's choices of products to sell (based on the cultural tastes of their clients) and consequently the customers they attract. These factors contribute to the reproduction of race/color and class stratification between black lower-class women and brown middle-class women at the flea market. They also reproduce subtle class and color distinctions between the market women and ICIs.

Family and Gender

Gender ideologies in Jamaica's racially segmented labor market and in family units complicate the work experiences of black Jamaican women even further. In addition to race and class, gender contributes to an overrepresentation of Afro-Jamaican women working in public markets and arcades. My research supports this conclusion: more than half the women reported going into higglering because there were no other options available to them, they were laid off, or their primary responsibility for taking care of their families required it. Of this group, more than half reported going into, and depending on, higglering because it helped them support their families. One woman argued, for instance, that higglering was important to her because "man run off all de time leaving women to support their family by themselves, so de business help dem out" (#35).

In Jamaica, twice as many women as men are unemployed, and more women than men are living in poverty, as mentioned earlier. This economic reality, however, does not change traditional gender norms: women are still expected to be primarily responsible for their households. In fact, the number of female-headed households continues to increase despite rising female unemployment and despite the racial, class, and gendered structures that organize Afro-Jamaican women's labor by limiting their employment options.[22] Where systems of race/color, class, and gender domination converge, then, we find that Afro-Jamaican women are burdened by unemployment, poverty, and household responsibilities. These factors lead large numbers of them into higglering.

Family and household responsibilities were major factors influencing the market women's and ICIs' decisions to work outside their homes. I asked every woman in the study to explain why she went into higglering.[23] More than half named their family responsibilities as the primary reason they engaged in higglering and said that they saw no other options available to them. Four women from this group (two market women and two ICIs) reported that they were laid off from their jobs in the formal economy and that this job loss, coupled with their responsibility for their families, made them choose higglering. Despite the limited options available to lower-class black women in the formal economy, then, they were able to fulfill their duty—taking care of their families. It was thus the informal economy that allowed these women the opportunity to earn an income and to fulfill their gender roles as primary caretakers in their households.[24]

The women in the study described another important relationship between families and informal economic activities: the intergenerational transmission of property. The property transmitted here is one's informal business and skills. Approximately one quarter of the women reported inheriting their business from their mother or grandmother.[25] When asked about their skills, roughly one-third of the women (thirteen market women and four ICIs) reported learning their higglering skills from their mother and grandmother as well. None reported inheriting their business or skills from their father or other males.

There is a general tendency to view the intergenerational transmission of property as a middle- and upper-class phenomenon. Patricia Hill Collins argues, however, that this legacy system also operates in working-class families, when working-class men inherit opportunities to earn a wage. Despite their inability to leave their sons large sums of money, business connections, or land, working-class fathers pass on their craft or their trade to their sons, which enhance their opportunities to earn a wage, according to Collins (1998). Here trade is understood as property. It is a resource having economic value and is therefore a source of wealth.

This transmission of inheritable property shows up among the women in my study. Not only did some of them inherit informal businesses, but also many inherited the trade. What is also significant is that this transmission of property is matrilineal. Mothers and grandmothers have passed on their businesses or trade to their daughters. Because higglering has been dominated by black women since slavery, it is not surprising that the transmission of this business and its skills would be from black woman to black woman. Fewer ICIs than market women inherited their businesses and skills from their mothers/grandmothers, a finding that makes sense in light of the much longer history of the marketing of fruits and vegetables than of modern higglering. This longer history has allowed more generations of market women to participate in this informal business and thus more intergenerational transmissions.

Gender, race, and class complicate the work experiences of black Jamaican women. In addition to contributing to their overrepresentation working in public markets and arcades, household gender roles impact their choice to work outside their homes: higglering gives them the time they need to fulfill their household duties. These roles also influence their decision about passing on their businesses to their children: deciding not to is tied to their responsibility to take care of their children's future as well as present needs.

Given this complexity, can we assume that higglering is simply a woman's domain? The experiences of Afro-Jamaican higglers reveal how intersectional structures and cultural ideologies around race, class, and gender have helped shape this occupation as the domain of a specific sort of woman—one who is lower class and black. This pattern is slowly changing, however, and today we find larger numbers of lower-class black men higglering as the Jamaican economy contracts, limiting employment options. Still, lower-class black women continue to dominate higglering, and the higgler is still imagined as a lower-class black woman.

3

"Bait of Satan"?

Representations of Sunday/Negro Markets and Higglering from Slavery to Independence

> Social spaces are not blank and open for any body to occupy. There is a connection between bodies and space, which is built, repeated and contested. While all can, in theory, enter, it is certain types of bodies that are tacitly designated as being the "natural" occupants of specific positions.
> **NIRMAL PUWAR,** *Space Invaders*

One explanation for the common understanding of higglering as a low-status occupation in the Jamaican economy and larger society is the predominance of women engaged in it, and its discursive construction as "women's work" (Bolles 1986).[1] Another is the hostility fueled by class tensions between higglers (or any other economic group) and traditional economic elites (LeFranc 1989). While both explanations are compelling, perhaps a more intriguing question is not why higglering is considered a low-status occupation but what this representation reveals about the social place of this practice in the Jamaican economy. Deconstructing public representations of higglering reveals that the real problem in Jamaica is that higglering boldly inserts itself—or intrudes—into economic spaces not intended for it.

In *Space Invaders: Race, Gender, and Bodies out of Place*, Nirmal Puwar (2004) discloses how social ideologies legitimize the organization of social space in ways that incorporate certain bodies and exclude others. One such space is the public domain, and various justifications have been applied to explain why this space is often imagined and experienced as masculine by nature. Women's presence in public spaces has historically been perceived as invasive, an idea that reinforces public/private distinctions that relegate women to the private domain.

Feminist scholars have long challenged these public/private distinctions, arguing that such binaries reinforce gender inequality (Acker 1990, 2004; Landes 2003). They have shown how meanings are attached to spaces that privilege the public as masculine, productive, and rational, and devalue the private as feminine, reproductive, and irrational. Feminists have actively deconstructed this public/private binary and have effectively blurred the boundaries between them in the literature. In practice, however, the distinctions have not been eradicated; they continue to shape in various degrees the distribution of bodies and human experiences in spaces.

For instance, Joan Acker has demonstrated that "gender is embedded in the structuring and ongoing practices of global capitalism," despite the insistence of many on viewing global economic processes as gender neutral (2004, 23). This presumed gender neutrality masks distinctions between commodity production and human reproduction that associate men with the former and women with the latter. Commodity production is linked to the public domain, the capitalist economy, while human reproduction is relegated to the private domain, the home, and tied to femininity. False notions of gender neutrality miss how these distinctions are reproduced in everyday life. More importantly, they ignore how these distinctions are hierarchically ranked: reproduction is devalued as unprofitable—and therefore unproductive—labor.

Neoliberal ideologies have reproduced these distinctions, which in myriad ways have "provided legitimacy for reducing welfare state programs and restoring corporate non-responsibility in most countries" (Acker 2004, 27). Indeed, welfare-state programs that address the reproductive needs of families are considered unproductive—unprofitable—and are usually the first to be eradicated in state and corporate financial restructuring plans. The effects of this ideology have been devastating to poor women, especially poor mothers in developing countries who disproportionately bear the brunt of neoliberal economic policies that absolve multinational corporations of the responsibility for providing living wages and employment safety nets. These policies also minimize, through structural adjustment programs, the power of local governments to provide social services to families, often leaving that responsibility to women (Moghadam 1999; Pettman 2006; Reddock 2000). Gender ideologies that separate the public/productive sphere from the private/reproductive sphere thus continue to shape global economic processes, creating hardships for poor women.

Public/productive versus private/reproductive divisions emerged as European capitalism developed, was transported to the colonial world, and was reproduced as part of its imperialist enterprise. These distinctions fragmented social spaces in the colonies. These spaces, however, were not simply gendered; they were also racialized and classed: a racial socioeconomic system developed in the colonies in which white elite male bodies had greater freedom of movement and dominance in the public/productive sphere than other bodies had. Their presence in the capitalist economy as owners and beneficiaries of various means of production was deemed a natural right within discursive frameworks of white supremacy and hegemonic masculinity.

For example, the colonial economy of Jamaica was highly stratified by class, race, ethnicity, and gender: wealthy, white English males were dominant actors as owners and beneficiaries of sugar production on rural plantations. This group owned vast acreages along with large numbers of chattel, and engaged in the cultivation and export of sugar. Their wealth and racial status elevated them to the colonial elite. Following this group—and occupying an ancillary role in the sugar economy—were penkeepers (owners of livestock) and coffee farmers, whose properties were moderate and less prosperous than those of sugar planters (Shepherd 2002). By the mid-eighteenth century, this group consisted of white men (and some free coloreds) of lower social status; class and occupation contributed to the racialization of this group as secondary whites. According to Verene Shepherd, penkeepers were primarily overseers and attorneys on sugar estates, jobs that kept them tied to the island. Their inability to become absentee owners—a marker of wealth—or to acquire large acreages like those of sugar planters contributed to their secondary status among whites (ibid., 154–57).

In the city of Kingston, white males were attorneys, clergy, doctors, and army officers, as well as storekeepers, wharfingers, manufacturers, clerks, and soldiers (Clarke 1975, 21). These occupations were among the most privileged, and these men were part of the urban elite both socially and economically. Jewish males were positioned slightly differently in the urban economy, where they predominated among merchants. They were powerful competitors as traders and entrepreneurs, making them a part of the urban economic elite. Although racialized as white, their ethnicity often penalized them, denying them access to the privileges accorded other members of the white elite, such as serving in political office (Douglass 1992, 98–101).

Lower-class white men, many of whom arrived in Jamaica as indentured servants, were also positioned differently in the economy. During the heyday of the sugar plantation, field work shifted from white indentured servants principally to slaves, yet class and ethnic differences between these servants and the white Creole elite placed them outside white elite society. After completing their indenture, a number of white immigrants gained access to landownership and became small planters (Beckles 2000a, 235). Others engaged in occupations in the city, such as carpentry and bricklaying. Many white ex-indentured women acquired positions in the lower segments of the economy as artisans, local traders, shopkeepers, yeoman farmers, and, along with their men, easily assimilated into the lower classes of white society (Mair 2006, 127) in accordance with deficiency laws aimed at growing and preserving the relatively small white population (Beckles 2000b, 2000c).[2] Access to public economic space was more difficult for white elite planter women, however; racialized gender ideologies relegated them to reproductive and domestic duties in their homes (Bush 1990; Mair 2006).

Barred from the plantations out of fear that their presence would incite slave riots, most free coloreds and free blacks migrated to the city. There they had restricted access to occupations in the formal economy, which were reserved for whites, forcing them to open petty huckster shops or to sell in the Sunday (then also called "Negro") markets (Clarke 1975, 20–22). The more fortunate free coloreds owned slaves, whom they hired out to other urban residents in order to earn an income. A smaller group of wealthier free coloreds used the inheritance from their former slaveholders to create their own businesses, such as lodging houses. Some were also penkeepers and were quite prosperous. In spite of their economic success, however, the colonial racial order restricted their economic endeavors and social standing. Enslaved black men and women were relegated to the lowest position in the plantation economy as objects of production (chattel) whose primary purpose was to labor for the benefit of their mostly white and male slaveholders. In the city, enslaved men engaged in manual labor at the ports; enslaved women, the majority of whom were colored, worked in the city as domestics or sold dry goods in the streets for their slaveholders (Bush 1990; Clarke 1975; Mair 2006; Welch 2003).

What all this demonstrates is that although production/reproduction, public/private distinctions structured social and economic spaces in the colonial capitalist economy, these ideological constructions contrast "with the actual organization of production and reproduction, as women were often as much 'producers' as 'reproducers'" (Acker 2004, 24). The blurring of these distinctions is evident when you factor in the combined effects of race, class, and gender on the experiences of secondary white women and especially of black and colored women, enslaved and free. Indeed, the lower-class status of secondary whites precluded these women from the life of leisure of their white elite counterparts. Many worked, in order to earn a living, either alongside their husbands on their own lands in the rural areas, or in the city as shopkeepers and traders.

Racial and gender ideologies helped fashion the organization of labor among slaves on rural plantations to illustrate what Barbara Bush calls the "corporeal equality of the sexes," as mentioned earlier (1990, 14). No differentiation was made between the physical bodies of black women and men; both were attributed masculine qualities of physical strength and, working side-by-side, engaged in backbreaking labor in the fields. Although most domestic workers were colored women, a significant number of colored women worked in the fields alongside their black mothers, or they worked in the towns. Enslaved black and colored/brown women were both producers and reproducers, and the products of their labor—human and nonhuman—circulated in the money economy. Despite the gender-coded separation of production/public/male from reproduction/private/female that prevailed in colonial formal economies and restricted white elite women to their homes, enslaved black and colored women and secondary white women were not constrained by these distinctions in the same way.

The presence of black women in the public sphere, particularly the formal economy, was constrained by race, class, and gender ideologies that legitimized their spatial relegation to the plantations, especially in the fields. Since white indentured servants were prevented from working in the fields, the physical space of the field and the labor associated with it in the public imagination became associated with black bodies. In the city, enslaved blacks and coloreds were similarly spatialized as domestic servants or petty traders for their slaveholders. Free blacks and coloreds, who fared a little better, were clustered around the fringes of the urban economy. These marginalized spatial locations helped reinforce the subordinate social and economic status of blacks, especially black women, and ensured the social and spatial dominance of whites, particularly white men, in Jamaican society and the economy.

Sunday (or Negro) Markets in Jamaica

The internal marketing system was a critical feature of urban space, and slave women were dominant actors in this semiformal/informal segment of the capitalist economy. Not only did Sunday markets provide slave women the opportunity to develop and exercise entrepreneurial skills, but, thanks to the efforts of slave higglers, such markets connected rural informal economies to urban economies—formal and semi-informal/informal—facilitating the smooth flow of slave provisions from one area to the next.[3] Sunday markets, then, provided a space for the blurring of formal, semiformal, and informal boundaries in the colonial urban economy.

Sunday markets were located in the city or towns as opposed to rural plantations where the provisions were grown and cultivated. It was quite common for slaves to travel every week from five to twenty miles each way to sell in these markets (Mair 2006, 261). That cities and towns were the spatial locations of Sunday markets is not surprising, since patterns of urban slavery marked a significant departure from plantation slavery in rural areas. In his groundbreaking study of urban slavery in Barbados, Pedro L. V. Welch (2003) demonstrated that urban slavery in the Caribbean differed significantly from rural/plantation slavery in several ways. First, the sugar economy dominated in rural areas, where large plantations were developed and operated, as opposed to urban centers, where commerce and trading played a more central role. As a result, the size of the slave population was much larger in rural areas.

Second, a high proportion of slave owners in urban centers were women—whites and free coloreds—not the case in rural areas. Most slaves were kept for domestic work or were hired out to other town residents so that these female slaveholders could earn an income. Third, the labor structure was more regimented on the plantations, where slaves were heavily disciplined so that planters could maximize their profits. The master-slave relationship was repressive on the plantations, since in the planters' view, a "productive body (producing labour that is) also had to be a subjugated body" (Bush 1990, 26). Labor organization was less regimented in the cities, where slaves were hired out to others or engaged in street vending for their slaveholders. Here, the labor structure was more flexible and urban slaves had greater freedom of movement. As a result, slaves enjoyed greater independence in the cities; they were not subjected to the kinds of surveillance by their owners that plantation slaves endured (Clarke 1975; Welch 2003). These factors, among others, mark significant differences in patterns of urban and rural slavery. Simply put, in the city, slaves had greater "room to maneuver" (to borrow Pedro Welch's phrase) within systems of constraints.

The less constricting conditions for slaves in the city gave them the opportunity to develop their own commercial enterprises, from which town residents benefited financially. Town merchants, for example, took advantage of the large crowd of potential shoppers, enslaved and free, who flocked to the markets every Sunday, opening their stores to sell or trade with slave higglers and their customers (Clarke 1975). Residents also benefited from increased access to the fresh ground provisions that they could easily obtain in the markets weekly, instead of having to wait for shipments from abroad.

The freedom and agency of urban slaves would have destroyed rural plantation economies, which depended on the complete subservience of its enslaved labor force. Some rural slaves could participate in this type of freedom away from the plantations, which required mobility beyond the spatial boundaries of the plantations and depended on securing a ticket from their slaveholders—and slaves did everything they could obtain one. Slaves who were not mobile exercised other freedoms on rural plantations. Provision grounds provided opportunities for them to develop into a proto-peasantry (Mintz and Hall 1960), growing provisions for themselves and, through their networks, transporting those provisions from their slave grounds to urban markets. Indeed, rural slaves who were tied to plantations were still able to participate in the urban commercial economy—but they did so indirectly. These slaves acted as suppliers of provisions for urban markets, while slave higglers acted as distributors and sellers of those provisions.

Representations of the Sunday Market: Space and Bodies

The Sunday (or Negro) market was a critical feature of slavery and urban life in the Caribbean, and by the eighteenth century these markets were an accepted and important feature of the Jamaican economy. As early as 1711, slave laws were created that recognized the right of slaves to sell (Norton and Symanski 1975, 463).[4] There was, however, ambivalence among white residents about the social place of the markets. Mrs. A. C. Carmichael, a planter's wife who wrote about slave society during her five-year residence in St. Vincent and Trinidad, described the reaction of white residents to Sunday markets: "The Sunday market I heard always talk of as an evil, neither did I ever in my life hear it vindicated in the abstract. To the white population it is a nuisance, and no advantage." Mrs. Carmichael, however, acknowledged the importance of these markets to black and colored residents on the islands. She explained that white residents were reluctant to interfere with the markets for fear of disrupting an uneasy peace between themselves and the larger black and colored population: "I conscientiously believe the white population of the West Indies are by no means advocates for buying and selling unnecessarily upon the Sabbath, but they must be aware, as residents on the colonies, of many difficulties and dangers in making any sudden change, of which those living in England can have no idea" (Carmichael 1834, 49).

Sunday markets were thus necessary evils in the white imagination. White residents were well aware of their smaller numbers in comparison to the black and colored population, and reluctantly tolerated Sunday markets for their importance not only to blacks and coloreds, but also to the overall stability of slave society.

Slaves and town residents who participated in the markets were often criticized for violating the laws of the Sabbath. In his discussion of the Sunday/Negro market Rev. Benjamin Luckock argued that one of the many demoralizing influences of slavery was teaching slaves "to profane and efface the very appearance of a Christian Sabbath, by employing that day as though it were 'a festival of hell'" (Luckock 1846, 119). He placed the blame for this irreverence squarely on planters who chose Sunday as the only day to relieve slaves from plantation labor, leaving them no option but to use that day to work on their provision grounds, engage in recreation activities, and sell "in the noisy traffic of the 'Sunday market.'" The result, Luckock said, was that slaves were "led to regard this day, as one which was to be devoted wholly to temporal pursuits. To the industrious, it was a time of labour; to others, of sport and recreation. Thousands on this day met in the public markets" (120). Quoting Bryan Edwards, a longtime resident and historian on the island, Luckock described activities around the public markets as "a kind of weekly carnival," because instead of worshiping, thousands of people converged on the marketplace buying, selling, and congregating (ibid.).

For Luckock, the Sunday market created disorder and indecency on a day that was meant to be serene and sacred. "The very streets and lanes in and about the towns," he lamented, "presented such scenes of riot and wickedness that scarcely a decent person dared walk out, even at noonday." Luckock described the early morning of the Sabbath, where "every road leading to the towns and market stations in the country, was crowded with negroes, carrying to the market heavy loads of ground provisions, wood, grass, etc. while the market itself baffled all description" (1846, 120). For him, the market space was indefensible because the vibrancy one encountered in it did not conform to the sense of discipline and serenity one would expect on a holy day.

The market also epitomized a space of evil for Luckock, for "every bad passion of the human heart was there seen in active operation. Covetousness exhibited itself under all forms; cheating, thieving, and extortion abounded on every hand; anger, jealousy, and revenge declared themselves by loud bursts of furious passion" (1846, 121). Although the market was a central feature of urban life, its presence created great anxiety for Luckock and other white residents not only because it operated on Sunday, a day when Christians were expected to exhibit piety, but also because it represented a space where individuals, enslaved and free, exhibited unrestraint from religious and wider social norms. The market, then, was spatially associated with deviance (and impiety) and was deemed not fit for decent persons.

Luckock's contempt for the Sunday market is consistent with earlier writings by white residents and visitors to the island. For example, in 1825 Rev. Richard Bickell also expressed his disapproval: the Sunday Market interfered with slaves learning the "proper ideas of the Christian religion." In his view, the market was "a bait of Satan" (1825, 68.) Moreover, it attracted individuals of low social caliber. Bickell expressed the "horror and disgust" he experienced as a passerby:

> It was on a Sunday, and I had to pass by the Negro Market, where several thousands of human beings, of various nations and colours, but principally Negroes, instead of worshipping their maker on His Holy Day were busily employed in all kinds of traffick in the open streets. Here were Jews with shops and standings as at a fair, selling old and new clothes, trinkets and small wares at cent. per cent. to adorn the Negro person; there were low Frenchmen and Spaniards, and people of colour, in petty shops and with stalls; some selling their bad rum, gin, tobacco, etc; others salt provisions, and small articles of dress; and many of them bartering with the Slave or purchasing his provisions to retail again; poor free people and servants also, from all parts of the city to purchase vegetables, etc., for the following week. The different noises and barbarous tongues recalled to one's memory the confusion of Babel. (66–67)

Bickell's inclusion of Jews, "low" Frenchmen, and Spaniards in his condemnation is significant given Jamaica's social hierarchy, where ethnic and class differences placed these groups among the lower echelons of white society as secondary whites.

Although most members of the Jewish community were economically on par with the white British elites, they were a devalued social minority group and faced discrimination in the Caribbean as non-Christians.

The "low Frenchmen and Spaniards" were part of the white immigrant population, many of whom were recent arrivals to the island, and were distinguished socially and economically from white British (Creole) residents. Colin Clarke reports that in Jamaica a "distinction was therefore made between established immigrants and newcomers, as well as between immigrant and Creole whites. A European club was formed in Kingston, the qualification for full membership being thirty years of residence in Jamaica" (1975, 21). Bickell linked these secondary whites with blacks and coloreds, and spatially associated all these groups with what he saw as the barbarity and confusion of the Sunday market.

Additionally, Bickell presented the activities of these groups—selling bad rum, bartering with slaves, purchasing slave provisions to retail again (to whites?)—as examples of poor moral values. Constructing Sunday markets in this way exposes a conception of respectability that privileges the social and cultural norms of the higher classes of white Creoles. By socially and spatially separating these groups from the Sunday market and its associated activities, Bickell, like Luckock, reproduced an image of white Creoles as respectable or decent persons, and the Sunday market as a space that these persons should avoid; in the process, Bickell represented the Sunday market as a deviant entity to be marginalized or, at best, contained in public space.[5]

The issue in these discussions, however, was not simply the pressing need of residents to respect the Sabbath. In fact, in Mrs. Carmichael's comments on the importance of religion to the white population in the Caribbean, she noted: "It seemed to me, that religion occupied very little, the attention of the great majority of society; and still there was little opposition to it. . . . I seldom or ever met any one who seemed ever to think at all seriously upon the subject of religion. I rarely saw any one read religious books, nor did there seem any desire to peruse works of this description" (1834, 47–49).

But these discussions of the Sunday market revealed other concerns, especially economic ones. In his condemnation of Sunday markets, Luckock admonished not only slaves but other residents as well: "It must be self-evident, that the slaves were not the only participators in these transactions. Had there been no free persons crowding into the markets, there would have been few purchasers of the articles brought for sale; while, if no shops and stores had been open, the slaves could not have carried back with them imported goods. Hucksters and private families would take these opportunities for making better bargains, in the purchase of provisions, and merchants would as gladly add to their weekly gains by the profits of the day" (1846, 121). As he scolded local residents and merchants, Luckock identified another important challenge Sunday markets created for town residents: the presence of these markets complicated market competition among local white merchants. Operating on Sundays, the markets placed white Creole merchants at a competitive disadvantage in the urban economy.

Ann Norton and Richard Symanski note that "because markets generate business for other local merchants, Sunday gatherings were a major issue in the slave period since Christian merchants could not take advantage of the market trade" (1975, 464). Protestant religious norms prohibited white Christian merchants, especially those from the respectable middle and upper classes, from taking advantage of the lucrative profits that could be made on Sundays, whereas non-Christian merchants were not so inhibited. Religious norms coupled with a social ethic of respectability created barriers to the economic involvement of white Christians in the Sunday market, and this in turn constrained their participation and competitiveness in the local urban economy.

A significant problem with the Sunday market, then, was that it was inserted by slaves into the urban economy and placed respectable white merchants at an economic disadvantage. Although markets had been established in the colonial economy by the late seventeenth and early eighteenth centuries (in fact, the first known market was established in Spanish town in 1662) and maintained by the colonial government, slaves originally participated in these markets in service of their slaveholders. Slave higglers quickly changed this practice, inserting themselves into the colonial economy as independent marketers and monopolizing the weekly markets by converting them into Negro markets. These Negro markets, then, became forces to contend with in the urban economy.

Representations of the Sunday/Negro market as deviant exposed assumptions that public economic spaces and opportunities naturally belonged to white Creoles. These assumptions operated within a broad framework of white (Creole) and male supremacy that privileged this group in the formal economy. Calls to contain and also to move the Sunday/Negro market to another day were frequent. Reverend Bickell insisted, for instance, that "the best day for the market would be Saturday for various reasons" (1825, 69). These calls usually fell on deaf ears, however, since moving the market to Saturdays would be disadvantageous to white rural planters, shortening the number of days that slaves worked on the plantations. Since the plantation sugar economy dominated the colonial formal economy, and many planters occupied powerful positions within the colonial government, its needs took precedence over the needs of smaller urban capitalists.

After emancipation, the colonial formal economy underwent a significant transformation from an economy driven by slave labor to one dependent upon wage labor. But converting newly freed slaves into a cheap and docile wage labor force was not easy. Shortly after August 1, 1838, when slaves became "full free" (at the end of the apprenticeship period, 1834–1838), their first response, especially that of the women and children, was to cease or substantially reduce their work on the estates and to turn their attention toward purchasing land. A small number of wealthier black and freed colored men entered the political system as members of the House of Assembly.

In his insightful study *The Problem of Freedom: Race, Labor, and Politics in Jamaica and Britain, 1832–1938*, Thomas Holt showed that as early as 1840 newly freed people purchased small plots of land averaging one to three acres, and the growth of smallholdings continued well into the following decades and beyond (Holt 1992). With this land, newly freed people increased their peasant production and marketing activities, and expanded their production activities to include crops for export. Because of the uncertainties that came with agricultural production (the unpredictability of weather, growth cycles of crops, etc.), large numbers of these peasant proprietors supplemented their peasant production with plantation wage labor. The combination of peasant production with wage labor, however, was a tremendous source of contention between freed people and planters, since peasant production "did not mesh well with plantation requirements" (ibid., 165). It was painfully obvious to planters that peasant production was a high priority to the workers. A common complaint among them was that the division of labor by workers typically favored their own grounds over wage labor (161).

Another source of contention was the loss of women—the primary source of field laborers prior to emancipation—from the available pool of wage laborers. According to Holt: "It seems clear that although women continued to give some work to the estates, a declining number gave their full time to wage labor. By the end of the first decade of freedom, the wage labor force was mostly male" (1992, 153). Fewer women in the wage labor force meant that planters had a smaller pool of laborers from which to draw, and this complicated efforts to keep wages at a bare minimum in the years immediately following emancipation. But perhaps more importantly, the departure of women meant that planters could no longer control the bodies and labor of a significant portion of the population—black women and their children—as they had before emancipation. Freed women and their children now controlled their own bodies and labor, and devoted most of their labor to their own peasant cultivation and marketing.

In other words, as opposed to the slave era when black men and women were positioned in the economy primarily as objects of production, their bodies subject to the power of planters (through labor coercion, punishment, torture, rape), freed men and women repositioned themselves in the economy primarily as independent peasant proprietors and marketers, and only secondarily as wage laborers. This repositioning radically shifted the relationship between freed people and planters. As Holt aptly puts it, freed people resisted becoming proletarians and embraced instead their autonomy (1992, 173). The significance of this shift is more striking for black women who, as field laborers and domestics, constituted the most exploited segment of the slave labor force both economically and sexually.

Although the Jamaican sugar economy had begun to decline for a variety of reasons prior to emancipation in 1838, it took a precipitous plunge in the post-emancipation era. Although the transformation of the labor force from slave labor to wage labor took its toll on the economy, other external factors played equal if not greater roles in this decline. One contributing factor was the passage of the Sugar Duties Act in 1846, a free-trade policy that essentially exposed the Jamaican economy to stronger competitors like Cuba, which remained a slave economy until 1880, where plantations were equipped with superior technology, and where the new railway facilitated the transportation of sugar (Williams 1984, 362). This meant that Cuba was able to produce large quantities of sugar efficiently and at low cost, thereby undermining the Jamaican sugar industry as well as other sugar industries in the British West Indies (369).

As the Jamaican sugar economy contracted in the post-emancipation era, the peasant economy, including higglering, blossomed. However, in spite of its vibrancy and economic potential, British and Jamaican authorities failed to nurture this segment of the economy or to seriously entertain it as a viable alternative to sugar production. Holt points out that shortly after emancipation, British policy makers and many Jamaican officials acknowledged the vibrancy of peasant production and trade, and seemed willing to entertain it as a sensible economic response to Jamaica's dire conditions. Their vision was quickly clouded, however, by their steadfast commitment to "estate agriculture as the mainstay of the Jamaican economy and avenue to civilization and culture for blacks" (1992, 280). "By 1865, Whitehall was deaf to any suggestion that peasant proprietorship might offer a road to economic recovery in Jamaica. That deafness reflected not only its commitment to capitalist agriculture in Jamaica but also its inability to even conceive of an alternate economy based on black initiative and enterprise" (279). The formal economy continued to be discursively produced and organized as the legitimate space for white creoles, and blacks were socially and spatially relegated to marginal roles, primarily as cheap and docile wage laborers.

Extant racist ideologies helped rationalize the continued marginalization of blacks in the formal economy. "Indeed, black was no longer a credible adjective to modify *initiative* or *enterprise*" (Holt 1992, 279, emphasis original). Instead, freed people were publicly imagined as having few aspirations for social and economic advancement, as being intrinsically lazy, and as preferring to simply live off the abundance of the land if not coerced to work. Such ideas gave legitimacy to the perpetuation of white privilege and colonial rule. In the end, "despite the decline of sugar, white economic power relative to the rest of the population did not diminish" (Bryan 1998, 117).

However, the emerging peasant economy and the expansion of Negro markets provided counterevidence to the presumed laziness of blacks. In the post-emancipation era, market days gradually shifted from Sundays to Saturdays, and the markets remained as vibrant as they were before emancipation, if not more so. Entire families worked to cultivate their lands, and women continued to market their provisions as they had during slavery. Holt noted: "Throughout the late nineteenth century observers commented on the energy and activity of the Jamaican markets. By Friday evening the roads were clogged with people on their way to town. They walked fifteen to twenty miles with a very small parcel of produce—bananas, coffee, chickens—in a basket on their heads. These were not a lazy people" (1992, 165). Indeed, the markets offered visual evidence of the industriousness and enterprising skills of freed men and women, yet the public image and discourse of them as lazy and backward persisted.

Negro markets continued to be represented as out of place in the white imagination. In a report by the Central Board of Health presented to the legislature in 1852, the authors argued for improved sanitation in the towns, including the markets: "The market places, situated in the most crowded throughfares, their sheds and buildings miserably ventilated and undrained, frequently tainted articles of food exposed for sale, contaminate the surrounding atmosphere with their putrid effluvia" (quoted in Sheller 2002, 12). According to Mimi Sheller, as they advocated for better sanitation, housing, and medical provisions, the authors "contrast[ed] the 'power of science' with the 'filthy' customs of the 'idle' lower classes" (2002,12). It is significant that filth, whether associated with lower-class customs or with market conditions, is socially and spatially linked with the marketplace, which is then configured as a contaminant and, by extension, a danger to the surrounding environment. This representation reproduces the image of the market as deviant and out of place, an intruder into or infector of the economy and larger society.

In a travel narrative published in *Harper's Monthly Magazine* in 1889, Howard Pyle draws a vivid picture of the market in Kingston in the post-emancipation era: "to understand and appreciate England, one must see London May Fair in the season; to understand and appreciate Jamaica, one must see Kingston market upon a Saturday" (1889–1890, 175). At the time, Mayfair was a fashionable residential district that catered to the well to do.[6] Pyle's selection of Mayfair as the epitome of England and the Kingston market as the epitome of Jamaica implies a stark contrast between the development and progress (that is, modernity) associated with England and the decay (that is, premodern) associated with Jamaica after the fall of the sugar economy. This sense of decay was evidenced in the physical landscape, in Pyle's view, by the tattered shops surrounding the market as well as the chaos, confusion, and sense of bewilderment one experiences in it.

> Directly one leaves the quiet court-yard of the lodging house and sets foot in the street, one steps as though by magic into the full clatter of life. It seems as though all Kingston was in the highways and in the byways. Nominally the markets are conducted in covered buildings set apart in two places for that especial purpose. But the measure of the covered market house is far too small for the life it was intended to hold. That life, so to speak, slops over everywhere. All along the street one passes rickety little tumble-down huts transformed into stores, where they sell cocoa-nuts, plantains, and yams. All along the walls one sees groups of negro women, sitting with piles of great pots and bowls and queer jars of red earthen-ware stacked around them to tempt the passer-by to purchase. (175–76)

Pyle finds the prospect at first nearly overwhelming: "Chatter, gabble, clatter! One stands in the market square bewildered at first; seeing so much that one sees nothing. One is glad to escape from the vortex of the confusion to the railed walls of the marketplace, where the older and less pushing women have drifted, and where they sit in long rows with baskets of oranges in front of them and piles of oranges around them" (176).

For Pyle, the market brims with life, energy, and disorder. It also symbolizes urban rot, representing Kingston and, by extension, Jamaica in ruins after the fall of the sugar kingdom.[7] Pyle describes at great length the history of Jamaica, from the years of the buccaneers to the slave era, denoting periods of great wealth and prosperity where mansions and other symbols of luxury dotted the landscape. He sees in a landscape now filled with "rickety tumble-down houses that helplessly crumble to decay in the heart of the town the same silent history of the days when those merchants entertained their guests with princely hospitality" (1989–1890, 178). In Pyle's view, the evils of slavery and pirating had sown the seeds of Jamaica's destruction; he believes that "Jamaica's own history has had to do with her town's decrepitude"(182).

I am particularly interested in Pyle's representation of the Negro market as a symbol of urban decay. The Negro market is intricately connected to peasant proprietorship and marketing/higglering. It serves in many ways as a measure of the health of the peasant economy.[8] To talk about the Negro market, then, is in some ways to talk about the peasant economy itself. Pyle describes the market as a site of confusion; it is noisy and filled with "chatter and clatter" that cannot be contained by its physical walls. His sense of bewilderment, which causes him to seek refuge outside the walls of the marketplace, echoes earlier descriptions of the marketplace and captures the attitude of many white residents toward the peasant economy and higglering as undisciplined and irrational. Of course, there were economic and noneconomic motives behind the participation of ex-slaves in, and the subsequent growth of, the peasant economy. In addition to market factors, ex-slaves understood peasant proprietorship and marketing as measures of their autonomy. Most planters failed—or refused—to recognize this viewpoint, however, and dismissed as irrational the choice of freed people to engage in peasant farming instead of wage labor (Holt 1992).

Pyle contrasted the disorder he encountered in the marketplace—and by extension, the peasant economy—with the quiet courtyard of the lodging house that was "a good exemplar of the better class of early Jamaican mansions" (1889–1890, 173). Here, the disorderly peasant economy contrasts with a sense of order and discipline dictated by imperial policies of mercantilism during the slave era that assured the commercial growth of Kingston—one of the apexes in the triangle trade. Kingston's role was "the import, storage and dispatch of slaves and British manufactured goods to the sugar estates and the collection, storage, and export of sugar to Britain. The growth of Kingston's economy was therefore geared to the growth of the island's economy" (Clarke 1975, 13). However, with the fall of sugar the policies were destabilized and the economy deteriorated, leaving behind a local peasant economy dominated by free black men and women who refused to accept their place as wage laborers. In Pyle's view, then, the chaos of the market symbolized an undisciplined population, a retrograde economy, a city in decay, and a country whose magnificence is lost.

I find it interesting that in 1872 the Victoria Market was built in Kingston on the site of the Sunday/Negro market. In the 1898 *Handbook of Jamaica*, the Victoria Market was lauded as a "remarkably handsome and very commodious structure," a rectangular space enclosed with iron railings on a brick wall. Entrances on all four sides allowed air to circulate, the principal one being on the western side from King Street. This main entrance was by an arched way between two rooms that served as offices for market clerks. The beauty of the market was further enhanced by a clock tower and a fountain opposite the main entrance. Inside the market were 92 benches where vendors could present their wares, "so arranged as to form lanes twelve feet in width running north and south for the public to circulate in. Between the backs of the ranges of benches a space four feet nine inches in width is set apart for the sellers. These spaces are so divided as to give 246 stalls with an aggregate lineal space of 1,840 feet" (*Handbook of Jamaica*, 1898, 440).

Not only was the new Victoria Market built on the site of the Sunday/Negro market, but also the orderly structure of the new market space replaced the presumed disorderliness associated with the old one and, by extension, higglering. The old Sunday/Negro market was frequently described by residents as extremely crowded. For example, one resident quoted in the *Columbian Magazine* in 1796 complained that the market was "so shut up with tables that in some places there is hardly six or thirty inches room for people to pass and repass" (quoted in Simmonds 1987, 34). Others complained that the market was so crowded it prevented decent persons from visiting it. The crowded and cramped spaces added to its disorderliness, and the newly built Victoria Market sought to correct this problem. Physical spaces within the Victoria Market, with its rows of vendors neatly organized, visually replaced and, in fact, disciplined the chaos, clatter, and disorder presumably embodied by the traditional Sunday/Negro market, and the activities associated with it, including higglering.

A strict spatial partitioning was built into the Victoria Market. The black bodies of vendors were spatially distributed behind rows of benches. Clerks governed the market from their offices on either side of its main entrance, keeping market sellers and buyers under strict surveillance. They also helped create a sense among the sellers of being surveyed—of being captured by what Foucault (1995) calls "panopticism," in which the arrangement of physical space serves as a means of disciplining bodies in the modern era.

When the market was opened on May 24, 1872, the Jamaican governor, Sir John Peter Grant, named it after Queen Victoria to symbolize the perpetuation of British hegemony under Crown Colony rule.[9] The placement of the Victoria Market on the physical site of the traditional Sunday/Negro market also signaled the containment of black agency and a resurgence of colonial power. The new Victoria Market was not just an orderly site where disciplined black peasants could engage in commerce; it also became a place for important social gatherings on holidays, particularly Christmas, which would be attended by Jamaicans of all classes, especially the white economic and political elites.

What is important to note here is that the Victoria Market was not built to aid or expand peasant marketing, higglering, and by extension, the peasant economy but to contain and discipline it. Indeed, little effort was made by colonial officials and planters to support and expand the peasant economy. By the 1860s, "all serious discussions of government assistance for growth and development focused on measures to assist the estates" (Holt 1992, 276). For example, road repairs occurred on roads serving the estates, not the peasant farmers. Main roads that did serve freed blacks on the way either to market or to work on estates charged tolls. The unequal treatment of peasant farmers in comparison to planters was further evidenced by peasant farmers having to pay higher taxes on food and clothing than planters, and "the tax on donkeys was more than on horses. Peasant carts which previously went untaxed were now charged eighteen shillings per year while plantation carts continued to go untaxed" (Sherlock and Bennett 1998, 252). Yet, in spite of having to pay taxes, peasants received no government support in return.

Whites maintained social, political, and economic hegemony on the island. This reality became increasingly clear to peasant farmers in disputes between themselves and planters. They quickly learned that "when the interests of the smallholders and those of the estates came into direct conflict, the government, predictably, sided with the latter" (Holt 1992, 276). This unequal and contentious relationship among the government, planters, and peasant proprietors contributed to the Morant Bay rebellion in 1865 and the subsequent installation of the Crown Colony government.[10] This relationship also disclosed the continued marginalization of the Sunday/Negro markets, higglering, and thus the peasant economy in colonial ideologies and policies. It bolstered the idea that economic spaces and opportunities rightfully belonged to white creoles in the post-emancipation era, as they had during slavery. This ideology was reinforced under Crown Colony rule: political power rested squarely in the hands of Britain (as opposed to local white creoles and a small representation of blacks and coloreds), and wage labor was perceived as a primary means of civilizing blacks.

In spite of its decline, sugar maintained its hegemony in the colonial formal economy until displaced by bananas beginning in the 1870s. Bananas had long been a part of the peasant diet and were grown primarily by black Jamaicans in their gardens and provision grounds (Holt 1992; Thompson 2006). The fruit was grown mainly for local consumption and was practically unknown in the United States and Europe (Thompson 2006, 48–49). In 1872, Captain Lorenzo Baker, a U.S. capitalist who owned a Cape Cod fishing fleet, visited Jamaica and encountered the delicious fruit. He returned to Boston with 1,450 bunches of bananas and made a small profit on them (49). Realizing the economic potential of this fruit, Baker started a small firm, the Boston Fruit Company, and developed his banana trade. By 1886 "he was shipping 42 percent of Jamaica's bananas" (Holt 1992, 350), and by 1898 he had shipped "over 16 million stems of fruit into the United States" (Thompson 2006, 49). In the late 1890s, after undergoing several organizational transformations, Baker's Boston Fruit Company grew into a multinational corporation, the United Fruit Company (Holt 1992; Sherlock and Bennett 1998).

In the early years of its development, Baker's company relied on peasant farmers to supply bananas for export. This relationship was economically fruitful for peasant producers but unfortunately short lived. As the company continued to grow, it acquired vast landholdings on the island, which allowed Baker and other planters who eventually saw the economic value in the "backwoods nigger business" to produce their own bananas using indentured labor from India.[11]

Bananas replaced sugar as a source of wealth and thus created opportunities for white planters to reassert their dominance in the economy by becoming part of a new agro-elite, which now included urban Jewish merchants. Then the balance of power between planters and merchants shifted. According to Lisa Douglass: "Jewish merchants as well as the brown intelligentsia were a combined demographic, economic, and social force that eventually overpowered the interests of the planters, who were enfeebled by world market conditions and the end of slavery"

(1992, 103). As mentioned earlier, Jewish merchants had long been part of the formal urban economy and enjoyed significant wealth as a result of their trading activities. Browns, largely descendents of slaves of mixed race, held privileged positions in the hierarchy of the slave plantations as skilled laborers. According to Don Robotham, this privilege carried over into the post-emancipation era and "provided one (but not the only) basis for the subsequent rise of the brown elite" (2000, 9). Indeed, many browns had access to colonial education and participated in politics in the post-emancipation era, especially before the implementation of Crown Colony rule. Their social and economic privilege facilitated their ascendance in the colonial color/class hierarchy, and the banana industry added to their wealth and social mobility. Verene Shepherd noted that the burgeoning banana industry helped speed "the emergence of a new class of land barons among people previously concentrated in commercial and professional fields" (Shepherd 2002, 162). This powerful group of Jews and browns were the genesis of today's white and brown economic elite in Jamaica.

The new agro-elite methodically pushed peasant farmers further to the margins of the economy, clearing the way for its own growth and development. For example, as the United Fruit Company's monopoly of the banana trade intensified, it shifted its relationship with peasant farmers by setting its own prices and trade conditions, leaving farmers little bargaining power: "By the early twentieth century . . . the Jamaican banana trade was controlled from production to marketing by one multinational corporation, rendering the former independent peasant cultivators a virtual proletariat" (Holt 1992, 356).

In the late nineteenth and early twentieth centuries, land in Jamaica was associated with bananas, and large acreages were concentrated into fewer hands. A general pattern emerged after 1880 in which the growth of the peasantry was drastically curtailed as peasants lost land they had once rented for farming to the banana estates (Holt 1992; Shepherd 2002; Sherlock and Bennett 1998). As peasant farmers lost their land, they were also losing the autonomy that they had fought so hard to obtain, and "the re-emergence of an influential plantation sector resulted in a return to dependence on the estate for labour at subsistence wages. This dependence on the estate led to destitution and poverty because wages were constantly reduced in an attempt to rationalize production and keep command over the labour force" (Shepherd 2002, 174). The development of the fruit trade paralleled, and in many ways triggered, the decline of the peasant economy. By the 1890s the fruit trade provided planters an alternative to sugar as a means by which they could generate wealth and reinforce their dominance in the formal economy. In the process, most black Jamaicans had to be repositioned in the formal economy as wage laborers, the peasant economy was relegated to a secondary role in the formal economy, and higglering remained a semi-informal/informal activity, barred from becoming a legitimate part of the formal economy. Indeed, the window of opportunity to elevate peasant cultivation and marketing was closed, and order in the economy was restored.

Most black Jamaicans responded to their proletarianization by engaging in resistance by flight, Phillip Sherlock and Hazel Bennett (1998) point out: black Jamaicans rejected corporate economic coercion and monopoly of land ownership by emigrating to areas such as Panama, the United States, and Central America. Those who could not travel abroad migrated away from estates to the city in search of higher wages; estate wages were vastly depressed as a result in large part of an indentured system. From 1881 to 1921, then, black Jamaican proletarians went in search of the best possible wages to improve their lives (Holt 1992; Shepherd 2002; Sherlock and Bennett 1998).

This migration had a significant impact on black Jamaican families and women's participation in the formal and informal economies. As most of the migrants were men, women were left to single-handedly take care of their households, resulting in an increasing number of black families headed by women as the primary breadwinner. We find women working as domestics, shopkeepers, and higglers to help them fulfill their responsibility as the heads of their households. Higglering flourished in the period between emancipation and independence, and became an important means by which women could support their families in the absence of male partners. Higglering income was also an important supplement to male incomes acquired through remittances or male employment in the formal economy (for those who could find employment). Higglering, then, played a vital role in sustaining black Jamaican families, as it had during the slave era. It was also an important means by which black women could maintain their autonomy as their economic conditions worsened, their employment options shrank, and their household responsibilities increased.

In the early 1900s the conditions for most black Jamaicans were grim. Changes in the world market, economic depression, high unemployment, reduced wages, intense poverty, and malnutrition plagued them, and by the 1930s these conditions became desperate. The first half of the twentieth century witnessed a series of labor rebellions in the Caribbean, including Jamaica, as World War I and the Depression years brought many workers to the brink of despair. Sugar prices fell in the world market and employment opportunities sank in countries like Cuba, where its cane fields no longer provided jobs for migrating Jamaicans. The demand for bananas fell, as the United States, a major consumer, participated in the war. Countries that had once provided jobs to migrating Jamaicans, such as Panama, Honduras, Cuba, and the United States, curtailed immigration as their economies contracted. This meant not only that black Jamaicans could no longer look to these countries for employment, but also that those already working there faced unemployment and returned home (Sherlock and Bennett 1998, 348–49). As Jamaican migrant workers returned home, black Jamaicans from rural areas continued migrating to the cities in search of work, producing a concentration of black poverty in the cities as the two groups competed for what little work was available in the urban formal economy. With few options in the formal economy, more and more Jamaicans turned to the informal economy, and petty trading/higglering became an important source of employment. Where in 1861 there were 431 documented petty traders, by 1921 the number of higglers had increased to 4,164 (Ulysse 2007, 67).

In April 1938, labor disturbances at the Frome Estate (one of two remaining sugar estates) in western Jamaica over the slow payment of wages grew into an islandwide rebellion against the harsh conditions of Jamaican workers and the poor, giving birth to Jamaica's modern nationalist movement, trade unionism, and catapulting two key figures into Jamaica's political history: Alexander Bustamante, a labor leader who later founded and led the Jamaica Labor Party (JLP), and Bustamante's cousin Norman Washington Manley, a lawyer who founded and led the People's National Party (PNP). Additionally, the labor unrest convinced the British Colonial Office to end colonial rule and initiate major constitutional reforms, which paved the way for Jamaica's independence from Britain in 1962.

What is critical to note here is that the color/class/gender hierarchy developed during the slave era did not dissipate with the dismantling of slavery and subsequent restructuring of the economy. Instead, this hierarchy was solidified in the post-emancipation era and beyond. In fact, the "hierarchy of shades" (Cliff 1985) took on greater significance as immigration of new indentured laborers from India and China, coupled with immigration of Europeans and Middle Easterners, complicated local racial hierarchies. These new immigrants helped reinforce the social distance between the white minority and black masses, and contributed to Jamaica's current racial/color/gender system. Although the formation of the peasant economy provided blacks an opportunity to reimagine and reposition themselves as independent producers and marketers, their efforts could not offset the solidification of white power over the political system, to which most blacks were denied access under the Crown Colony system. Nor could they offset white-brown economic power, which was strengthened by the fruit industry. The expansion of the immigrant population created greater distance between blacks and these centers of power.

Additionally, the massive black rural unemployment of the 1920s and 1930s that spurred the rapid migration of black Jamaicans to the cities was not caused solely by changes in the world market, but was also the "result of economic and social policies adopted by the colonial government in alliance with a white-brown upper class" (Sherlock and Bennett 1998, 351). This reality was made painfully clear in a report by the royal commission organized by the British government and directed by Lord Moyne, a colonial secretary. The goal of the commission was to assess conditions in the region shortly after the labor riots of the 1930s, but its report was in effect an indictment of Crown Colony rule (Heuman 2006; Sherlock and Bennett 1998). The Moyne Commission's report confirmed charges made by black leaders like Marcus Garvey that blacks were being oppressed by the white and brown ruling classes:

> Through the policies they followed, the government and the upper middle class discouraged industrialization and manufacturing, used systems of taxation that burdened the poor and eased the prosperous, denied educational opportunity to the lower class, the blacks, and created a type of caste system that kept blacks at the base of the social pyramid. These measures, designed to retain a low-cost black labour force, burdened the available land with too many people and increased rural unemployment. Crown colony and upper-class rule created the urban slums. (quoted in Sherlock and Bennett 1998, 352)

The economic and social policies created by the colonial government in alliance with the white-brown upper class intensified the rapid urbanization of the black population, which in turn made the racialized class hierarchy clearly visible on the physical landscape of the city. The black poor were concentrated in the downtown areas of Kingston, while the rich and powerful white and brown minority lived uptown in the surrounding hills. Perhaps more importantly, these policies reveal that public economic spaces continued to be imagined as the natural place for white and brown bodies as dominant actors, whereas blacks continued to be discursively produced and managed as cheap labor.

In the 1960s—the era of independence—Jamaica experienced rapid economic growth based on bauxite, tourism, and light manufacturing. The problem, however, was that these industries, especially bauxite and tourism, were foreign owned (Heuman 2006). As the economy grew, the benefits of its growth were concentrated in fewer hands. The distribution of income was highly uneven, and increasing levels of illiteracy and unemployment were compounded by inadequate housing, especially among the poor living in western parts of Kingston (Heuman 2006, 156). The racialized class hierarchy that was solidified in the post-emancipation era flourished in the era of independence as well. Despite the fact that blacks constituted roughly 90 percent of the population, "it was local whites, light colored browns, Jews, Lebanese and Chinese who dominated the economy" (156)—a reality that did not go unchallenged by the black population.[12]

Today in Jamaica the so-called twenty-one families—prominent members of Jamaica's white wealthy capitalist class—and their allies control the private sector and wield substantial economic, social, and political power (Douglass 1992; Phillips 1977; Reid 1977). Although these families dominate the private sector, members of the brown economic elite control most local large-scale businesses, such as the tourist industry, and wield tremendous influence in the political system. In the post-independence period, factions of the brown elite, which includes ethnic minorities such as Jews, Lebanese, and Chinese, have had considerable economic and political power. Although we see a significant development of a black bourgeoisie, browns and the twenty-one families continue to occupy dominant positions in the formal economy.

Global economic processes have contributed to a contraction of the formal economy and the subsequent expansion of the informal economy, yet higglering continues to occupy a marginal position in the formal economy in spite of its expansion and modernization. Higglering has grown and includes a new set of traders, informal commercial importers. And yet their assigned place in the Jamaican economy—shaped by ideas of race/color, class, and gender—remains. Public acknowledgment of this business in the 1980s by the Jamaican government with the assignment of the title informal commercial importers suggested on some levels an attempt to include this type of higglering as part of the formal economy. But the lived experiences of informal commercial importers provide evidence to the contrary. The treatment of ICIs by the government sends a clear message that these women and their business continue to be imagined as out of place (see Chapters 5 and 6).

Representations of Sunday/Negro markets as necessary evils and as spaces that embody deviance and disorder discursively constructed these sites and the activities associated with them—higglering—as out of place and out of order, constructing an image of the formal economy as disciplined, orderly, and most importantly, legitimate. This juxtaposition helps legitimize the containment of higglering and its related markets in order to secure the positions of formal economic businesses and merchants, and perhaps to shield them from the competition these activities potentially generate in a developing economy. Indeed, these representations reinforce the spatialization of higglering to the margins of the formal economy—the position it occupies today.

Although the Jamaican economy underwent significant transformations over decades, dominated first by agriculture, then manufacturing, and now a service orientation, the marginal position of higglering has not changed. It continues to be discursively produced and managed as out of place. Indeed, representations of higglering disclose broader assumptions of public formal economic spaces as racialized and gendered, and a somatic norm that privileges white and later brown male bodies as natural inhabitants of these spaces. By representing higglering as out of place, a construction of public economic space as white, brown, and male is envisioned yet unspoken.

4

"Natural Rebels" or Just Plain Nuisances?

Representations of Higglers from Slavery to Independence

> [Huckstering] allowed [enslaved black women] to possess and, later, own property, which in itself represented an important symbolic offensive mission against the established order.
> **HILARY BECKLES**, "An Economic Life of Their Own"

Caribbean historian Hilary Beckles succinctly captures the symbolic significance of the business of higglering/huckstering as it flourished throughout the slave era (Beckles 2000c, 733). This semi-informal/informal economic activity afforded slaves the opportunity to produce and sell their own foods, while marketing allowed slaves "to own and possess property in a system that defined *them* as property" (Beckles 1989, 73, emphasis original). Slave higglers were "natural rebels"—typical women whose everyday experiences represented a culture of refusal and resistance (Beckles 1995, 137). Through higglering, these slaves transformed themselves into economic *subjects* within a broader social and economic context that defined them as objects. Their participation and dominance in the colonial internal market economy as commodity producers and distributors—not as *objects* of production for colonizers—challenged a colonial system that defined public economic spaces as the natural site for distinctive (racialized and gendered) bodies.

Black Women and Sunday/Negro Markets

In a slave economy that relegated black men and women to the lowest strata as objects of production, Sunday/Negro markets afforded slaves, especially enslaved black women, the opportunity to convert their status—albeit temporarily and in the contained spaces of urban markets—from economic objects to commercial subjects.[1] Urban Sunday markets provided an alternate space where rural slave women could re-imagine and present themselves not as economic objects for the sugar economy, but as economic subjects for their own and their families' well-being.

Slave women's mobility from rural plantations to urban markets symbolized the transgression of a spatial association of enslaved black women with plantations and fields. Field work was discursively constructed as the natural domain of enslaved black women, as we have seen (Bush 1990). Their bodies were perceived as biologically structured for this type of labor; in slave auctions the highest value of an enslaved black woman was normally attached to a strong and able field worker, in contrast to a man, whose price instantly rose as he acquired a trade (Mair 2006, 205). The presence of enslaved black women in urban markets as commercial subjects was, in many ways, unnatural, since it contradicted the prevailing view that their rightful place was in the fields as exploitable laborers.

Not only was the presence of enslaved black women in urban markets inconsistent with colonial ideology, but their activities in these spaces—higglering—pushed the limits of the white colonial imagination. In the markets, enslaved women set their own prices and bartered with customers and local merchants for products. As Lucile Mathurin Mair notes (drawing from writings of observers in the 1830s), slaves apparently had no "regular price for anything, but asked as much as they could get." Women were considered "more eloquent in making bargains." As a consequence, "the greatest numbers are Women that one sees on the Market" (2006, 261). In the markets, interactions between slave women and their customers, including white residents and merchants, were not based on a master-slave relationship determined by the complete subservience of slaves. Instead, the relationship was based on bartering, which implies an exchange or trade between two subjects. Slave women repositioned themselves in these market exchanges as economic agents, and the profits and income generated from their sales belonged to them, not their slaveholder. In fact, at one point, slave higglers controlled most of the coins that circulated on the island (Clarke 1975).

Slave women also re-presented alternate self-identities in the markets through their bodies.[2] According to Mair: "Women allocated a fair portion of the returns from their creative/productive/marketing activities towards purchasing their clothes and finery. The colour and flair of black women's fashion attracted regular attention from contemporary observers. They bought out of their private earnings dresses 'of a very superior description' and wore their hats, handkerchiefs and gold and coral jewelry with striking style, to market, to church and on holidays" (2006, 263). Through higglering, slave women became consumers—a privilege denied them as objects of production—and used the power of consumption to create alternate identities. Higglering provided a means over and beyond the rations given them by slaveholders by which slave women could acquire clothing.[3] Most clothing given to slaves was made of osnaburg, a coarse fabric that was inexpensive and could withstand the wear and tear that came with rigorous plantation labor (Buckridge 2004, 30). Gender distinctions were not made in the selection of this fabric for slave clothing; enslaved men and women all wore (or were expected to wear) this coarse fabric, which was not only uncomfortable to the skin but also helped reinforce a sense of sameness among them. Although planters' selection of osnaburg may have been based primarily on economic factors, this material, in effect, served as one way in which gender distinctions were visually suppressed among slaves.

As this fabric helped suppress gender distinctions among slaves, however, it illuminated and reinforced distinctions between slave women and others, especially white elite women, who often wore clothing of fine silk and lace. In *The Language of Dress: Resistance and Accommodation in Jamaica, 1750–1890*, Steeve O. Buckridge reports that silk was a marker of high status and wealth, and had long been considered the fabric of the elite and rulers in many societies. In the Danish West Indies, for instance, slaves were forbidden to wear silk, as well as gold, silver, precious stones, lace, and other expensive items, and it is highly probable that similar restrictions existed in the English territories (2004, 31). Colonial constructions of slave women as unfeminine associated certain fabrics and styles of dress with that presumed lack of femininity so much that enslaved women in dresses "of a very superior description" caught the attention of whites.

Higglers used their purchasing power to create alternate—feminine—identities, thus engaging in nonverbal resistance to colonial ideologies that discursively constructed them as unfeminine. "Dress and the body as signifiers of contrasting and complex meanings," Buckridge comments, "enabled oppressed people (including slaves) to symbolically and covertly resist, to make satirical and politically subversive statements about their identities in relation to the dominant power" (2004, 78). Thinking about dress in this way enables us to understand why slave women allocated large portions of their earnings to purchase fine clothing. Within colonial society, where racialized gender systems excluded

FIGURE 3. *Female Negro Peasant in Her Sunday and Working Dress.* From James M. Phillippo, *Jamaica: Its Past and Present State* (London: John Snow/Paternoster, 1843), 230. (Manuscripts, Archive, and Rare Books Division, Schomburg Center for Research in Black Culture, The New York Public Library, Astor, Lenox, and Tilden Foundations.)

black women from dominant conceptions of femininity, dress became a way in which they could contest those discursive frameworks (see Figure 3).

These contestations continued well into the emancipation era and still occur today.[4] Buckridge shares a story, for instance, about a street vendor in 1891 who was overheard saying to a friend, "When I lick on me silk frock and fling me parasol over me shoulders and drop into Exhibition Ground, you will know wedder I is a lady or not" (2004, 172). Higglering, then, provided black women, enslaved and free, a means by which they could "fabricate identities" outside the oppressive slave system, and the Sunday/Negro market (including churches and festivals) provided a space where those alternate identities could be exhibited and performed (Bakare-Yusuf 2006).

Representations of Slave Higglers: The Formal/Informal Economic Divide

White residents were ambivalent about the social place of Sunday/Negro markets, which were discursively constructed as out of place because they presumably embodied deviance and disorder, as we have seen. Not only were these market spaces perceived as deviant, but the activities associated with the markets were deemed out of order. White residents were also ambivalent about the women who sold in these spaces. Barbara Bush notes that "whilst recognizing their economic importance, planters were worried by the entrepreneurial independence they fostered. Market women/higglers were often described as clever, cunning and untrustworthy" (1985, 41).

In her essay "Slave Higglering in Jamaica, 1780–1834," Lorna Simmonds shared a letter to the editor from the *St. Jago Gazette* for July 11–18, 1829, in which a resident in Spanish Town claimed:

> The undue advantage which the higglers in the market at present possess, and, at a time of such scarcity as we are now laboring under, has operated greatly against the poor of this community. —I had occasion to pass through the market yesterday when I saw a woman sitting on the ground, and several persons collected around her. I heard a great noise as if they were quarrelling. Curiosity led me to the spot to see what was the matter, but, instead of a fight, the woman I saw on the ground, had taken possession of a bag of provisions that belonged to a country negro, and would not allow him to sell any one of the bystanders as much as 5d. worth of the provisions, as it was her intention to purchase the whole bag, and thereby obtain a monopoly in the market. This practice, I am told, is pursued by the higglers generally. Should such things be permitted, Sir, when provisions are so scarce? (quoted in Simmonds 1987, 36)

The question of whether "such things [should] be permitted" is significant not only within a context of scarcity but also in a context of market competition. Here black market women, enslaved and free, were not only seizing scarce produce but also capitalizing on this scarcity and using it to gain a market advantage in order to maximize their profits.

In another letter to the editor, published in the *Royal Gazette* of July 13–20, 1816, a Kingston resident complained:

> The parochial enactments against higgling were never more deserving of serious attention than at the present moment—[the October rains having] destroyed two-thirds of the vegetable provisions, throughout this part of the island, and caused an alarming scarcity. The very scanty supply lately brought to this city is chiefly intercepted and bought up by negro and mulatto higglers in the town, principally slaves, and many no doubt, runaways, before it reaches the proper and legal market-place, and these locusts thereby levy a contribution of 75 to 100 percent in profit upon the inhabitants, and at the same time defraud the industrious and praise-worthy planters of small properties, the mountain gardeners and the industrious slaves, who cultivate these provisions and vegetables, of a great proportion of their hard-earned and just profits. (quoted in Simmonds 1987, 37)

Higglers exhibited an uncanny understanding of market conditions, that is, trends in production of provisions and in consumption demands. Moreover, higglers knew how to manipulate these conditions to secure a competitive advantage. This is a classic capitalist strategy. The problem with these women in the discourse, however, was not that they supposedly defrauded industrious slaves and praiseworthy—white—residents, but that they boldly occupied public commercial spaces and acted in ways that violated colonial norms. That is, dominant gender and racial norms dictated the social and spatial location of black women, enslaved and free, to the margins of the public sphere, especially in the formal economy. Yet higglers inserted themselves into the urban economy as entrepreneurs and at times had a competitive advantage. The assertion that many of the higglers were "no doubt runaways" speaks to the writer's assumption that not only were their activities improper, but also the women themselves were illegal. The description of these shrewd businesswomen as "locusts" speaks powerfully to a presumed invasion of these women—physically and economically—into a space not meant for them. Indeed, these women were out of order.

In times of scarcity, customers, including white residents, had little bargaining power, and their whiteness could not shield them from this disadvantageous position. The monopoly some higglers had in the internal market system signaled an inversion of social and economic power in a context where black women's bodies, especially those of the enslaved, were products that were sold at prices determined solely by slaveholders for their own gain. In these economic exchanges, slaves were silenced. In the Sunday/Negro market, however, this silence was shattered. Here, black women named their prices, which allowed them to exercise control over their products and, by extension, their personhood.

The commercial savvy of the higgler—her knowledge and ability to acquire produce at reasonable prices from rural slaves to resell in towns and to maximize their profits—thus marked her as deviant. Blacks, enslaved and free, were not expected to exhibit this kind of capitalist knowhow. For this affront, higglers were denigrated; they were represented in the public discourse as aggressive rogues who took advantage of others. In a letter to the editor in the *Watchman and Jamaica Free Press* in 1831, the author described higglers as follows:

> Having occasion to go to the Beef Market on Sunday last, I was not a little astonished to find it infested by a number of black females, well known by the name of "Higglers" (most of them free), who monopolize everything. The poor country negroes have scarcely time to put down their loads, before they are surrounded, and in a thousand instances robbed by these women. It is a well known fact that these Higglers take every possible advantage of the poor negroes, who, for the advantage of a better market, and with the hope of obtaining higher prices, travel upwards of forty miles from their homes to this town, with ground provisions, etc. etc. (quoted in Sheller 2002, 11)

Higglers as infestations not only monopolized the market but also robbed poor country slaves of their goods. Again, illegality is mapped onto the bodies of these women.

An interesting urban/rural distinction is established in these letters, with country higglers represented as disciplined and trustworthy, urban higglers as aggressive and deceitful. In the post-emancipation era, the colonial government capitalized on this image of country higglers—market women—as industrious and disciplined, and used it to establish its own legitimacy as well to encourage the development of the economy through tourism and foreign investment. This urban/rural distinction, and subsequent privileging of the country higgler, is replicated in modern Jamaica, where market women are associated with a folk culture with characteristics that include industry, discipline, temperance, and respectability (Thomas 2004), as opposed to modern higglers—informal commercial importers—who, according to Gina Ulysse, represent the "ultimate rude gal" (2007, 48). These contrasting images influence the choices of brown middle- and upper-class customers to interact more frequently with market women (especially those at the Papine Market in uptown Kingston) than with ICIs, as I have pointed out.

The letters dismiss the entrepreneurial skills of higglers and present these women as aggressive and deceitful. Representing higglers in this way reinforced the idea that these black women did not conform to the societal racial and gender norms that required their docility. These women also transgressed an established economic order, and public reactions disclosed a colonial framework that defined the economy as the natural domain of white men. In the admonition of higglers and their economic activities, a somatic norm was implicitly constructed in public discourse that privileged whiteness and maleness in the economy and larger society.

The devaluation of higglers in public discourse discloses processes of boundary construction between legitimate and illegitimate businesses. We see the emergence of this boundary construction during the slave era when white citizens recognized a growing population of slave higglers in the city. Indeed, the growth of street vending during the slave era was matched by constant efforts by town authorities to regulate it. As today, the government built markets in an effort to remove higglers from the streets and to generate revenue from these lucrative businesses.

Public narratives around higglering throughout the slave era constructed higglers' physical presence as an infestation that contaminated city space and, by extension, the local economy. In the *St. Jago Gazette* of November 9–16, 1822, "an inhabitant of Spanish Town complained of 'having observed, for some time past, the streets of this Town to be greatly infested with a set of Hawkers, Peddlers, &c. from Kingston to the great injury of the trading part of the community and in the very eye of the Police." For this inhabitant, higglers' physical presence in the city threatened formal economic businesses, and "he felt compelled to call upon the magistrates to take steps to counteract this 'growing evil' which would eventually ruin the 'fair trader' who is obliged to contribute to the public revenue" (quoted in Simmonds 1987, 34). There is an interesting juxtaposition here. Higglers and, by extension, the business of higglering are represented as growing evils compared with formal economic business people, who are represented as fair traders. In this period, most merchants and traders were whites or secondary whites, and higglers were black slave women who were often associated with evil.[5] The description of an infestation of higglers, then, has not only an economic dimension but also a racial and, by extension, moral one.

Caribbean slave society thrived on distinctions of race, class, and color. In this system, race mixing was perceived as a threat to the small white population.[6] Many pro-slavery advocates claimed that race mixing fostered infertility, because brown or mulatto people—the product of race mixing—were thought to be infertile, and they spoke out vehemently against it. The large influx of slave women into the cities and in close proximity to whites would have been troubling to many whites who were already disturbed by a growing population of colored or mulatto people. Higglers, then, posed a double threat to whites in the cities, particularly white business owners or "fair traders." Their physical presence threatened the reproduction of the white population, and their economic success threatened white economic power, especially that of white merchants and traders.[7]

A petition by the white inhabitants in the town of Falmouth, published in the *St. Jago Gazette* on September 27, 1817, powerfully illustrates this point:

> The inhabitants of this town [Falmouth], and we understand, most of the other towns in the County of Cornwall, are preparing petitions to the Honourable House of Assembly, against the prevailing practice of vending all kinds of Merchandise and Stores upon Sugar Estates, and other Plantations . . . the Managers of which it would be supposed would suppress this trade as, this practice is permitted, must soon destroy the Establishment of the Regular Trader, and consequently ruin the Towns, which in cases of internal commotion, exclusive of their importance in other points of view, afford the best protection to the inhabitants. And, in order also to put a stop to the present extended system of higglering Dry goods of every description about the country, by hired Negroes and others, the magistrates of Trelawney are determined rigidly to enforce the Law in all cases. (quoted in Simmonds 1987, 35)

White traders perceived higglering as a serious threat not only to their businesses but also to their towns. Since higglering provided stiff competition to formal economic businesses, the worry was that if these formal businesses failed, higglering would become the major means of commerce in the cities, leaving the inhabitants vulnerable to the whims of slaves. To control these businesses, measures used against slave higglers were equivalent to the penalties used against runaway slaves. In addition, laws were created to stifle the competition of higglering by regulating this type of trade (Sherlock and Bennett 1998, 173–74; Simmonds 1987).

A commentary published in *Columbian Magazine* in 1798 addressed this issue of slave higglering providing stiff competition to formal economic businesses:

> Kingston at this time pays one hundred pounds yearly to a police officer, who, as a retail shopkeeper himself will feel the force of what follows. If in the course of his rounds he should remark, that the poor inhabitants who pay rent for their shops—their share of pool and parish taxes—honestly buy from the merchant and endeavor to be punctual in their returns: if he should observe that this useful and deserving class of citizens, have their trade interfered with by shoals of idle and disorderly slaves who infest our streets and lanes, obstruct the common pathway and keep extensive shops in the piazzas, (to the constant annoyance of foot passengers and the peace of the inhabitants) for the sale of beef, pork, herrings, . . . and every possible article of edible commerce—even to our horses' grass—how can this hired officer pass by such flagrant breaches of our laws without the remembrance of his duty? The miscreants here described, who live free from rent and taxes, and who frequently recruit their stores with the spoils of the night, can well afford to undersell the honest white traders. Negroes, in general, will most assuredly prefer that mode of purchase where tenfold advantages offer, that is, in buying stolen goods from their own colour, rather than give a full and fair price to the merchants of this commodity. (quoted in Simmonds 1987, 36)

This lengthy passage bears a striking resemblance to present-day narratives around higglering in which businesspeople are constructed as law-abiding citizens who are victimized by lawless higglers (see Chapter 6). Higglers are also portrayed as victimizing pedestrians, as they block the sidewalks and make it difficult to pass. White inhabitants of the slave era perceived higglers' physical presence as contaminating the local economy, placing legitimate merchants at an economic disadvantage. In these narratives, the value of higglering as an economic enterprise is summarily dismissed as idleness, disorder, and criminality, and higglers are reduced to mere infestations of city space and the formal economy.

The writer of this passage compares "poor and honest inhabitants" and "useful and deserving citizens" to "idle and disorderly slaves"; "Negroes" and "miscreants" to "honest white traders." Blackness is associated here with deviance. This is not surprising. In the Caribbean, the colonial and postcolonial regimes established a color/class hierarchy in which "hegemony was legitimized in terms of the superiority of all things European, the inferiority of Africa and African-derived traditions" (Robotham 2000, 9).

The comparisons in the narratives are an effective means of constructing whiteness in the public imagination.[8] In the discourse around higglers in the slave era, two narratives were told. The first, and explicit, narrative described formal economic or legitimate businesses being threatened by higglers. The subtext, however, is more complicated. By constructing boundaries between "honest inhabitants," "useful and deserving citizens," and "honest white traders" and "Negroes," "miscreants," and "idle and disorderly slaves," categories of whiteness and blackness took on meaning and a racial/color hierarchy was established. Categories of citizen and noncitizen were also constructed, placing in the former category whites, who used this construction to assert, implicitly, their rights.

The subtext in the public discourse of that time was that the established color, gender, and class hierarchy was being threatened by the large influx of black slave higglers in two ways. First, they diminished the economic power of white urban traders and merchants by taking away their black customers (slaves and freemen), who converged on the towns by the thousands on the weekends. Second, this large black female presence in the towns, where many whites lived, presented the opportunity for increased incidents of miscegenation that would compromise the survival of the small white population.

In a society with an economy dominated by white men and dependent upon slave labor, higglers posed a quandary. The economic power large numbers of slave women wielded through higglering must have been disconcerting for white merchants, many of whom were losing their business to these slaves. White merchants and other white citizens perceived these black slave women's economic power as undermining the racial, gender, and class hierarchy upon which the colonial regime depended. White demands to suppress higglering were attempts, on one level, to protect this hierarchy.

Visual Representations of Higglers: Bodies in/and Space

Images of higglers in paintings, sketches, and photographs provide us with visual interpretations of the transgressions of black women in the formal economy. For example, a painting by Agostino Brunias entitled *The Barbados Mulatto Girl*, dated around 1780, depicts the color and class hierarchy among women in the colonial era (see Figure 4).

In this painting we observe three women on the roadside, a mulatto woman positioned between her servant and a higgler (Mohammed 2007). She is taller than these women, and her facial features are clearly defined, while the features of her dark-skinned counterparts are hidden, a contrast that draws the viewer's gaze immediately to the mulatto figure. The black women disappear into the background. The artist thus visually creates an image of beauty and sexuality that mulatto women were believed to embody. Although this painting depicts Barbadian women in the colonial era, the image represents the construction of mulatto women as desirable throughout the Caribbean (Mohammed 2000, 2007).

I am interested in the servant and higgler in this image. The stark color contrasts between the three women coupled with the height difference between the lighter-skinned woman and the black women accentuates the pervasive color hierarchy in colonial society. The mulatto woman is elegantly dressed in European-style clothing, jewelry, and an exaggerated head wrap; of her darker-skinned counterparts, one is partially dressed with a piece of fabric wrapped around her waist, and the other wears simple work dress. The differences in clothing draw attention to class distinctions among the three women. As opposed to the elegantly dressed mulatto woman, the seminude body of the servant along with her head wrap, which appears to be held together with a piece of fabric, clearly marks her as enslaved and extremely poor. In comparison, the higgler is better dressed in her work clothes. It is possible that while the higgler and servant are both enslaved, the higgler, through her earnings, was able to acquire better clothing, which distinguishes her from the servant and places the higgler in a better economic position. The clothing of the higgler could also be indicative of her status as a free person (Mohammed 2007). However, the bare feet of all three women symbolize their subordinate status in colonial society, which is represented by the plantation house in the far right background of the image.

The image of the three women represents the correlation of color and occupation in colonial society, where physical labor, especially that required of field work, is associated with black bodies, while nonpraedial

FIGURE 4. *The Barbados Mulatto Girl,* by Agostino Brunias. From a print. (Courtesy of the National Library of Jamaica.)

tasks are associated with brown (and white) bodies (Bush 1990; Mair 2006; Mohammed 2000). The image of the mulatto woman reinforces a gender ideology that represents privileged women, especially those of lighter complexion and higher class, as frail and incapable of the kinds of physical labor associated with field work. These privileged women are assisted by darker-skinned women who carry out labor-intensive tasks such as carrying heavy baskets.

The correlation of color and labor is rendered by the positioning of the hands of the three women. The black women are shown holding or carrying something in their hands—one holds a basket, while the other holds a piece of produce that she is selling. These hands are for labor—are used for productive purposes. But perhaps more importantly, the hands are positioned as serving the mulatto woman. Patricia Mohammed argues that in many of Brunias's paintings, it is common for black bodies to be configured in poses of serving or deference (2007, 15). We see it here in this image, where both black women are lifting items—a basket presumably belonging to the mulatto woman and a piece of produce for her to view. In contrast, the mulatto woman's right hand lifts the outer layer of her skirt, perhaps to cool her legs from the island heat. Her hands are for leisure—for ease and comfort. Her left hand is extended, almost as if she is dismissing the advances of the higgler. The mulatto, as consumer, is clearly in charge. By centering the mulatto woman and placing her higher than her black counterparts, this painting visually connects color privileges with consumer privileges (linking color and class) and blackness with labor.

A comparison of the two standing figures in this image reveals a powerful juxtaposition of the dark seminude body of the servant with that of the mulatto woman. This contrast underscores an oppositional relationship between constructs of respectability and high culture and presumed savagery and low culture. As Steeve Buckridge explains: "Many Europeans had long believed the racist propaganda of the period that African people were all naked savages and thus incapable of any great accomplishment" (2004, 25). The seminude black woman in this image in contrast to the elegantly dressed mulatto woman reproduced the presumption of the backwardness of blacks and reinforced the presumed backwardness of Africa: the exposed, seminude black body versus a civilized Europe represented by the European-style clothing that covers the mulatto woman's body. In spite of her mixed race, the European-style clothing that covers the mulatto woman's body serves to discipline her to conform to European standards and norms. In effect, it civilizes her. Indeed, the layers of European clothing that cover the mulatto woman's body are not appropriate in the tropical heat, yet European norms of respectability and femininity—symbolized, in part, by the clothing—confines the mulatto woman to lifting the outer layer of her skirt as the only means to cool her body, and aligns her with colonial gender norms.

The unflattering images of the black women in comparison to the mulatto woman signal their presumed violation of colonial gender norms: their working bodies are presented as undesirable and unfeminine within the colonial discursive framework of a racialized femininity, apparent when we compare the mulatto woman's dress with the higgler's simple work dress. Like the servant's body, the body of the higgler, though clothed, is not presented as desirable: she wears no jewelry and her clothing lacks ruffles, lace, or color that would enhance her femininity. Moreover, the higgler's body is marginalized in the image, which shifts the viewer's gaze away from her. The marginal position of the higgler's body suggests that her body is not an object of desire. Instead, both the higgler and servant are used in the image to exaggerate the privileged status of the mulatto woman as desirable. At the same time, the positioning of the mulatto woman exaggerates the devalued status of the higgler and servant. The unflattering image of the laboring women sends a message of the devalued status of this particular kind of work and workers.

The distancing of the mulatto woman from the sitting higgler in the painting signals their opposing worlds within colonial society. That the mulatto woman does not return the gaze of the sitting higgler with fruit in hand speaks to the vendor's diminished importance. The mulatto woman's gaze is directed instead toward her servant, whose labor caters directly to her daily needs. Both black women are indeed present in this image, but at the same time their bodies and labor are made invisible and insignificant. Their work fades into the background as the viewer's gaze is drawn to the mulatto lady of leisure, and the power of the consumer is illuminated. In this way, an image of the island as a space of leisure where black bodies are available to serve the white and colored elite, and also British visitors, is powerfully depicted.

Another painting by Agostino Brunias, entitled "Domestic Scene—Two Mulatto Women and Child and Seated Negro Woman" (undated), reproduces the devalued status of higglering and higglers. In this painting, the mulatto women take center stage and draw the gaze of the viewer away from the higgler. The standing mulatto woman is dressed in a colorful European-style dress and a necklace, while the sitting mulatto woman wears a plain dress with one breast and leg exposed, signaling her femininity and sensuality (see Figure 5).

The facial features and skin color of the mulatto women are clearly defined, in contrast with the higgler, whose features are indistinguishable. Her blackness blends into the background, making her almost invisible. The seated position of the higgler on the ground places her on the lowest level in the image in comparison to the mulatto women. She appears as if she is serving the other women, which reinforces her sub-

FIGURE 5. *Domestic Scene—Two Mulatto Women and Child and Seated Negro Woman.* (From the Barbados Museum. Courtesy of the Peter Moores Foundation.)

ordinate status. The mulatto women appear not to look at the higgler—the seated mulatto woman looks past her—and this contributes to the higgler's invisibility.

The image displays a racialized gendered division of labor that spatially relegates mulatto women to the domestic sphere and to child care, as opposed to the higgler, whose work takes her outside the domestic space. The spatial positioning in this image of the mulatto women also contributes to their femininity and sensuality, as their bodies are connected to the home and bedroom. Separating the higgler from domestic space adds to her representation as deviant, as she does not adhere to gender norms that require women to take care of their households and children. This separation further masculinizes the higgler.

Moreover, the image reproduces a racialized gendered division of labor in the positioning of the hands of the women. The higgler's hands disappear into her basket of produce, which physically connects her body to her basket and, by extension, to agricultural labor. The tallest mulatto woman in the center of the image holds a piece of produce that she is presumably purchasing from the higgler. The artist constructs this woman as the consumer of her household who is purchasing not only for herself but also for her child, who clings to her leg. This mulatto woman is a homemaker. The hands of the second mulatto woman lift her skirt, exposing and gently rubbing her leg. Like the mulatto woman in Figure 4, the hands of this woman create ease and comfort. These hands are not associated with physical labor, in contrast to the higgler, whose connection to the basket (designed to be lifted) and produce (harvested) links her body with physical labor. As in Figure 4, then, a correlation between color and occupation is depicted in this image.

The clothing and positions of the three women symbolize on some levels the roles black and brown women were assigned in slave society: as mothers, concubines, and workers. The tallest woman embodies a conception of motherhood espoused by colonial society. The child by her leg and produce in her hand symbolize her role as mother and caretaker of her home—respectable roles within European gender paradigms. The mulatto woman's European-style dress and her central location in the image serve to valorize European norms of femininity and respectability. Her clothing (which is similar to the mulatto woman's in Figure 4) symbolizes her conformity to middle-class European ideals. The covering of the mulatto woman's entire body by European-style clothing—leaving nothing exposed but her hands and neck—symbolizes her being disciplined or civilized by European customs and norms in spite of her mixed race.

The second mulatto woman symbolizes the hypersexuality often associated with mulatto women. Her exposed breast and leg present her as an erotic and exotic figure. Unlike the other mulatto woman, whose entire body is covered, this woman does not represent European gender ideals of respectability. Her exposed body parts emphasize her sexuality and thereby relegate her (and those like her) to the role of concubine in colonial society, her primary purpose to satisfy the sexual desires of white colonial men. The mulatto woman's plain dress distinguishes her from the mulatto mother figure and locates her outside respectable society in spite of her color privileges. In other words, although both mulatto women are presented as feminine and desirable in comparison to the higgler, ideas of respectability (which is tied to motherhood) are mapped onto their bodies, differentiating the two.

The higgler in this image is represented as a worker and as such outside European gender norms of femininity. The blurring of her facial features renders her and her labor invisible. She is represented as neither a respectable mother nor a sexual figure. Her subservient position in the image, along with her work dress, is consistent with a discursive construction of black women in colonial society as workers first, mothers and sexual objects last.

Higglers are subdued in these two images. In fact, the paintings discipline higglers' bodies. In her study of visual representations of the Caribbean by tourism promoters during the colonial period, Krista Thompson notes that "one aspect of the island's picturesque image that promoters had to maintain was precisely the colonies' reputations as disciplined societies. The medium of photography itself became central in the perpetuation and maintenance of this disciplined image; it served as a form of discipline." Thompson points out how photographers selected parts of the Caribbean landscape along with its inhabitants and positioned them to fit into a disciplinary framework; the resulting photographs were used to represent the Caribbean as tamed and safe for European visitors (2006, 17).

Higglers are similarly disciplined in these paintings, which impose a colonial framework of discipline and social order shaped by race, class, and gender, and position the female figures to fit into this framework. The hard work and agency of higglers are made invisible and insignificant in these visual images; the artist represents them as docile. Their black female bodies are passive, restrained, and unthreatening, which reinforces the racialized, classed, and gendered hierarchy pervasive in colonial society and ignores the relative power and monopoly they wielded in the markets.

The critical point here is that the racial/gender/class hierarchies created during the slave era were reinforced in a variety of ways throughout the colonial period.

Indeed, unflattering images of higglers continued to be reproduced in the post-emancipation era. For example, in a sketch by Gilbert Gaul entitled "A Fruit Vendor," published in April 1897 in *Century Illustrated Monthly Magazine*, an older black woman sits on a box on a sidewalk next to her basket of fruit (see Hawthorne 1896–1897a). Her surroundings give the impression of urban decay. What appear to be fire hydrants lean sideways. The street is unclean, and the higgler is surrounded by trash. Her facial features are partially defined. She rests her chin in her left hand, and her expression reflects weariness and perhaps frustration (see Figure 6).

The higgler is presented as asexual and unfeminine. Her hands are

FIGURE 6. *A Fruit Vendor,* by Gilbert Gaul. From Julian Hawthorne, "Jamaica: Summer at Christmas-Tide," *Century Illustrated Monthly Magazine,* November 1896–April 1897. (Courtesy of Cornell University Library, Making of America Digital Collection.)

rough from the hard labor associated with higglering, in contrast to the hands of the mulatto women in previous images, soft and fine in texture. Her facial features appear coarse and wrinkled, as opposed to the mulatto women, whose features are fine and smooth. The unhappy expression on the higgler's face as she sits beside a basket full of produce suggests the possibility of failure in her business.

This image accompanied a description of the city as having straight streets, two-storied houses that appear to lack paint and varnish—a place where "there were negro women in light colored frocks of calico, with bandanas on their heads, smiling black faces, and round, shining eyes, which could give most significant glances, for there is a universal capacity for flirtation among these jolly damsels" (Hawthorne 1896–1897a, 432). The author of the article, Julian Hawthorne, writes that "it was market day and steamer day, and the following week was to be race week, and Christmas was only a little way off; so the gaiety of Kingston was at its height" (433). He makes no reference to this higgler. His only associated comment is that "fruit was for sale on every corner and on every woman's head" (432). The higgler was visible and yet invisible. Her work, her life, and her value were irrelevant to the author and the artist. Her image does not correlate with the description of "jolly damsels" nor do her facial expressions and body language suggest the gaiety of the season. Instead, she appears miserable.

Although the image of the higgler does not fit Hawthorne's description of the city and its inhabitants, this representation corresponds with a larger discursive framework of Jamaica as ruined by emancipation. In the image, trash and deteriorating structures surround the higgler, associating her body and labor with urban decay. She is not shown actively selling her fruits to customers, nor do her surroundings suggest commercial success and profitability. Instead, the surroundings appear desolate. This image reinforces a perception of higglering as devalued labor and of higglers as deviants. Here, higglering is not portrayed a profitable, legitimate, or even desirable business. Instead, it is visually presented as part of the country's demise.

Hawthorne's article, "Jamaica: Summer at Christmas-Tide," in which this sketch was featured was written for an American audience. As the Jamaican sugar economy contracted and transitioned to bananas, efforts were made by the British government along with British and North American corporations to reimagine and re-present the island as a viable tourist attraction and site of foreign investment (Thompson 2004, 2006). To attract potential investors and to stimulate white migration, it was critical to re-present the island as orderly and disciplined, especially after emancipation where free blacks vastly outnumbered whites, and where memories of black rebellions were fresh in the white imagination (Thompson 2004, 2006).

Hawthorne's article is consistent with this re-presentation. It offered detailed descriptions of the city of Kingston, the island, and its climate, and presented a picture of Jamaican society as quaint and orderly, its inhabitants friendly:

> The English administration in Jamaica is a thing to be thankful for: there are law and order, excellent roads, comfortable houses, adequate police, lawn-tennis and cricket, plenty of manly, companionable English army and navy officers, and a governor who is strong, able and genial. At the same time it would be folly to maintain that the island is producing a tenth part of the wealth that is latent in the soil and atmosphere, or that most of the wealth that is beginning to make its appearance is due to anything so much as to the American enterprise and capital which are opening up railways and cultivating fruits. (1896–1897a, 429)

Hawthorne alleviated a potential tourist's and investor's fears of post-emancipation Jamaica with the assurance that the British government has successfully created order under its Crown Colony system. His description of adequate police and significant British army and naval presences on the island sent a clear message that the island was safe and secure, and that its inhabitants were disciplined.

Additionally, Hawthorne presented the island as a gold mine for any foreign (i.e., white) investor—a diamond in the rough, so to speak—that it would be a mistake to preclude from reaching its full potential. Hawthorne gives the reader an impression of Jamaica as resource rich and yet underappreciated and underdeveloped by its local (perhaps backward) inhabitants. The potential contributions of free blacks—who were already developing their local peasant economy—as a means of economic development are ignored. Instead, market activities and higglers, and by extension the peasant economy, are presented as part of the island landscape for tourists' and investors' consumption (Thompson 2006).[9]

What interests me about the image of the higgler is that the article not only presents her in an unflattering manner but also fails to offer her independent business, and by extension independent peasant production and marketing, as a viable option for economic development in post-emancipation Jamaica—despite the fact that peasant production of ground provisions constituted around 50 to 55 percent of total agricultural output at the time, making it possible for the island to become less dependent upon food imports (Satchell 1995, 218). Indeed, peasant production and marketing helped the island become more self-sufficient in food, but this is not represented in this image of the higgler. Her slumped back, hand on cheek, and facial expression suggest failure. Placing her body in the midst of decay reinforces a dominant view in colonial society that peasant proprietorship cannot (or should not) offer a road to economic recovery. Instead, the only means of economic success is through the development of the fruit industry, tourism, foreign investment, and the transformation of black bodies into low wage laborers.

These representations help reinforce racial, gender, and class hierarchies in the construction of public economic spaces as the legitimate or natural domain of white, wealthy men, and the spatial location of black women on the margins. The visual depiction of higglering as a failure in the white imagination leaves wage labor as the only alternative for developing the economy and civilizing blacks in the post-emancipation era.

There are less unflattering representations of higglers, however. For example, in the same issue of *Century Illustrated Monthly Magazine*, April 1897, a sketch by Gilbert Gaul entitled "On the Way to Market" captured three women on their way to the market carrying baskets on their heads (see Figure 7).[10] This image accompanied a description of the activities of the inhabitants of Jamaica, who cultivate their grounds, in the post-emancipation era. The description of the women represented in this image is telling: "On market days the women put in a basket whatever surplus is not needed for the family consumption, and walk down to Kingston with their baskets on their heads, sell their produce and walk back again at nights with the same springy tireless step. . . . It is a primitive and healthy life, and superb specimens of smiling ebony womanhood most of these mountain nymphs appear" (594). Although "superb specimens of smiling ebony womanhood" may appear to be a flattering description, the women are quickly objectified as "mountain nymphs," which affiliates their bodies with nature in the construction of the island as a tropical paradise. Krista Thompson suggests that black market women, "more than any other human presence, entered the representational frame as the visual companion of tropical nature" (2006, 103). In these images, black market women served as part of a backdrop to an image of the Caribbean as a safe tropical paradise available for tourist consumption. Indeed, in promotional images for tourism in the Caribbean, black inhabitants were viewed as the natural companions to a tropical landscape and "black market women, frequently depicted

FIGURE 7. *On the Way to Market,* by Gilbert Gaul. From Julian Hawthorne, "A Tropic Climb," *Century Illustrated Monthly Magazine,* November 1896–April 1897, 593. (Courtesy of Cornell University Library, Making of America Digital Collection.)

balancing fruit on the crowns of their heads, especially completed and proffered the island's tropically abundant image" (107). Like the previous image, this drawing is not meant to celebrate the value of higglering or higglers to the local economy but is created principally for the tourist gaze.

This image also sends the message that the island's inhabitants are disciplined and industrious. The bodies of the two higglers in the foreground, who stand erect, arms at their sides, like soldiers, symbolize discipline and order among the black inhabitants. The industriousness of the three women is captured by their carrying heavy loads on their heads with relative ease. Images like this played a critical role in the post-emancipation era; they served as counterevidence to common perceptions in the United States and Britain that freed blacks were lazy and unproductive, and that British colonial policies had failed to civilize Jamaica's black population (Thompson 2006).[11]

There have been numerous instances throughout the eras of slavery and colonialism in Jamaica when white residents and visitors marveled at the ability of black women to carry heavy loads on their heads. For example, in a November 18, 1859, *New York Times* article headlined "Emancipation in Jamaica: Its Results upon the Present and Future Welfare of the Island," the author strongly contested commonly held views among a U.S. audience that blacks were lazy: "No sight is more novel to the stranger than is presented on market morning, on any road leading from the seaport towns. A procession of women, miles long, lines either side of the road. They stride along, with even and steady step, bearing on their heads wooden trays filled with yams, cocoas, and other products of their mountain gardens, all hurrying to the market." The author explained that the inhabitants of the island were entirely dependent upon these women for their supply of fruits and vegetables, and this made them valuable assets to society. Furthermore: "If you take one of those trays and lift it, you would find it no easy job to carry it two hundred yards; yet these women have borne that burden in some cases six and eight miles. Such cheerful toil excludes at once the statement that laziness is a characteristic of the Jamaica negro." Although the author praises the women for their work, he glosses over the real difficulty that comes with higglering along with its value to the local economy. Put simply, he ignores the intrinsic value of higglering as a legitimate business and higglers as entrepreneurs. Instead, the value of these women's work is that it provides strong evidence of the success of British colonial rule.

In spite of this praise, however, images of higglers have accompanied strong indictments of black *men* as lazy. For example, in his article in *Harper's Monthly Magazine* in 1889, Howard Pyle asserted: "All the vendors of fruit and produce are women, and nearly all those whom one sees marching along streets and roadways with great heavy-laden baskets poised upon their heads are women also. In Kingston, the negro men turn their heads to work, but in the country districts they seem to lay the burdens of life upon the other sex." He then described a young man on a road riding a donkey, while an elderly black woman, barefoot and carrying a basket on her head, followed behind holding its tail. Pyle was intrigued by this scene. "No doubt the peculiar inversion of sex responsibility that makes the woman the laborer and the man the consumer is a relic of a former barbarism of the African bush, when the men fought and the women worked. The need for fighting seems to have passed away; the necessity for work remains" (1889–1890, 176, 177).

Indeed, the hard labor of higglers has been used as evidence of the inversion of gender roles among blacks. What this view exposes is a presumed gendered division of labor and space that relegates men's work to the public sphere and women's work to the private sphere. There is also a gendered construction of consumption that assigns this role to women as part of their domestic duties. We see this construction visualized in Figures 4 and 5, where mulatto women occupied this role in relation to higglers, which reinforced their femininity in comparison to higglers, whose labor in public space renders them unfeminine.

Higglers continued to capture the imaginations of white residents and visitors throughout the colonial era. According to Krista Thompson, the higgler was "one of the most persistent icons in colonial Jamaica. Indeed, by the end of the 1920's the market woman figuratively embodied Jamaica" (2004, 3). As opposed to the eighteenth and early nineteenth centuries, when market women played a peripheral role in visual representations of the island—usually as part of the tropical landscape—these women assumed a more prominent role in the late nineteenth and early twentieth centuries (Thompson 2004, 2006). The prominence of market women in visual representations of Jamaica correlates with the developing tourist trade and the colonial civilizing mission (Thompson 2004, 4). Numerous images that featured market women circulated in tourism-related literature and pictures; "within these representations," according to Thompson, "an iconography of the market woman as a type emerged, one that emphasized her tropical, primitive, yet industrious characteristics" (5). The growing tourist industry paralleled the developing fruit trade, and companies like the United Fruit Company actively participated in tourism, using their ships for transporting tourists as well as fruits. The merger of these two interests—tourism and the fruit trade—was beneficial to the United Fruit Company, as tourists became targeted consumers of its fruits (Thompson 2006).

In addition to symbolizing tropical characteristics of the island, however, representations of the labor of higglers sent a clear message to potential investors that there was a reserve army of disciplined laborers ready at hand. Colonial authorities and fruit-industry promoters had an investment in presenting images of the island's inhabitants as hardworking and industrious—an image that would resonate favorably with potential investors and would speak to the successes of Britain's civilizing mission through colonial rule (Thompson 2004, 7). Images of laboring black women, especially market women, served this role. In these images market women were frequently depicted as workers—carrying baskets, standing or walking alongside donkeys on their way to market, or sitting next to or carrying produce. They are not represented or described as entrepreneurs. These representations reinforced a perception of the Jamaican people and economy as eager for and in need of the guiding hand of British and American interests for the island's economic development.

Although these images represented black Jamaicans as industrious, they also reproduced and reinforced a construction of racialized femininity created during the slave era that excluded black women—a perception of higglers as women rather than ladies. Images of the laboring bodies of higglers reinforced perceptions of them as unfeminine. Ideals of femininity, fueled by constructions of gender, race, and labor, are depicted in these images by the absence of white and brown women, and by the presentation of higglers' bodies for utilitarian purposes—as evidence of the success and necessity of British colonial rule, and as part of the tropical landscape. These laboring bodies were not presented for pleasure or desire.

Like most black Jamaicans, higglers were placed outside colonial constructions of beauty and femininity and were not framed as worthy of art (Thompson 2004). That role, and the constructions of femininity and beauty associated with it, was reserved for white and colored women, especially those from the leisure classes.

Indeed, while images of higglers circulated in tourist literature to represent the tropical landscape of the island and the industriousness of its inhabitants, other women were used to represent femininity and beauty. We see this quite clearly in national beauty pageants that consistently excluded black Jamaican women, including higglers (Barnes 1994; Ulysse 2007). According to Gina Ulysse, the earliest winners of Miss Jamaica contests, which began in the 1940s, represented a white bias and excluded other racial and ethnic groups on the island (2007, 36). Other contests were organized in the 1950s in an attempt to be more representative of the racial and ethnic diversity of the population. For example, the Ten Types, One People contest organized in 1955 tried to be racially and ethnically inclusive. However, it "took this multiracial approach for blackness to be publicly treated as beautiful, but only with chemically treated hair" (ibid.). In other words, although blackness was presented as beautiful in this pageant, its beauty was associated with its proximity to whiteness.

This privileging of European features over African features continued well into the period of Jamaica's independence in 1962, and beyond. National beauty pageants in the post-independence era replicated the celebration of brown women as the beauty ideal. Despite two black women with natural hair winning the crown in the late 1960s and early 1970s, brownness continued to represent beauty in these pageants and in the wider society (Barnes 1994; Mohammed 2000; Ulysse 2007).[12]

So while the market woman figuratively embodied Jamaica by the 1920s, images of her by the colonial government were scripted. Images of market women in tourism literature were used to construct the tropical landscape, as well as to represent to a foreign (U.S. and British) audience the industriousness of black Jamaicans and the power of British colonial rule. We see variations of these images of market women in tourism literature in the Caribbean today, in which the produce the women carry represents the abundance of the island, their smiling faces represent the island as a happy and carefree place to vacation, and their laboring bodies represent black industry in the service of whites—tourist and otherwise.[13] What is not represented in these images, however, are the market woman's entrepreneurial skills and the value of higglering to her, her family, and the local economy. Indeed, as in Brunias's paintings, higglers are visible and invisible in colonial and postcolonial representations, thus establishing their status as outsiders in the formal economy and wider society, and reinforcing color/gender/class hierarchies.

Representations of higglers, then, disclose racialized gender norms that black women violate by working in public spaces, because they occupy positions reserved for white men. Although enslaved black women were already working in public spaces—that is, in the fields—higglering represented a deviation from this norm: black slave women occupying public commercial spaces dominated by white men. Enslaved black women's activities in these commercial spaces were perceived as a transgression of racial norms, as they at times wielded economic power over their white customers via the power to set their own prices and to make bargains. But perhaps most importantly, enslaved black women transgressed racial, gender, and economic norms in public commercial spaces that defined them as objects of production to be traded by slaveholders. Through higglering, these presumed objects of production became commercial subjects and this violated a fundamental premise of the slave ideology and economy.

Black women in the post-emancipation period continued to be represented as violating racial, class, and gender norms in public space. Their continued presence in public markets and streets as higglers was viewed as a violation of the gender and economic norms that relegate women to the domestic (reproductive) sphere, and white and black men to the public (economic) sphere. They also violated racial norms, as these black women, like their enslaved counterparts, at times wielded significant economic power in the markets over other racialized groups, including whites. In other words, higglers' economic power allowed them to invert—albeit temporarily—relationships of domination and subordination shaped by race, class, and gender.

As the formal economy transitioned to bananas and tourism, images of higglers were co-opted and used to promote Jamaica as fertile soil for foreign investments and tourist consumption. The laboring bodies of higglers were used to represent a disciplined labor force for potential (that is, white) investors, as well as the success of the British colonial project. There were deafening silences and omissions in these representations. Higglers' labor and marketing activities were re-presented as valuable assets for foreign capitalists in search of a disciplined labor force. In other words, higglers were discursively produced as disciplined wage laborers, not microentrepreneurs.

These images reinforced color, class, and gender hierarchies. Representations of higglers disclose a somatic norm that privileges white—and later, brown—male bodies as natural inhabitants of public economic spaces. By representing higglers as deviant, public economic space as white/brown and male is constructed in the public imagination. The commercial activities of black women in public spaces are imagined as unnatural within a broader discursive framework of race and gender, which implies that these activities are rightfully suited to white and, later, brown men.

Today, higglers continue to grapple with the challenge of making a living within a public economic space that historically has excluded them, or has assigned them to the primary role of low-wage labor. They also struggle against public representations that continue to identify them as deviants, socially and economically.

5

Higgler, ICI, Businesswoman
What's in a Name?

> To raise the question of identity is to reopen the
> discussion on the self/other relationship in its enactment
> of power relations.
> TRINH T. MIN-HA, "Not Like You/Like You"

In an editorial titled "On Higglers" in the *Jamaica Gleaner* of August 10, 1986, Morris Cargill, a white Jamaican journalist, ponders a question about the bodies of higglers: "Considering that so many Jamaican girls are slim and pretty one is bound to wonder whether higglers are the result of selective breeding. To begin with, few seem to weigh less than 250 lbs. They are also a special shape, sticking out back and front simultaneously; huge protruding bottoms and equally huge tops, both of which they use as battering rams."[1] Cargill's invocation of Jamaican higglers with huge breasts and protruding bottoms battering unsuspecting bystanders carries a racial connotation that relies on a stereotypical image of the black mammy figure. We see this image reproduced in various artistic representations of the Jamaican higgler. Her head is wrapped. Her breasts are large. And her bottom protrudes. But most importantly, she is represented as asexual—her body is not to be desired.

In fact, Cargill writes, it is "worse still [to] have [a higgler] run up against you and you soon know that there is no soft flabby fat there, but solid muscle." He likens higglers to Russian weightlifters who do what they do "because they happen to be built like that in the first place." As Cargill writes years later under the subhead "Bras with Cement," in another *Jamaica Gleaner* editorial, "Bleaching, Etc.," this one published July 29, 1999: "In the case of the higglers, . . . cleavages are not for sex but for storage." He constructs higglers as unfeminine, asexual women who take advantage of ordinary citizens and the Jamaican authorities, and this construction legitimizes his call for their containment by the Jamaican government. The image of the black mammy as higgler serves Cargill's purpose, justifying their removal from public spaces.

Cargill's unflattering construction of higglers draws from a representational frame that defines these women as deviants and their work as devalued labor—a frame well established during the colonial era. Indeed, Cargill's description of higglers' presumably large and unattractive bodies in contrast to "so many Jamaican girls [who] are slim and pretty" reproduces that era's comparisons of higglers and more feminine (soft-featured, genteel) women, including brown/mulatto women. Not only do Cargill's descriptions of higglers' bodies serve to construct these women as unfeminine, but also their presumably large bodies indicate their lack of control, that is, self-control and control by the state. Cargill employs unflattering descriptions of higglers' bodies—their appearances and actions—to call on the state to discipline these workers. In doing so, he reinforced the formal/informal, legitimate/illegitimate divides in the economy and society, and the relegation of higglers to the informal and illegitimate.

In the August 15, 1986, *Daily Gleaner*, members of the Higglers Association in uptown Kingston responded to Cargill's editorial, demanding an apology. In "Higglers Blast Cargill Article As 'an Insult to All Women,'" Mrs. Williams-Edwards, president of the association, described Cargill's statement as insulting not just higglers, but all women, and attributed his views to "a growing class prejudice which articles like Cargill's only served to worsen." She proceeded to defend higglers: "Are we being likened to cows, or some other animal, which is classed as a special species? We are not of any different breeding" Williams-Edwards dismissed allegations implied in Cargill's editorial that higglers were lawless and were taking advantage of ordinary citizens and the government. She produced several customs receipts to prove that higglers, and ICIs in particular, were law-abiding citizens who paid duties on their imports like every other citizen.

Williams-Edwards went on to explain that higglers were the "backbone of the society" and had helped sustain the Jamaican economy, "since they have to pay the taxi man to transport the goods from the airport, the handcart man, and the man who services the stalls. They also pay women to sell their goods for them. Higglers are not a menace, as Cargill is suggesting, but rather an industry." These remarks are significant, given the current state of the Jamaican economy. The imposition of neoliberal policies by the IMF on the Jamaican government, which minimizes its role in the local and global economy, coupled with a national debt that has reached unprecedented levels, has weakened the economy and the state's ability to provide for the basic needs of its citizens. The rate of unemployment in the formal economy has contributed to the expansion of the informal economy, and higglers, as Williams-Edwards suggests, provide employment opportunities to poor Jamaicans at a moment when the state is unable to.

After quoting her defense of higglers and the legitimacy of higglering, the article explains that Mrs. Williams-Edwards took "exception to the name 'higgler'" and suggested using an alternative term, "vendor," which carries less-negative class connotations. In her view, the adoption of the label "vendor" would help higglers avoid the negative stigma associated with their informal work, and the public could perceive them as respectable businesswomen. Today, few women use the term "higgler" to describe their work.

What is particularly interesting about Williams-Edwards's response is her presentation of Cargill's ridicule as an insult to all women, not just higglers. This is an important strategy, because if Cargill's remarks were read simply as an attack on higglers, the Jamaican public would be less outraged by them, since these remarks are consistent with a general perception of higglers, and of poor black women in general, as deviant. Recasting Cargill's commentary as insulting to all women, across class and color, carries greater meaning. If the more respectable women in Jamaican society, especially brown and white elite women, are vulnerable to insults like Cargill's, the public is more likely to take them seriously. Williams-Edwards's response reveals her keen understanding of these color and class dynamics in Jamaica that privilege a middle-class femininity and respectability, and her ability to draw on those dynamics in order to address this attack on higglers.

Williams-Edwards's suggestion to replace the label "higgler" with "vendor" is another example of her awareness of a predominant middle-class notion of respectability and her attempt to reimagine higglers as respectable women through renaming. In other words, Williams-Edwards attempts to manage the stigma of higglering through a process of redefinition and in doing so provides an opportunity for higglers to disassociate themselves from the negative stigma attached to higglering in the public discourse and to re-present themselves as respectable workers.

Higglers' attempts at stigma management are the central focus of this chapter. I examine the self-identities of forty-five higglers and suggest that these women's constructions of themselves and bodily performance of their work in the informal economy exemplify contestations and negotiations of hegemonic discourses of race/color, class, and gender in Jamaica. Higglers contest negative discourses using various stigma management techniques, and thus illustrate their agency within a context inhibited by a myriad of discourses that constrain and limit their possibilities for economic success and general social acceptance.

Of course, identities are not static, abstract, one-dimensional conceptions of self. They are not finished products, but are produced and reproduced through our multitextured bodies and our performances (Butler 1990). Identities, then, are understood as what we do. Through our performances, they are constantly reproduced, and that reproduction occurs within specific social, spatial, and historical contexts that influence, and are potentially changed by, those performances. For instance, public constructions of femininity that are simultaneously racialized, classed, and sexualized influence how one perceives or identifies oneself as a woman/lady and feminine. These constructions of femininity also shape and constrain our behaviors, that is, how we *do* femininity, especially in Jamaica where constructions of femininity embodied by the Jamaican lady preclude her from wearing clothing that exposes her body and sexuality in public spaces. She is relegated to spaces where behaviors that involve flaunting one's sexuality are not deemed appropriate. However, a person who resists the construction of the Jamaican lady may go scantily clad anywhere in public, whether in the dance-hall space, the front yard, or on the streets.

Identities, then, are not produced in a vacuum. Lise Nelson argues, for instance, that "subjects continually perform identities that are prescribed by hegemonic discourses" (1999, 336).[2] The hegemonic discourses around higglering influence the identities and behaviors of higglers. These constructions are then reproduced through their performances. Those performances perpetuate or reinforce public constructions of, say, femininity, but they also (potentially) change those constructions by negotiating and contesting them.

Identities are also relational. That is to say, the formation of identities includes broader social relationships (Knowles 1999). As relational constructs, one's identity, or a "me" (to borrow from Toni Morrison), is often accompanied by a "not me" that serves as a subtext (Morrison 1990). The public construction of higglers, with all its color, class, and gender connotations, serves as a marker of otherness. Higglers represent the woman who is unfeminine, nonbrown/white, poor, unlawful, indecent, and undisciplined.[3] This symbolizes for the brown/white middle and upper classes (and those who aspire to this status) the "not me." The invocation of these images plays an important part in their identity formation, because as the public images of higglers are constructed, images of the brown/white middle and upper classes are projected.[4]

Labels used in the Jamaican public discourse on higglering serve to locate women in the social order as well, ranking them relative to others. Labels such as "lady" are used as indicators of a person's prestigious position and high social value, whereas labels such as "woman" and "higgler" indicate a person's low prestige and social value. Of course, such descriptions impact an individual's self-identity. Indeed, a "person's public identity consists of the names by which they are known" (Pfuhl and Henry 1993, 160). Such labels, however, do not determine a person's identity. In the process of identity formation, labels change and are contested over time. Subjects, then, are not solely determined by hegemonic discourses. Instead, they exercise some agency, through negotiations and reflexivity, within those constraints and eventually can bring about change. I am particularly interested in ways in which these women exercise their agency by negotiating hegemonic discourses around higglering. One way in which they do this is through stigma management.

In *The Deviance Process,* Edwin H. Pfuhl and Stuart Henry describe stigmas as "marks or brands placed on people (e.g., slaves, criminals and others) to indicate their low social position and their status as outsiders" (1993, 157). Stigmas serve to pinpoint people's spoiled identities (their social undesirability) and take precedence over other nondeviant qualities they may have. Individuals are then rejected on the basis of those spoiled identities. The label "higgler" has often been used in this way in Jamaica's public discourse. Many times the label "higgler" is used to identify a person as socially undesirable and an outsider. With this label, a higgler's presumably objectionable conditions are publicly known.

Although many people who are labeled deviant accept the associated stigma and shame, others attempt to minimize the negative impact of their stigma by managing it.[5] The goal of these stigma-management techniques is to "reduce the relevance of the 'known' stigmatized condition by attempting to maintain a positive, if not normal, self-image and identity." One tactic used is destigmatization: "the process used to regulate or expunge a deviant identity and replace it with one that is essentially non-deviant or normal" (Pfuhl and Henry 1993, 198).

We see this attempt at destigmatization in Mrs. Williams-Edwards response to Cargill's statements, in which she called for the replacement of the label "higgler" with "vendor." Through this renaming process, Williams-Edwards attempted to disassociate higglers from an identity presumed deviant in the public imagination and to replace it with one that was nondeviant or more respectable. What has happened in the public discourse, however, is that the stigma associated with the label "higgler" has been transferred to the label "vendor" (or street vendor);

it is quite common to see the terms used interchangeably. The women in my study use other labels, and other management techniques, aimed at destigmatizing their identity.

Destigmatization does not depend solely on changing labels. Behaviors have to be changed as well: socially acceptable behaviors replace ones that are stigmatized. A person's performance plays an important role here. As one attempts to reconstruct or negotiate her identity within the constraints of hegemonic discourses, it is important that she replace behaviors presumed to be deviant with nondeviant ones. These performances, critical in the negotiation or contestation of identities, are clearly evident in my study of higglers.[6] They utilized stigma management techniques; they described presumably deviant behaviors among fellow higglers, culturally distancing themselves from those behaviors; and perhaps most importantly, they performed their own identities as nondeviant.

Higglers' Self-Identities

To get a sense of the self-identities of the forty-five women in my study, I asked: "Based on the kind of business you operate, would you consider yourself a (a) higgler; (b) market woman; (c) ICI; (d) vendor; (e) entrepreneur/businesswoman?" Of 45 women, 44 answered this question. One-third of the market women identified themselves as higglers, one-third as entrepreneurs or businesswomen, and only three as vendors.[7] Among the ICIs, only one identified herself as a higgler. Another woman claimed that "higgler and ICI are both the same" but identified herself as an ICI (#39). Although this woman did not elaborate on why she believed higglers and ICIs were the same, she implicitly addressed the way in which they are constructed in the public discourse, where no distinctions are made between them. Both are perceived negatively.

Overall, the ICIs were less likely than the market women to identify themselves as higglers or vendors. Instead, almost all the ICIs identified themselves as either entrepreneurs/businesswomen or as ICIs. The educational differences between the two groups of higglers are important in shaping their identities as either businesswomen or higglers. The ICIs were more educated than the market women. Two-thirds reported having at least a secondary/high school education or higher, as opposed to half of the market women. More ICIs than market women were educated beyond high/secondary school. The difference in education level and occupation is an important indicator of class differences between the two groups of women, associating the market women with the lower and peasant classes, and the ICIs with the working class.⁸ These class differences along with the connection of market women to the peasant economy influence their identities as "higglers" or "entrepreneurs." These identities reflect an urban/rural distinction as well. Whereas market women have greater ties to the agricultural/rural sector, ICIs are connected to the urban sector; their self-naming reflects those distinctions.

The pattern of responses also demonstrates that despite a public discourse that uses the terms "higgler" or "vendor" in a way that collapses ICIs with market women, these distinctions are important among these women. Four ICIs argued, for instance, that they were not higglers, because higglers sold food, whereas they sold foreign items. Although the market women had a wider range of responses to the identity question in comparison to the ICIs, none identified themselves as ICIs. This demonstrates that the women emphasized the distinctions between the two groups of informal workers in spite of the tendency in the public discourse to collapse the two groups.

I asked all the women if their businesses and higglers in general were respected, to get a sense of these women's awareness of the public discourse around higglering and the public perception of higglers. I posed these questions: (1) Do you think your kind of business is highly respected/valued in Jamaica? (2) Do vendors/higglers generally get a lot of respect in Jamaican society? Explain. (3) Do you think you get the same kind of respect as businesspeople who have stores in the Plazas? The women's responses revealed that more than half in each group believed that their businesses were highly respected. When asked to explain her answer, one market woman declared that her business was respected because "we keep the country!" (#1). In the midst of economic decline, this market woman saw that higglering generated income for the nation's poor, provided employment, and kept the country's economy running. Another market woman explained that higglering was respected because it "keep you from begging" (#14). An ICI declared that her business was respected because "vendors employ people" (#35). Another stated that higglers' businesses were respected because "we can help ourselves and don't ask for handouts" (#39). The general feeling among the women was that respect was accorded their business efforts because they helped sustain Jamaica in dire economic times.

In a context of economic decline and a weakened state, higglers perceived their work as respectable because it allowed them to be self-sufficient. This rationale is consistent with a vision of progress and respectability that has been firmly rooted in Jamaica's cultural ethos since the post-emancipation era and has been espoused by Jamaica's political and economic elites during the period of independence and beyond. This notion of respectability emphasizes, among many things, education, thrift, self-sufficiency, independence, and self-improvement through individual initiative. Furthermore, principles of egalitarianism and meritocracy embodied in Jamaica's Creole nationalist motto, "Out of many, one people," are advocated among the brown elite, who assume an open system where one's conditions can be improved with individual effort, not necessarily with structural change.[9] The women I interviewed interpreted their business endeavors as attempts at self-sufficiency and as alternatives to "begging in the streets." More than one-third explicitly stated that their businesses were respected because they could be self-sufficient. For some women, their businesses allowed them to build their own homes, manage their households, and employ other people, all of which led the women to believe that their businesses were respected.

I also asked the women if vendors or higglers themselves were highly respected. More than half the market women believed that vendors and higglers were respected. One market woman said: "Many people respect higglers. I've seen a lot of higglers uplift themselves" (#15). Another said: "Yes, higglers are respected, because I can manage my home" (#16). These responses are similar to those regarding public respect for the business of higglering in ways that are consistent with the Jamaican ethos of self-sufficiency and individual initiative. However, more ICIs than market women believed they were not respected. One ICI reported that only "people who know how hard you work" respected higglers (#45).

Specifically, half the ICIs and a third of the market women believed higglers in general were not respected. More than half the market women (thirteen) and roughly a third of the ICIs (eight) believed that vendors and higglers were respected. Two market women and one ICI argued that higglers were respected, but that respect depended on "how you treat people" (#5, #6, #37). The other higglers in the sample simply said yes (they were respected) and offered no explanation.

In sum, although half of both groups of higglers believed their businesses were respected, a larger number of ICIs than market women reported that higglers themselves were not respected. Of great significance are the ICIs' explanations as to why they believe this is the case. An ICI asserted, for example, that higglers are not accorded respect, because "you are not looked upon as a businessperson" (#42). As evidence of their lack of respect by the public, most of the ICIs noted being forced to pay higher duties in comparison to formal sector businesses (or so they believed) and being targeted at customs. For these women, ICIs were not respected as legitimate businesspeople. One ICI explicitly stated that lack of respect show up in the public's attitude: "ICIs are treated as higglers" (#29), that is, not as legitimate businesspeople. As higglers, these ICIs experienced differential treatment in comparison to the more respectable formal businesspeople. The ICI confirmed this when she noted that the "government believe higglers are the low-low class of people. Higglers are associated with drugs." In her view, there is a sense of illegality and illegitimacy associated with higglers, and their differential treatment reflects and reinforces this perception.

One ICI described being targeted by customs and having to pay unfair duties: "Higglers get no respect. Customs handle you bad. You have to pay high duties. They just treat you bad" (#38); she believed Lebanese/Syrian businesspeople received better treatment than higglers. This comparison is significant because this ICI attributes her differential treatment not only to the informal status of her work but also to class and color differences between herself and Jamaicans of Lebanese/Syrian heritage, who are not only giants of retail, tourism, horse racing, industry, and manufacturing in Jamaica but also part of Jamaica's white economic elite.

These ICIs' remarks may appear paradoxical: more than half reported that their businesses were respected, yet half believed higglers themselves were not. These remarks, however, make sense in light of their lived experiences. In 1983 the Jamaica government officially recognized higglers who specialized in foreign trade by giving them the official title of informal commercial importer (ICI), not only to recognize this trade but also to regulate it by imposing quotas on the amount of goods and foreign exchange brought into the country. Special areas were organized at custom offices at airports, where ICIs had to pay custom duties and taxes.

The official recognition of ICIs by the government served to locate these women among a group of businesspeople who are also formally recognized. ICIs, then, use formal economic businesses as a point of reference in their self-evaluations and perspectives on the treatment of women like themselves. I found, for instance, that their self-identity as either ICIs or entrepreneurs/businesswomen were shaped by the tendency to associate and compare themselves with other formal economic businesses instead of with higglers, which reinforced their sense of legitimacy. For example, one ICI argued that she was a businessperson like Mr. Issa, a major businessperson of Lebanese/Syrian descent on the island. She suggested that a person like Mr. Issa would not be considered a higgler, and because she viewed her business as legitimate—formally recognized by the government and charged customs as well as stall fees—she is more like Mr. Issa and is therefore not a higgler. Other ICIs made similar comparisons with formal economic businesspeople and disassociated themselves from higglers.

For the ICIs, official recognition by the government is a source of empowerment but also a source of pain. Their official recognition is empowering because it gives the women a sense of legitimacy as businesspeople in comparison to women involved in traditional forms of higglering. This sense of empowerment and legitimacy is evidenced in their self-identities as entrepreneurs/ businesswomen or ICIs, and influences their evaluation of their businesses as respectable. The ICIs' sense of pain, however, is evidenced in the contradictions in these women's treatment at customs, for instance, compared to the treatment of other formal businesspeople. These contradictions influence their evaluation of higglers as not respected; they are not given the respect that is expected by legitimate businesspeople. Their treatment reinforces their outsider status in the economy in spite of their official title.

Most ICIs asserted that they did not receive the same respect as people who worked in the Plazas in uptown Kingston. One ICI stated, for instance: "We don't get the same respect as the people in the Plaza. The people in the Plaza don't feel you are capable, they feel they are better to run their business" (#37). Another ICI remarked that "Mr. Ammar's buyers don't get the same treatment like ICIs and higglers" (#29). Mr. Ammar is of Lebanese/Syrian descent and a member of Jamaica's white economic elite; like the Issas, he is a major retailer on the island and a dominant player in the private sector. This ICI's reference to Mr. Ammar is significant because not only was she describing the differential treatment accorded formal and informal sector businesses but also, by specifically identifying Mr. Ammar, she implied that this differential treatment was influenced by the color and class differences between the two business owners—her and Mr. Ammar.

The class privileges of Mr. Ammar and Mr. Issa intersect with other privileges, namely, color. Both are descendants of Lebanese/Syrian immigrants who are part of Jamaica's white economic elite. Their status as white and upper-class formal economic businessmen, and as members of prominent families on the island, gives them access to privileges that black lower-class ICIs do not have. One of those privileges is public respect. As members of the brown economic elite, the Ammars, Issas, and those associated with their businesses enjoy a sense of legitimacy in the public imagination in ways that this ICI or her employees would not. Her specific reference to Mr. Ammar, then, points to those privileges that go far beyond his formal economic status.

The idea of differential treatment of brown/white middle- and upper-class and black lower-class business owners was echoed by two other ICIs. One ICI from the Constant Spring Arcade described what she perceived as the government's preferential treatment of the Chinese: "The Chinese don't pay as much fees and duties as vendors; we get less breaks. The Chinese get the loans, they don't re-invest in Jamaica, they take their money to China. The Chinese get the shops, while ICIs get stalls" (#25). An ICI at the People's Arcade in downtown Kingston declared that Jamaican government policies "encourage the Chinese and other foreigners over vendors" (#36).

The ICIs described differential treatment not only of formal and informal economic businesses, but also of middle-class brown women who engaged in similar informal work. Explaining why ICIs were not respected, an ICI from the Constant Spring Arcade compared the respect received by middle-class brown women who sold at the Lady Musgrave Flea Market to that accorded the predominantly working-class black ICIs in the arcade: "ICIs are treated as higglers. In the flea market, doctors, nurses, teachers, and bankers are like ICIs. Bankers are like ICIs, but ICIs are treated as higglers and handled like higglers. Higglers are associated with drugs" (#29). This ICI made a clear distinction between the treatment of women engaged in similar informal work who differed by color and class from the ICIs: the privileges enjoyed by middle-class brown women protected them from social degradation. Her remarks disclosed her recognition of the complex ways race/color and class impact how she conducts her business and how others treat her.

This ICI's comments are significant because she worked in the Lady Musgrave Flea Market as well as in the Constant Spring Arcade and was able to observe firsthand the differential treatment and level of respect accorded both groups of informal workers. The ICI made another distinction between the flea market and the arcade: "Sellers harass customers in the arcade. They don't do that in the flea market" (#29). She identifies the behaviors of ICIs, along with the association of higglers with drugs in the public imagination, as part of the reason they are handled like higglers.

Further probing into the ICIs' open-ended responses revealed that they often used the behaviors of higglers to explain the lack of respect they receive from the public. For example, two ICIs at the Constant Spring Arcade described higglers as "hooligans who will cuss [curse] you out if you don't buy their goods!"(#1, #2). Another ICI explained that higglers "act bad," and added that "sometimes higglers and ICIs run their customers [away] with their bad behaviors" (#34). An ICI from the

People's Arcade claimed that "some of the higglers are fussy [cantankerous]—you can look at them and tell" (#36). One ICI who identified herself as a businesswoman argued that ICIs were not respected because of "how they carry themselves. We get no respect because you are not looked upon as a businessperson. You can talk but your voice isn't heard. You don't have the caliber of people to talk for you. ICIs and Higglers aren't that caliber. An ICI would be irated [irate] and shout. They don't know how to talk when they are irate. They are aggressive and that's part of their problem" (#42). Higglers, she said, were "not educated to deal with pressure." Their behaviors, in other words, made them unsuitable examples of businesspeople, which accounted for their lack of respect from the wider public.

This ICI conceived of a businessperson or a professional as educated, articulate, and capable of "carrying themselves" properly in the presence of other (legitimate) businesspeople; the presumably aggressive behaviors of ICIs and higglers contradict a professional image and contribute to their lack of respect in the public eye. This emphasis on the so-called bad behaviors of higglers and ICIs was a common theme raised by the ICIs in our conversations at the Constant Spring Arcade. These explanations are consistent with the public belief that the conditions of higglers are, for the most part, self-imposed.

Among the market women, a common argument was that higglers were not respected because their businesses are not as financially successful as in the past. These women, and most of the women I interviewed, described their businesses as "very slow" (not financially prosperous) and attributed their lack of respect to that fact. They believed that to be respected, one had to have money. This sentiment is consistent with a general focus in the public discourse on class position as affecting social experiences and relationships, or more specifically, the association of respectability with the middle class.

Whether or not the claims of the women are accurate, the perception of their differential treatment relative to that accorded formal businesspeople, and their assessment that their treatment is to some degree of their own doing, are significant for two reasons. First, these perceptions are consistent with public discourses around higglers as deviant; second, these perceptions affect the women's identity constructions. Our discussions reflected the women's keen awareness of the public discourse around higglering and higglers as deviant. They were also aware that the public construction of higglers as deviants placed greater emphasis on their behaviors, and higglers received differential treatment and respect based on those behaviors.

In my interviews, then, higglers were aware of the social context within which they conducted their businesses. Many of the market women who believed their businesses were respected, for instance, often qualified their claims, stating that their respect depended upon how they treated their customers. Many of the women embraced principles of egalitarianism and meritocracy and believed that one's treatment and level of respect depended, for the most part, on one's own achievements. These principles are consistent with ideologies in the broader Jamaican society.

Many Jamaicans believe that the "responsibility for a person's situation, or for its transformation, lies in the effort, striving and disciplined behavior of the free individual, not in the power relations of the social order at large" (Douglass 1992, 9–10). With this principle in mind, the women, especially the ICIs, argued that the treatment higglers received was to some extent of their own making; their presumably bad behaviors were major contributing factors to their treatment. The women's responses demonstrated that many of them have internalized, to some extent, the racial, gender, and class logic that justifies the unequal distribution of prestige and power among Jamaicans. By attributing the treatment of black lower-class higglers to their supposedly deviant behaviors, the women drew from predominant racial/color, gender, and class discourses, which portray black women as vulgar and aggressive and reinforce an ideology of a culture of poverty. The problems of higglers, then, are individualized; they are not issues of social structure.

I found in my interviews that if the issues of social inequality were raised at all, the women would describe class inequalities and overlook inequalities based on gender and color. One ICI, for instance, described the higher import duties she believed ICIs had to pay in comparison to formal businesses as an example of "class oppression" (#35). Other women described class, instead of gender or color, as a factor affecting one's ability to advance in Jamaican society.[10] There is a general reluctance among Jamaicans to speak about inequalities based on gender and color. These women were no exception.

The women I interviewed, then, were situated within discourses of egalitarianism and meritocracy, and constructions of higglering and higglers as deviant. These hegemonic discourses influenced how they viewed their work. Dominant discourses of egalitarianism and meritocracy, for instance, influenced most of the women to view their businesses as respectable. Because they believed their decision to work was consistent with an ideology of self-sufficiency and self-improvement (as opposed to begging in the streets), these women viewed higglering as respectable.

The public construction of higglering, with its color, class, and gender connotations, was also at work in these women's description of higglers and ICIs. Their attention to the behaviors of higglers as aggressive, vulgar, and uneducated was consistent with discourses that associated these behaviors with a degraded black lower class. The women also tried to account for the differences between them and others in racialized terms. One ICI argued: "Blacks don't help each other. We see other colors over us." She then described with some admiration what she perceived as a sense of community among the Chinese, and she attributed their financial success to their cooperation with each other (#25). A market woman made the same argument: "Chinese people help each other. Black people don't" (#20). These accounts are connected to an ideology of meritocracy and support the idea that the majority of black Jamaicans (as opposed to browns and whites) are poor because they are undisciplined, uneducated, and uncooperative.[11]

These dominant discourses also influence the self-identities of the women I interviewed. The ICIs were particularly interesting in this regard, because unlike the market women who identified themselves as either higglers or businesswomen, most of the ICIs identified themselves as businesswomen, as we have seen. When asked to explain their answers, the discussions that emerged revealed the influence of public discourses around higglering on these women's identity constructions. The woman at the Constant Spring Arcade who identified herself as a "businessperson" revealed interesting color and class dimensions when she explained her self-identity: "I am a businessperson because we wouldn't call Mr. Issa a higgler. Mr. Issa would be a higgler. Higglers sell food; I sell like the stores. The Issas and retailers are like higglers, but we don't consider them higglers, so why should I consider myself a higgler? I am a businessperson" (#25). This ICI rejected the label "higgler" and identified herself as a legitimate businessperson like the Issas, who are members of the white economic elite. She challenged the application of the label "higgler" to women like herself, not only because higglers sell food, but also because this label would not be applied to formal retailers nor would it be applied to people of higher social and economic status (i.e., brown/white and middle/upper class). Here, she illuminated the racial and class connotations of the label "higgler" and its application in the public discourse only to the black lower class. She then rejected the label and redefined herself as a businessperson, thus constructing her identity as legitimate and respectable.

Other ICIs constructed their identities as legitimate by distancing themselves from higglers as they are publicly imagined and represented.

An ICI at the Constant Spring Arcade declared: "I am an entrepreneur. People look at higglers as the worst level. They comb their hair on the plane and carry on bad" (#34). This sentiment was echoed by another ICI at People's Arcade: "I am an entrepreneur. I am not interested in higglers, because of their behaviors and drugs. When higglers talk, they brawl and are loud. I don't mix with them" (#37). She thus not only identified herself as an entrepreneur, but also explicitly stated that she does not interact with higglers.

Two other women from Constant Spring described themselves as ICIs because "higglers sit down with their legs wide open. We don't do that" (#1, #2). These women, like the others, appropriated the public discourse around "higglers as deviants." Their utterances—"We don't do that" or "I don't mix with them"—explicitly disassociated them from the stigma of higglers as they engaged in their own identity construction. These ICIs revealed not only their awareness of the public image of higglers as deviants, but also their understanding that these constructions are centered around the presumably deviant (unfeminine, vulgar, undisciplined, indecent) behaviors of these women. The public image, then, influences these women's self-identities because they serve as examples of what the women are not to be. Here again, we see the predominant racial/color, gender, and class discourses that portray lower-class black women as vulgar and aggressive at work in the ICIs' identity constructions. The ICIs internalized yet resisted or managed the racial, gender, and class logics that describe black women's behaviors as deviant.

In addition to disassociating themselves from higglers, two ICIs at the Constant Spring Arcade in uptown Kingston established uptown/downtown distinctions between themselves and ICIs and higglers who worked downtown. Uptown and downtown are not solely geographical identifiers but also indicators of social position, as mentioned earlier. Uptown is associated with the respectable brown middle class, and downtown with the black poor. One ICI stated: "I don't like downtown. It is too crowded and the people there are too terrible" (#31). The other identified herself as an entrepreneur and disassociated herself from ICIs who worked downtown by describing them as "illiterate confusing idiots," playing on the acronym ICI (#34). These uptown and downtown distinctions are consistent with the public discourse that associates uptown with privilege and propriety, and downtown with poverty and impropriety. By distinguishing themselves from downtowners, the uptown ICIs attempted to position themselves in a better social location relative to downtown ICIs, and to establish their sense of propriety. I did not encounter these uptown/downtown distinctions among the ICIs at the People's Arcade in downtown Kingston. Their focus, instead, was on separating themselves from higglers.

The market women did not exhibit the desire to distance themselves from the term "higgler" that I found among the ICIs. For example, at Papine Market, one market woman who identified herself as a businesswoman simply said: "This was something I've always wanted to be" (#9). Another identified herself as a "market woman" because "I sell from my own farm; higglers buy what they sell" (#7). In part, reasons for this difference among these market women have to do with the status they occupy within their own communities. Despite the overall low status of higglering in the public discourse, market higglers "perform essential services for which they gain not only cash income, but also self-worth and status in their local communities" (Durant-Gonzalez 1983, 3). Many of the women perceive higglering as a preferable option or advancement in relation to domestic work because a higgler is independent. Because the educational levels of this group of women are lower than that of the ICIs, many of them would have turned to domestic work, given the constraints of the economy. Higglering, then, is a better option and, as an independent business, it carries higher status.

At Papine Market, three market women reported that they were domestic workers before they turned to higglering, but "work out don't pay the bills; its better to batter [hustle] for yourself" (#3). Another said: "I don't want to work for others. I did domestic work but wanted to work for myself" (#7). The third woman said that she always wanted to become a successful businesswoman—for her, like other market women, higglering was a preferable option and carried greater status because it was an independent business.

In contrast, three ICIs turned to higglering after they were laid off from white-collar jobs (one described working in an office doing accounting). For this group of women, generally better educated than market women, higglering was an alternative to unemployment, not an advancement in their careers. Five ICIs went into this business after leaving factory work that, they said, offered low pay. The move from a factory job to higglering, however, is different, from a social status viewpoint, than a move from domestic work to higglering. The latter is a vertical move, whereas the former is a lateral move at best, especially since business has been very slow and these ICIs have been unable to generate substantial earnings. Higglering, then, would not have the same impact on the ICIs' status within their local communities that it would for the market women.[12]

The general public image of the market women at Papine in uptown

Kingston as nonthreatening, respectful peasants also contributes to the women's lack of desire to distance themselves from the term "higgler." In Jamaica the rural peasant is often seen as embodying respectability, self-sufficiency, and autonomy (Thomas 2005). We see this construction reproduced in images in the *Daily Gleaner* of market women at the Papine Market that portray them as pleasant, courteous, and cooperative in comparison to market women at the Coronation Market in downtown Kingston. Coronation Market is often described in the newspapers as "chaotic" and "gritty," and its higglers as "rough."[13] Even though higglers in general are devalued in the public discourse, the more favorable images of the higglers at the Papine Market reinforce uptown/downtown distinctions among them.

Two market women argued, for instance, that they chose to work at Papine instead of Coronation Market because "Papine is peaceful and safe" (#14, #16). Another chose this site because "I prefer Papine because there is cooperation here" (#15). A fourth stated: "I started out at Coronation, but the people there are too rough. I came to Papine instead" (#19). These women's descriptions of Papine Market as peaceful and safe and the people as cooperative and not rough are consistent with public images of this marketplace, along with the spatial location of uptown (versus downtown) and the bodies that navigate these spaces. The work site of the Papine Market helped lessen the stigma associated with higglering and the women who worked there.

The identity constructions among the ICIs were significant in that their subtexts were projections of "not me." That is to say, as the ICIs constructed their identities in the interviews, two stories were being told. As they identified themselves as ICIs or entrepreneurs, the ICIs were also telling me who they were not. The ICI at the Constant Spring Arcade who declared that she was like Mr. Issa told me by the subtext that she was not that degraded, vulgar, undisciplined higgler who appears in the public discourse.

The ICIs' identity constructions also revealed their attempts at stigma management. The women tried to destigmatize their work by identifying themselves as entrepreneurs/businesswomen or ICIs, titles that gave them a sense of legitimacy and respectability while they participated in work that is publicly devalued. In this way, the women attempted to negotiate their public identities. This negotiation also involved ICIs' disassociation of themselves from higglers through their behaviors. By constantly identifying the stigmatized behaviors of higglers, the ICIs implied and at times asserted that these were the kinds of behaviors they did not imitate.

The ICIs performed their identities as entrepreneurs/businesswomen and ICIs by refraining from the stigmatized behaviors of higglers. Throughout the time I spent at the Constant Spring Arcade, for instance, I did not hear the women use vulgar language or curse at customers. Quite often, many ICIs brought to my attention that they did not harass their customers or me; they stressed that customers were free to look at their goods without any pressure. The women were respectful to their customers and used proper English instead of patois. Not only did the ICIs identify themselves as respectable businesswomen, then, but also they performed that respectability in their interactions with customers. By doing this, the ICIs attempted to negotiate their public identities by adopting a nondeviant label for themselves, disassociating themselves from the stigma associated with higglering, and performing their identities as respectable businesswomen.

Despite the difference between the identity constructions of the ICIs and market women, they shared one commonality: they were providers for their families. Although I asked the women to identify themselves based only on the kind of business they operated, their responses to why they engaged in higglering and why higglering was important to them revealed another telling aspect of their identities: their business assisted them in their gendered identity as provider for their homes and families.

Most of the women reported either being the primary wage earner in their household or sharing that responsibility with a partner, and more than half named their family responsibilities as their primary reason for higglering. One market woman described her business as important because it helped "put food on the table" (#5). Another said: "It school my children and I can keep a home going" (#16). An ICI regarded her business as very important because "I can take care of my house" (#31). Another said it was "the best way to support my family" (#35).

Here, we find that most of the women have internalized gender norms that assign women the primary task of caretaker of their household. Through their businesses, both groups of women perform that task and construct their identities as providers and mothers.

More than half the women in the study reported that their business was important to them because it helped them take care of their families. One market woman argued that her business "help mek up to pay school fees" (#7). This woman's children attended prep school; her business paid not only for her children's school fees but also for school uniforms.

A few women explained that their business gave them the time needed to take care of their children. Said one ICI, for instance: "My business is important because this is my money. Nobody can push me around. It give me more time to do my housework and time to take my son to the [U.S.] embassy [to apply for a travel visa]. If I was working for someone, I wouldn't be able to do that." Furthermore, "when you work for someone, you have to be there by eight o'clock in the morning. That mean you have to catch the bus by seven. But if your children have to go to school, you can't be there to help them get ready and send them off. When you work for yourself, you can open your stall at any time you want. That give you the time to take care of your children in the mornings" (#31). Through her informal work, this ICI garnered a real sense of freedom. Her business not only provided much-needed financial resources, but also enabled her, through a flexible schedule, to be a mother to her children. A market woman stated: "This business is very important to me because it help me achieve. It help me grow my children, build my house, and now I am trying to help my grandchildren" (#15). These informal businesses, then, are important for economic reasons and for the freedom they give Jamaican women, ironically, to conform to established gender norms and to perform their identities as responsible, even respectable, mothers and household heads.

Although the women in my study benefited from a business that allowed them to earn a wage in a constricting economy and to fulfill their gender roles, most did not wish to pass their business on to the next generation. Among the market women who either inherited their business or learned the skills from their mother/grandmother, only three said they would encourage their daughters/niece to take up the business. Among the ICIs, only two said they would so encourage their daughter/niece. One of these was a second-generation ICI; she and her daughter were operating their business together in the Constant Spring Arcade. Her case was an example of three generations of women (her mother, herself, and her daughter) engaged in this informal business.

The reluctance of most of the women in the study to encourage their daughters or nieces to go into higglering was attributed to bad (slow) business, the low status associated with this business, and their desire for the upward social mobility of the next generation. (This reluctance is consistent with findings of other studies; see LeFranc 1989; Macfarlane-Gregory and Ruddock-Kelly 1993.) The women who would so encourage their daughters/nieces based their approval on the sense of independence that came with this business and the potential profits that could be gained. Many of these women, however, stressed that their business was not as profitable as it used to be (one woman (#27) declared, "We have more sellers than buyers!"), which made them a bit ambivalent on this issue.

Almost half the women who would not encourage their daughters into the business wanted to pass greater educational opportunities on to their children, not their business. Four ICIs, for instance, insisted that their daughters received a good education so that they would not have to work in the arcades like they did. Although the market women did not specifically mention education, seven of them insisted that their daughters or nieces should "do better" than their generation. One ICI said that she wanted her daughter to be "computer literate." Another said she would encourage her niece to engage in higglering, but only as a stepping-stone to nursing school. One market woman said she wanted "the next generation to do differently," and another reported using her business to send her five children to school in the United States. Most of the higglers described their business as too "rough," "hard," and "slow," characterized by heavy lifting and dirty markets or arcades. They would not encourage their daughters to take up this business because, as one market woman put it, "the next generation must move up." (These findings are consistent with those of earlier studies on higglering; see Abbensetts 1990.)

Here again, we see the women in my study fulfilling their gender roles as caretakers of their families, particularly of their children. Their decision to not pass on their businesses and skills to their children was based on their concern for their children's futures: their desire for their children to be socially mobile. These women used their informal business to provide a good education for their children with the hope of giving them greater opportunities—opportunities many of these women did not and do not have.

When I compared the ICIs and market women, I found that for both groups family responsibility was a primary factor in their decision to engage in higglering. It was also a primary reason why they viewed their work as important. Here we see gender norms influencing these women's work experiences in similar ways. Informal economic activities gave them the means to perform their primary role as caretaker of their household and their identity as a good mother and head of household.

My interviews reveal, then, that higglers appropriated the public discourse on higglering; at the same time, many negotiated the discourse in their identity constructions. The understanding of many of their work as respectable (as opposed to begging in the streets), their constructions of themselves as respectable businesswomen, and their active efforts to disassociate themselves from "deviant" higglers and behaviors were examples of negotiating, for the most part unconsciously, dominant discourses about them and their work. They were aware of these public discourses but negotiated their positions within them as a way of gaining a sense of legitimacy in themselves and their work.

The behaviors of the women are examples of deviance as politics—part of "an ongoing power struggle in which competing interests vie with one another for an official stamp of legitimacy" (Pfuhl and Henry 1993, 229). There is indeed a power struggle between higglers, the government, formal economic businesses, and citizens. The experiences of these groups reflect the unequal distribution of power in Jamaican society, with higglers having the least. The construction of higglers as deviant has less to do with the desirability of the women themselves (pace Cargill) and more to do with social organization, that is, more to do with maintaining color, class, and gendered hierarchical structures. The stereotypical images of higglers in the public discourse provide a subtext about constructions of race/color, class, and gender. Constructing higglers as deviants reproduces images of whiteness, of brownness, of the upper class, and of femininity that draw from historically created racial/color, gender, and class hierarchies. These images are produced and espoused by a brown middle class, and by those who aspire to this class, to secure its place in this privileged position, and to differentiate the white and brown economic elite from the black masses.

Ironically, many higglers have adopted the negative images of higglers and have used them in their own identity constructions. This was especially true of the ICIs at the Constant Spring Arcade, who used these images to differentiate themselves from higglers in general and from ICIs and higglers who worked downtown. These ICIs used the negative images of higglers to re-present themselves as respectable. The uptown ICIs have also used these images to establish a sense of propriety among themselves in relation to degraded ICIs and higglers, especially those who work downtown.

The women I interviewed were (and are) engaged in a power struggle for a sense of legitimacy as they engage in work historically represented as illegitimate. These higglers are also engaged in a struggle for space in an economy that has always tried to marginalize them. This struggle has intensified as the Jamaican economy continues to contract and the distribution of wealth continues to be concentrated in fewer hands. Even though higglers exist and work within a set of dominant discourses that devalue them, they simultaneously engage and negotiate those discourses, producing a rich life transcript that has captured the imagination of Jamaican society.

6

Dirty and Dis/eased

Bodies, Public Space,
and Afro-Jamaican Higglers

> As we know it, dirt is essentially disorder. There is no such thing as absolute dirt: It exists in the eye of the beholder. If we shun dirt, it is not because of craven fear, still less dread of holy terror. Nor do our ideas about disease account for the range of our behavior in cleaning or avoiding dirt. Dirt offends against order. Eliminating it is not a negative movement, but a positive effort to organize the environment.
>
> MARY DOUGLAS, *Purity and Danger*

Most cities in developing and developed countries contain dual and interrelated economies: formal and informal.¹ Socially formed meanings of markets and market activities in each economy vary, often privileging formal markets as more legitimate than informal markets. In Jamaican society, the informal economic activity of higglering is generally perceived as a low-status, illegitimate, or illegal occupation. Higglers have also been constructed as deviants in the public imagination; Richard Burton notes, for instance, that the higgler is "regarded with ambivalence by the wider society: admired for her 'manlike' autonomy and assertiveness, she is also derided on account of her often invasive physical presence, her loud dress, and her even louder demeanor and language" (1997, 64).

One can account for this ambivalence when one understands that public representations around higglers in Jamaica have focused on their laboring bodies, constructing higglers as unfeminine while simultaneously presenting them as an ideal source of cheap and disciplined labor for potential investors, as mentioned earlier. So the higgler's praiseworthy autonomy and assertiveness are associated with her ability, through hard labor, to fend for herself and her family (and make her a valuable resource for capitalist investors). At the same time, the higgler's labor helps place her outside racialized and classed norms of femininity. A conundrum, indeed.

The issue I address in this chapter is how public representations of higglering and higglers affect the ways in which these microentrepreneurs experience their work in the informal economy, evidenced primarily in newspaper articles and letters to the editor published from 1980 to 2006 in two of Jamaica's most popular newspapers, the *Daily Gleaner* and the *Jamaica Observer*.[2] These news articles addressed, among many issues, tensions between the Jamaican government, the formal economic business community, uptown city residents, and higglers over the removal of these informal economic activities and workers from city streets.[3]

Cities and Markets: Constructed and Produced

Markets are lived experiences that are embodied, as I have suggested in the preceding chapters. We cannot reduce our conceptualization of formal or informal markets to a series of abstract economic processes and impersonal exchanges, because to do so conceals complex operations of power, especially power shaped by race/color, class, and gender. Markets are indeed a set of relations that occur in particular social, economic, and geographical contexts and involve the experiences, practices, and embodiments of everyday social actors.[4] The bodies of particular kinds of women (brown and black), for example, and the spaces in which they engage in informal work influence how that economic activity is conceptualized and experienced. Public discourses regarding higglering, then, shed light on lived experiences of markets because these discourses feed into the practices of everyday commercial life.

An explosion of informal economic activity has occurred in the city of Kingston over the last several decades, as Jamaica continues to grapple with economic decline and all the challenges associated with it. The struggles between higglers, the formal business community, uptown city residents, and the state reveal a relationship between city imaginaries and the spatial organization of Kingston within this context of acute economic and social challenges. My interest lies in the racialized/colored, classed, and gendered dimensions of those imaginaries, and how they are re/produced and negotiated through struggles over city space.

Understanding cities as both physical and imagined helps illuminate ways in which "differences are constructed in, and themselves construct, city life and space" (Bridge and Watson 2002, 507). One feature of city spaces is their high population density and the likelihood of encounters with difference. These differences help shape and are shaped by social relations in city spaces and by the spaces themselves (Fincher and Jacobs 1998). Sophie Watson points out that "space is both produced and consumed within relations of difference where women and black people are often at the bottom of the pile. And these differences, in part, are a product of the social imaginary, which classes these categories of people as subordinate" (2000, 103).

Because city spaces are infused with relationships of power, an analysis of a city must take into account "how networks of power differentiate space unequally, or how the social imaginary is translated into spatial hierarchies within which the city becomes socially polarized and fragmented" (Watson 2000, 103–4). Power is evidenced not only in the ways in which difference and hierarchies are re/produced in city spaces, but also in the ways in which those hierarchies are contested, negotiated, and transformed through the use of those spaces by various bodies.

In her analysis of how public space in urban society becomes semiotically encoded and interpreted reality, Setha Low distinguishes what she calls the "social production of space" from the "social construction of space." The social production of space "includes all those factors—social, economic, ideological, and technological—the intended goal of which is the physical creation of the material setting; . . . the social construction of space is the actual transformation of space—through people's social exchanges, memories, images, and daily use of the material setting—into scenes and actions that convey symbolic meaning" (1996, 861–62). Low's distinction is useful in understanding the battles presently being waged between higglers, the business community, uptown residents, and the state over the use of public urban space, which transform a physical setting into an arena for the contestation of symbolic space. In this context, race/color, class, and gender relations are re/produced and contested in a physical urban setting for economic and ideological reasons.

A distinctive feature of the city of Kingston is its division both physically and conceptually into uptown and downtown, as we have seen. This division is in large part the result of class- and race/color-based social and spatial polarization in the 1960s and 1970s in response to the high population density that resulted from an explosive rural to urban migration (Clarke 1975; Portes, Itzigsohn, and Dore-Cabral 1994). This race/color and class spatial polarization configured the city into what Alejandro Portes, Jose Itzigsohn, and José Carlos Dore-Cabral describe as an "upside down ice cream cone," with the predominantly poor black masses of Jamaicans concentrated in downtown Kingston and the small brown and white elites uptown (1994, 18–19).

Although migration patterns have changed since the 1970s and satellite cities have developed to relieve Kingston's population density, those uptown/downtown distinctions have largely remained. Brown and white economic elites remain overrepresented in uptown residential and business areas in Kingston, and although pockets of poor housing settlements are located uptown, poor black Jamaicans continue to dominate downtown. Moreover, Kingstonians use uptown/downtown distinctions to indicate social standing. To belong uptown or downtown signifies one's membership in a particular racial/color/class group. When one is identified as an "uptown lady," for example, certain expectations follow (Douglass 1992; Ulysse 1999, 2007), just as when a woman belongs downtown, an expectation about her comportment follows, as we will see.

The social production of space, then, involves a geographical location and its meanings (uptown/downtown distinctions on the physical landscape of the city). The social construction of space involves those symbolic interpretations that emerge out of the everyday use of a physical setting; it is the symbolic construction, identification, and performance of one's social standing, which may be tied to their physical location.[5] The social construction of space also involves the delineation of boundaries (social and spatial) that emerge through people's everyday practices, particularly through their struggles over the use of that physical location. It is in these practices that we find the distribution of social honor that leads to the reproduction of what Max Weber (1993) calls a "status order." Urban landscapes thus are not blank places upon which everyday practices simply unfold; these landscapes shape and are shaped by those practices and imaginaries.

In many practices of boundary creation and in the reproduction of a status order, we find ideas of pollution, disease, and dirt used to signify anomalies in an existing system. As Mary Douglas argues in her classic text *Purity and Danger,* dirt is "matter out of place" that "implies two conditions: a set of ordered relations and a contravention of that order. Dirt then, is never a unique isolated event. Where there is dirt there is a system. Dirt is the by-product of a systematic ordering and classification of matter, in so far as ordering involves rejecting inappropriate elements" (2002, 44). Ideas of dirt often legitimize the expulsion or containment of anomalies, which if successful fortifies existing boundaries and re/produces a preferred social and spatial order. Over the last few decades, the business of higglering has often been associated with pollution, dirt, and disease. It is essential that we examine these representations and responses to them, for they reveal, often with disturbing clarity, a presumed social and spatial order in Jamaica that is racialized/colored, classed, and gendered.

The Problem of Higglering

After Jamaica gained its independence in 1962, political and economic power was transferred from a white British elite to a brown/white economic elite. This economic elite, which is made up of people of mixed heritage, as well as ethnic minorities such as Jews, Lebanese, and Chinese, remained in power until 1992, when P. J. Patterson became the first prime minister to self-identify as black and engaged in projects aimed at "blackening the nation" (Brown-Glaude 2006; Robotham 2000; Thomas 2005). A budding black professional class controlled the political process in Jamaica until September 2007, when it shifted back into brown hands with the victory of the Jamaica Labour Party under the leadership of Bruce Golding. It will be interesting to see how this shift in political power will unfold, given that the black professional class has been in power for fifteen years. But even during that period, the brown/white economic elite controlled the economy and enjoyed local economic wealth, and it is likely that they will continue to do so.

Like many Caribbean and Latin American nations, Jamaica has since its independence pursued an economic development model that has, in effect, entrenched the economy further in a dependent relationship in the global market (Portes, Itzigsohn, and Dore-Cabral 1994; Huber and Stephens 1992). The devastating effects of structural adjustment policies that have undermined earlier solutions to urbanization and economic development; reduced government employment; weakened the purchasing power of local wages; and drastically curtailed public services, health, and welfare programs have produced incredible hardships for Jamaicans, especially the poor. The economic elite and middle classes have fared better, maintaining their privileged positions in society and expanding in spite of structural adjustments (Clarke and Howard 2006, 109–14).

Over the years, the economy has contracted under pressures of increasing debt, both foreign and domestic. To manage this debt, almost half the national budget has been earmarked for debt servicing. For example, in the 2010–2011 fiscal year, debt servicing will consume roughly 48 of the national budget (see, e.g., "Government Slashes Debt" 2010)—a drastic improvement from previous years when budget servicing consumed 60 to 70 percent of the national budget.[6] One of the outcomes of Jamaica's debt challenges is the drastic reduction of jobs in the formal economy, resulting in an unemployment rate of about 14.5 percent. This situation is particularly difficult for Jamaican women, who have experienced almost twice the level of unemployment in comparison to men, as we have seen. What we find since independence is a rapid expansion of the informal economy as the formal economy contracts. As a response to deteriorating economic conditions, limited formal employment options, and their responsibility as the primary support of their households, many Jamaican women turn to the informal economy, particularly street vending. Today half of Kingston's male labor force and more than half of the female labor force consist of informal workers (Clarke and Howard 2006, 110).

As the informal economy expands, the formal business community and uptown city residents express anxiety over the presence of higglers on the streets of Kingston, and each year a struggle ensues over the use of city space. Public perceptions of higglers are fraught with contradictions. On the one hand, higglers are admired for their ability to survive in the face of great adversity; they are thought to exemplify the strength and resilience of Jamaicans. On the other hand, higglers are scorned for their presumed indiscipline and vulgarity. These perceptions often fuel public debates that call for the government to contain the ever-expanding informal economy—particularly the business of higglering. Efforts by the state to restrict the activities of higglers include the use of agencies like the Kingston and St. Andrew Corporation (KSAC) and the Metropolitan Parks and Markets (MPM), along with local police to relocate them from the streets to designated market places.[7] These interventions sometimes result in the destruction of higglers' property and their means of generating income.

Although struggles over city space occur throughout the year, they tend to intensify around Christmas, the busiest shopping season. In an editorial entitled "The Drama of Christmas Vending" published in the *Daily Gleaner* on December 10, 2003, Peter Espeut argues that the Christmas trade is so lucrative that profits made in this season can carry the business sector financially through most of the following year. So much money is to be made at Christmas, he asserts, that each year it "draws every higgler and would-be higgler on to the streets and sidewalks of every city and every town in Jamaica to get a piece of the action." He adds that some Jamaicans who have migrated abroad return to Jamaica at Christmas to sell on the streets.

Indeed, the informal economy and higglering in particular represent real competition to formal economic businesses, especially during this season. Public debates about higglering reveal, on one level, anxieties by the business community over this economic competition. In these discourses, social and spatial boundaries between formal and informal, legitimacy and illegitimacy, are created that preserve the privileged positions of formal-sector businesses in Jamaica's weakened economy. These boundaries are also supported by many uptown city residents and are re/produced in their ways of talking about higglering in the city. A close examination of these views, however, suggests that such boundary constructions do not simply reinforce formal/informal economic divisions, but also re/produce and reinforce racialized/colored, classed, and gendered boundaries of exclusion and inclusion that are mapped upon and negotiated by bodies—particular bodies, at that—in city space.

Higglers versus Formal Businesses

Articles in the *Daily Gleaner* and *Jamaica Observer* reveal narratives of higglers getting out of control and taking over city streets and sidewalks. Higglers are also imagined as public nuisances and an unfair threat to legitimate businesses. "Vending: The Bigger Picture," published in the *Daily Gleaner* on December 28, 1999, for example, described the practice of street vending, as old as civilization itself, but pointed out that a major problem is "its unfair threat to store-based businesses."[8] This "unfair threat" includes triggering a decline in the profits of formal economic businesses. For instance, on December 18, 1999, as reported in "Sellers Squabble over Space," Michael Ammar Jr., then vice president of the Jamaica Chamber of Commerce and a prominent member of Jamaica's economic elite, told the *Daily Gleaner* that stores that were blocked by higglers (who sold on the sidewalks in front of them) reported a 30 percent drop in business, and that their customers complained of jostling to get in and out of them. He added that in order for the downtown business district to be restored, the "problem of illegal vending" must be addressed: "I think it is fair to say that the private sector has done more than its fair share to try to restore downtown Kingston. However, without the rule of law and order, our investments are all at risk."[9] In this and other narratives, higglers are associated with lawlessness and disorder. What exactly is being disordered by higglers? Their activities signify the disruption of a spatialized economic order firmly in place since the colonial era (Clarke 1975)—an economic order that secures greater access to economic resources for formal businesses in a weakened economy.

The economic order's formal sector is dominated by members of the elite classes, who are predominantly brown and white. This economic order then is also racialized, classed, and gendered. Higglers are aware of this racialized/colored/gendered economic order and their less privileged positions within it, insisting in our interviews that the Chinese, browns, and whites "sell in stores that's rented," or "own the stores," or "have their own business enterprises" and are not found higglering. These responses obviously signify the perceived presence of a racialized/colored and class division of the economy, in which Chinese, brown, and white Jamaicans—members of the elite—occupy privileged segments (as formal-sector store owners) and are not found higglering, whereas poorer black women tend to be relegated to the informal sector and are likely to be found higglering.

Although it is no surprise that we are more likely to find more lower-class women than women from higher social classes in the informal economy, the movement of higglers' multitextured bodies, when read in this broader spatialized context, takes on greater significance. Their movement into more exclusive spaces in the economy suggest a transgression, consciously or unconsciously, of this racialized/colored and classed economic order on city space. The public responds to such transgression by admonishing higglers for disrupting law and order in the city.

The disorder to the business world signified by higglers extends to the city as a whole; their undisciplined bodies pose a threat to general city life. "Congested Streets of Downtown Kingston," a news article in the *Daily Gleaner* of September 1, 2000, notes congestion as a major problem in downtown Kingston and describes Princess and Beckford Streets, which "rank as the most congested in the downtown business district. These sidewalks are sandwiched by stalls, permitting pedestrians single-file access only. As noon approaches, the pavement and sidewalk of Beckford and Princess streets disappear under a veritable sea of humanity as thousands converge on the area. The vendors settle on the sidewalks, and spillover into the road making it almost impossible for vehicles to traverse the street. Traffic is a clumsy snail of delivery vehicles, taxis, bicycles, handcrafts and people." The physical presence of the higglers—their bodies and businesses—is judged disruptive of the general flow of city life. Their presence creates "congestion," which suggests that these informal businesses have been inserted into a physical space that originally was unable, or unwilling, to accommodate them; now this space has to be shared.

Similar descriptions exist of higglering on other parts of the island. In Mandeville, higglering was "posing a serious problem for vehicular traffic and also with the pedestrians who are forced to walk in the middle of the street," according to "Street Vending Wrecking Mandeville," in the *Jamaica Gleaner* of February 4, 2002. "Vendors Evicted Permanently," in the *Jamaica Gleaner* of February 16, 2000, describes May Pen street vending as "one of the main causes of traffic congestion in town." The same article reports a meeting of Clarendon Parish Council, where attendees heard of the "total take over by vendors of the sidewalk, the post office, and the town's square, resulting in round-the-clock traffic jams." Language of higglers "taking over" streets and sidewalks appears in a significant number of articles and suggests a perception of higglering not only as contaminating cities but also as having a predatory quality. That is, the insistence and persistence of higglers to insert themselves into public spaces that were not created for them is interpreted as an invasion not only of public spaces but also of the rights of law-abiding citizens.

On May 14, 1994, an article titled "Monday Is D-Day for Vendors" described plans by the Metropolitan Parks and Market (MPM) to remove vendors from the streets and sidewalks of downtown Kingston. A press release given to the *Daily Gleaner* by the MPM described the problem of higglering, the article reported: "The crowding caused by street and sidewalk vending has also provided cover for criminal activity. The release said that all law-abiding citizens are being urged to ensure that the city returns to some semblance of decency." The news articles often associate higglering with criminality, because higglers often have their goods exposed on the open sidewalks, which makes them easy targets for thieves. The article on congestion in Kingston cited earlier includes an accusation that some higglers themselves are criminals; a businessman explained: "Because the street is congested, the delivery trucks cannot carry the goods to the doors of the store, so you have to pay the cart men to carry it up, and then the same vendors in the streets tief [steal] the goods and sell it back." On March 16, 1994, in "Businessmen Renew Call for Vendor Removal," the *Daily Gleaner* reported a businessman and member of the Jamaica Chamber of Commerce, Milade Azan, was injured and his employee accidentally shot and killed in downtown Kingston after a dispute between two male vendors over a selling spot on a sidewalk. On June 17, 2000, in "Police Arrest 48 Montego Bay Vendors," the *Daily Gleaner* reported a pedestrian in Montego Bay fatally stabbed by a male vendor on whose feet he had accidentally stepped while walking along the piazza. Although the vendors in these cases were males and such events are rare, they further tainted the public perception of higglering and reinforced the idea that higglering was not only a nuisance, but also dangerous and in need of control.

What is interesting to me in many articles is the invocation of categories of decency versus indecency, which are notions intimately tied up with bourgeois ideas of manner and morals. In the congestion article, for example, a businessman stated in frustration: "Indiscipline is indiscipline, it is not culture. This is no longer even about business—this is about common decency. Why do Jamaicans do this to themselves? A crowd doesn't mean good business, the more people in the street, the less money they can make because people can't spend in that sort of chaos." The narrative around the criminality of higglering reinforces the dichotomy of law-abiding versus lawless, discipline versus indiscipline, decency versus indecency, with higglering and other kinds of vending believed to encourage behaviors that threaten the well-being of Jamaican society, narrowly understood.

Publicly constructing higglering and higglers in this way justifies their physical and sometimes violent removal from city streets by soldiers and their relocation to designated markets and arcades. On D-Day in Kingston, the day of vendors' removal, for instance, the MPM destroyed vendors' stalls, the *Jamaica Gleaner* reported on May 17, 1994, in "MPM Smashes Vendors' Stalls." Although the removal of the vendors brought great relief to formal-sector businesspeople, the destruction of the vendors' property sparked large protests; vendors took to the streets, attempting to block the intersection of West Queen and Princess Streets in downtown Kingston. When the vendors threatened to sue the government for their losses, their claims were settled soon after for an undisclosed amount, as the *Jamaica Gleaner* reported on May 21, 1994, in "Vendors to Sue Government for Smashed Stalls," and on June 6, 1994, in "Vendors' Claims Settled."

An editorial in the *Daily Gleaner* on December 2, 2003, in support of the removal of higglers from the streets described their presence as "hold[ing] the city of Kingston ransom for yet another Christmas season." Titled "Vendors Must Obey the Rules," it applauded the KSAC's attempts to enforce a set of rules in order to create "civil order" while allowing higglers to sell in designated areas. It was expected, however, that higglers would protest their removal, and these protests were perceived as indicative of their indiscipline. "The infection of indiscipline is beginning to spread among the vendors," the editorial went on, expressing support for the mayor to take a "zero-tolerance" stance against them. Describing higglering as "a subset of squatting" that had gotten out of hand, the editorial claimed that "many vendors are much more affluent than they make out to avoid paying taxes on their profits. Their wholesale capturing of the streets of downtown Kingston is an affront to law and order and a stop must be put to it once and for all. This will call for a mix of force and tact but unless the authorities prevail the city will fall victim to incremental chaos." Here, the social imaginary of the city as an ordered space is revealed, an order that socially and spatially fragments city space to contain the infection of undesirables.

Historically, downtown Kingston was polarized, relegating black, poor Jamaicans to West Kingston (contributing to a concentration of racialized poverty and unemployment in this area) and formal businesses to East Kingston (Clarke 1975). Higglers, however, have actively transformed the downtown city space, expanding it—particularly the streets—into a site of economic opportunity for larger numbers of Jamaicans, especially the poor. The presumably infectious indiscipline of higglers, then, signifies their refusal to use city space passively in accordance with established rules created by authorities and supported by social groups that benefit from those rules—especially those from the well-off classes, many of whom have investments in the downtown area.

What interests me about these narratives are the ways in which the city becomes a metaphor for the economy through which the boundaries of legitimate and illegitimate, lawful and lawless and, perhaps more importantly, formal and informal are constructed. The expansion of the informal economy is evidenced on city space through the proliferation of street vendors, and their presence is thought to signify urban and, by extension, economic decay. Concerns about the capture of city streets by higglers merge with concerns about their competition in the economy. To create order within city space, then, is to create order in the economy, that is, to contain the informal economy and its social pollution by removing the competition it creates for formal businesses.

In these narratives, the formal economy occupies a privileged position, as it is associated with—and indeed defines—legitimacy and lawfulness. Yet the formal economy is described as vulnerable in relation to the informal economy due to the unfair practices of illegitimate businesses. Implied is that fairness is denied the law-abiding citizen—formal business owners—which raises questions about the government's ability to protect its citizens effectively, enforce law and order in the city, and resuscitate a failing economy. These questions are especially significant given the government's diminishing role in the economy as part of IMF-imposed structural adjustment policies and its adoption of a neoliberal economic framework that minimizes its power—factors that have contributed to a loss of confidence in the government in the minds of many citizens.

There are, however, interesting racial/color, gender, and class dimensions at work in these narratives as well. Lower-class black Jamaican women dominate the business of higglering. The public discourse describes their presence on the streets and in economically viable spaces in downtown Kingston as contaminating or disrupting an economic order that privileges formal-sector businesses dominated by the brown/white elite. The public maps social pathologies onto these black female bodies and casts them as threatening an established social and economic order. Disruptions of city space by lower-class black female bodies thus symbolize anomalies in the established racialized/colored economy. In other words, higglers' bodies are out of place. The narratives create a sense of moral panic and help legitimize the government's control, and sometimes its violent removal of these workers from city streets.

On November 2, 2001, for instance, the *Gleaner* reported under the headline "The 'Dons' Set the Stage" the successful removal of higglers from the streets of downtown Kingston with the assistance of area drug dealers, commonly referred to as "dons": "Some people have been marveling at the silence and docility of the usually vociferous vendors in downtown Kingston, whose stalls were smashed, reportedly by MPM workers on Monday night, in preparation for the Government-ordered removal of sidewalk vendors by Sunday, November 4. Investigations by *The Gleaner* revealed that the removal of the street vendors is actually being overseen by the two ranking 'dons' of downtown Kingston, hence the dutiful compliance of the normally aggressive and hostile vendors."[10] The same article reported that although some members of the public marveled at the success of this removal effort by the government, some members of law enforcement and other observers were concerned that the use of dons by government agencies was a mistake. Some members of law enforcement asked: "What is going to happen when these people [the dons] take it on themselves to exercise authority in other spheres and elsewhere?" They concluded that "the precedent is bad. Civil society can't operate in that way."

What is interesting about this report is the overwhelming silence by the public over the government's violation of higglers' rights by using drug dealers to intimidate them. One source quoted in the same article said that the higglers "know if they breathe a word in protest, they would have to face the consequences. It's not good." Nothing, however, was said about the use of dons as being a violation of higglers rights as Jamaican citizens. Instead, the concern was with the possibility of the dons exercising their authority in other spheres. That is to say, some were concerned that the dons would exercise their authority on other law-abiding or legitimate citizens. Indeed, the use of dons against the higglers was publicly sanctioned. The public construction of higglers as deviants justified the government's use of these extreme disciplinary measures against these women. If these removal efforts were successful, lower-class black female bodies would be kept in their place and the established racialized/color, classed, and gendered economic order fortified.

These removal efforts, when successful, benefit formal businesses. For instance, a news article in the *Jamaica Observer* of December 21, 2003, reported that formal businesses, especially those uptown, were doing better during the Christmas season than those downtown. Informal businesses, particularly higglering, were the least successful, as a result in large part of relocation efforts and heavy policing by the state. In "Uptown Businesses Outdoing Downtown," the *Observer* reported that "while some businesses in the downtown shopping area also reported brisk sales, vendors, recently removed from the shopping districts and sidewalks, say their source of income has all but dried up. 'We a suffer down here, from them move us off the streets we a dead fi hungry like dog [we are dying of hunger like a dog],' a licensed higgler in the Buck Town vendors arcade on Peters Lane said." Meanwhile, storeowner Michael Ammar Senior reported, the removal of higglers had enhanced his business. "Business is not bad. Better access to the sidewalk brought back some of our old time customers who are happy to know they can return downtown." It is very likely that the customers Ammar refers to are uptowners, as poorer black customers were already shopping downtown in significant numbers because of more affordable prices. With the help of local police, then, formal businesses were protected from competition with higglers and able to capture a lion's share of the profits earned in the lucrative shopping season.

What these public narratives also illuminate is the relationship between city imaginaries and the spatial organization of Kingston. In a capitalist economy, most informal businesses are marginalized, as evidenced by their concealment from public view and from government records. Although street vending in Jamaica is not concealed from public view, its marginalization is evidenced in the treatment of higglers and their relegation to markets outside the central business district and in areas not conducive to good business.

Higglers feel this marginalization in their day-to-day work experience. In my interviews, all forty-five higglers reported that the government was unsupportive of them. But even more telling is the sense among most that higglers do not receive the respect they deserve. Three market women described the squalid conditions of the market in which they worked as evidence of this lack of respect: "The market is dirty. If we talk, the head of the market don't like it. We get no support from the government. The market want to look after and the government don't do anything" (#17). It was common to see piles of garbage and puddles of mud and to experience foul stenches in the air when you entered these markets, as opposed to the plazas. The state of the markets along with the unsanitary conditions of the bathroom facilities were common complaints among the market women, who intimated that I would not encounter these conditions at the plazas (and I did not). An older market woman argued that "there is no security here in the market and the sanitary conditions are nasty. No, we don't get the same respect as the plazas" (#1). In this way, socially polluting higglers are both symbolically and spatially put in place by being relegated to the filthy places of the city—their physical environs, in effect, reflected how they were generally perceived and valued.

These sentiments were echoed by the ICIs. One remarked, for instance, that the "government believe higglers are the low-low class of people" (#29). Another stated that higglers get no respect, because "you are not looked upon as a businessperson." One ICI described being targeted by customs and having to pay unfair duties. She stated, "Higglers get no respect. Customs handle you bad. You have to pay high duties. They just treat you bad" (#38). This ICI compared her treatment to that of formal-sector businesspeople, particularly Syrian/Lebanese (racialized as white), who she believed receive better treatment. As with the market women, the idea of preferential treatment for formal businesses in the plazas was common among the ICIs.

Although the higglers in my study viewed their businesses as a source of great pride, since it helped them support their families and gain a sense of independence, higglering was also a source of pain, as noted earlier, because of the differential treatment and disrespect they believe they receive in comparison to that accorded formal businesses. In some ways, many higglers felt betrayed. One ICI remarked: "We don't get respect again like we used to. In the 1980s when big businesses left, vendors stayed here and kept the country going, but we don't get respect now. Jamaica encourage foreign business and not encourage vendors. They encourage the Chinese and other foreigners over vendors. Chinese sell what the vendors sell and undercut their profits. I wonder if the Chinese pay duties" (#36). In spite of this sense of betrayal among many, higglers continue with their businesses, partly out of necessity but also out of pride in their work.

Higglers have challenged their marginalization by refusing to remain in the markets and continuing to sell on the streets. They have used various strategies of resistance, ranging from engaging in a "cat-and-mouse" game with local authorities to directly confronting the police and business owners. On December 6, 2001, for instance, Petulia Clarke reported in the *Daily Gleaner* under the headline "Cat-and-Mouse Game Downtown Kingston" that despite the KSAC's zero-tolerance approach toward higglers, "street vending in the commercial district remain as hectic as ever with a few new twists." Higglers, determined to profit from the busy Christmas season, remained constantly mobile, moving from one street to the next, to avoid getting caught by the authorities. Some higglers had also hired watchmen to alert them of approaching authorities so that they could clear the streets before they arrived.

Many higglers have complained not only that the government-appointed markets were unclean but also that many were located in unprotected areas too far removed from the public, hindering their ability to attract customers. This gets even more complicated when we factor in the spatial division of downtown Kingston into political factions that violently clash with each other daily, especially during election years. These political factions are often tied into Kingston's drug culture, in which an area drug leader, or don, presides over each faction and demands loyalty from area residents. One vendor complained that a designated market was located in an area outside their political territory, where conducting business would be risky, even deadly. "The arcade full and that a 'shower man' turf. That might nuh healthy fi we [might not be healthy for us]. Sometime war start and we might can't cross the border," said the vendor, quoted in the December 12, 2003, *Jamaica Observer* under the headline "Kingston Vendors Stay off the Streets." In the name of safety, then, many higglers' turn to the streets and continue to sell there in spite of the risk of getting caught by government agencies.

Higglers have also engaged in direct confrontations with local authorities and businesspeople. On December 9, 2003, higglers chanting, "No vendors! No stores!" gathered in front of the KSAC and stormed businesses in major shopping areas, forcing many to pull down their shutters, the *Jamaica Observer* reported in "Vendors Protest . . . But KSAC Vows Not to Back Down." In another protest a few years earlier, the article reported, higglers had marched on formal-business stores downtown, drawn down their shutters, and shouted, "If we caan [can't] sell, then nobody will sell," forcing local authorities and businesses to negotiate with them for space to sell. In both instances, higglers challenged attempts to push them out of economically viable spaces simply by using their bodies to avoid detection by authorities or by directly confronting them. Here, the multitextured bodies of higglers purposely create disorder instead of being or embodying disorder. Instead of passively accepting their marginalization, higglers use their bodies to actively contest it and at times have been successful in their struggles—if only for a moment.

Higglers versus Uptown Residents

Not just formal businesses but also local residents are constructed in the public discourse as victims of higglering. On November 16, 1986, the *Daily Gleaner* published an article by Dawn Ritch, a popular columnist and member of the brown elite, titled "No Such Thing as a Happy Higgler: "They Are Spreading like a Disease into Every Residential Area." Ritch bemoaned the encroachment of higglers into uptown residential areas: "They've oppressed and endangered the environment, and the country's public health standard. They are spreading like a disease into every residential area, and will continue until stopped. What was once quaint is now a morass of indiscipline because higglers want to make money but don't display the responsibility that usually comes with earning it. Higglers are just too bright for their own good. And I don't believe in appeasing them because there is no such thing as a happy higgler." Ritch's assertion that "higglers are just too bright for their own good" interests me. In Jamaica, telling someone they are too bright for their own good suggests that the individual has crossed an unspoken boundary and is out of order (in fact, a contemporary Jamaican saying is, "You too out of order!"). Higglers are thought to be crossing not only a physical boundary with their physical bodies into uptown residential areas, but also an economic boundary by encroaching on the profits of legitimate businesses. For Ritch, higglers have also crossed social boundaries by introducing indiscipline into disciplined areas. In her view, higglers are out of order, as well as out of place, physically, economically, and socially.

Higglers are also too bright (smart) and out of order in an epistemological sense. By describing higglers as too smart for their own good, Ritch speaks to these women's ability to understand their economic situation, which allows them to subvert resources given to them by the government, and to manipulate the system in their favor. Ritch reports in her article that higglers were provided arcades in order to conduct their businesses. Local merchants and the Jamaica Chamber of Commerce (formal-sector businesspeople and organizations) financially supported the construction of these arcades for the purpose of removing higglers from the streets. According to Ritch, however, this plan backfired, because many higglers used these arcades as "head offices" and storage facilities. She claimed that the arcades were often used as a "business base" to promote the expansion of these microbusinesses. These bases became central distributive points from which other microbusinesses, run by higglers' family members and friends, were organized. Instead of containing the microbusinesses of higglers, then, the arcades were used by these women to facilitate their expansion, which intensifies the competition between these businesses and those in the formal economy. Ritch interprets higglers' resistance to these attempts at containment as indicative of their indiscipline, and she declares that the "time has come to see the higglers for what they are, . . . a highly articulate, highly organized group of traders who want to have their cake and eat it."

Ritch's use of the metaphor "disease" speaks volumes about the ways in which higglers are imagined. Social pathologies again are mapped onto the black poor female bodies of higglers, who are figured as contaminants. Their movements into uptown residential areas signify "dis-ease," since long-established patterns of racialized and classed residential segregation are challenged by their very presence there. Ronald Sundstrom reminds us that "when we sort people by categories, we do so spatially; with race come racialized spaces." He insists that we take seriously the relationship between social space and human categories, because "who we are is bound up with place" (2003, 92). Among Kingstonians, uptown (like downtown) is not simply a geographic identifier but also signifies one's social standing, as pointed out earlier. The social standing of the brown elite is bound up with uptown residential space. Higglers' presence uptown, then, not only disrupts spatial boundaries but also has the potential to change the meaning of uptown space and jeopardize the social standing of browns. To put it bluntly, if uptown is now dominated by poor black female bodies (that signify social pathology and degradation in the public imagination), that circumstance alone could change the meaning of uptown and impact the social standing of brown residents. In Ritch's view, the presence of these predominantly black, lower-class higglers in previously restricted uptown areas signifies a contamination that must be removed so that the social order (racialized/classed residential segregation) is restored and, I might add, the social standing of the brown elite is protected.

Yet many uptown residents purchase locally grown produce from market women, especially on Saturday mornings.[11] I saw such transactions at the Papine Market in uptown Kingston. But these spaces and workers are spatially contained. With the deterioration of the Jamaican economy and the expansion of the informal economy, informal business spaces are expanding and privileged spaces of the brown elite are not easily insulated. Higglers, then, take up too much space, in the view of many uptowners, as these black women move into previously restricted areas in search of new customers.

The themes of contamination and the construction of higglers as public nuisances occur in other letters to the *Daily Gleaner*. For example, in a letter to the editor published August 20, 1999, under the heading "Illegal Street Vendors," a woman discussed what she considered "the ridiculous situation existing in our city today, where higglers and vendors selling their wares have taken over the streets." She described "the growing problem at the Barbican round-a-bout": "It is bad enough that the fruit sellers there have total control of the public sidewalks, forcing the pedestrians to take to the roads. But now every person who has anything to peddle has put up a stall." She admitted that her letter was sparked by two instances where she almost hit male vendors as they ran out into the streets to sell to motorists, and who subsequently cursed at and threatened her. The woman wrote in frustration: "I am sick of the conditions we have to live under in this country. Where are the laws to get these dangerous illiterates off the sidewalks?" She questioned whether street vending was legal and suggested that the government was not doing its job in controlling vendors who, in her view, were not making any contribution to the country; she assumed they were not paying taxes. The woman concluded her letter in a tone that suggests a sense of defeat on her part: "Well, this 'black gal' doesn't want to have her head 'chapped' [chopped] open so I have decided to drive another route, despite it being much longer and inconvenient. Chalk up another victory for indiscipline and criminality."[12] From her vantage point, higglers and vendors are unruly, disrespectful, uneducated, and even dangerous.

Although this woman's letter was triggered by her encounters with two male vendors, her anger was directed toward all vendors, including women. She signed the editorial "Victimized Black Gal," implying her own spatial (being forced to take a detour to avoid the vendors), economic (having to pay taxes while higglers don't), and social (racialized gender) victimization. The public narrative around higglering, then, describes it not only as threatening legitimate businesses but also as contaminating uptown residential areas: higglers take advantage of the generosity of the government and business sectors and victimize law-abiding citizens. These narratives reinforce constructed boundaries of lawful versus lawless and legitimacy versus illegitimacy, but extend those narratives beyond the business community to add ordinary, law-abiding citizens to the list of victims.

The complicated ways these narratives use racial/color and class codes are especially telling. Uptown Kingston—a middle- and upper-class area—is imagined as lawful, proper, and clean. The intrusion or infection of higglers represents a transgression of class boundaries that involve racial markers. This way of talking about higglering, for instance, generates endless oppositions that come to be connected in public discourse (e.g., lawful/ lawless, legitimacy/illegitimacy, sanitary/unsanitary, literate/illiterate, white-brown/black). Particularly interesting to me are the ways these oppositions provide a context in which the invocation of one word—say, "lawlessness"—calls forth a range of other meanings, such as race/color. This is one way of grasping what Stuart Hall refers to as "the over-determined complexity of the whole" of Jamaican society (1977, 154). In other words, the woman's sarcastic use of "victimized 'black gal'" exposes, however subtly, the complex way race/color operates in these exchanges.

In a letter to the editor published in the *Daily Gleaner* on March 26, 2000, entitled "The Making of a Slum," John H. Williams, a resident of the primarily upper-middle-class, uptown Kingston 8 area, describes the "deteriorating condition of Manor Park." He holds that "Manor Park should be a prime and pristine residential area. It is now deteriorating into a 'slum.' At the foot of [Stony Hill] which was once a large green common area is now taken over by higglers, taxis, and an assorted bunch of idlers who have now turned the once lovely green area into a filthy wasteland." Williams writes of bus sheds being "taken over by higglers and idlers making the pedestrians and buses fight for space in the middle of the road." Of the Constant Spring Market, where higglers sell: "Its ghoulish shoddy ambience contributes greatly to the general chaka chaka [chaos] of Manor Park. This entity is completely out of place and should be removed." Formal businesses in Manor Park need to be "relocated or moved back so that the roadways can be widened." The general breakdown "makes the place look like a growing holocaust and creates traffic jams even on Sundays."

What interests me about this letter is Williams's suggestion to remove completely the Constant Spring Market and, for that matter, higglers, because they are "out of place," yet he wants formal businesses only to be "relocated or moved back." Higglering is not perceived as suitable for that upper-middle-class area, even if higglers conduct their business in the designated marketplace. Williams has a definite idea about what is appropriate for this geographical area: his concern is not simply the aesthetics of Manor Park but the social meanings attributed to this upper-middle-class space—what kind of place it is and what kinds of people live and work there. Williams's description of Manor Park's deterioration and its being "taken over" by higglers, idlers, and taxis carries subtle and not so subtle racial/color and class meanings, as these activities are dominated by the black poor. The use of the term "slum" operates similarly. Like the terms "ghetto" and "urban neighborhoods" in the U.S. context, "slums" represent the social and spatial location of the black poor (Sundstrom 2003). By claiming that Manor Park was deteriorating into a slum and associating higglers with filth and waste, and a source of this deterioration, Williams uses race/color and class symbols to generate moral panic among Jamaicans, particularly uptown residents.

Williams also uses gender symbols against class and race/color: "What kind of country is this where higglers and idlers easily capture every inch of space? Where is the town planning department, the security forces, the KSAC, the Member of Parliament? Are all these paid entities afraid or impotent?" With Williams's questioning of the impotence of government agencies, he challenges structures of masculinist power, identifying its inability to control the poor in general and poor black women in particular. What, for instance, would "potency" mean? Here it seems to involve not only protecting law-abiding citizens by controlling the black poor and women, but also having the power to restore a presumed social and spatial order structured by race/color, class, and gender.

The use of gender symbols against class and race/color is also evidenced in public constructions of the Jamaican lady and woman, and the placement of higglers among the latter. In her study on the Jamaican white elite, Lisa Douglass makes a clear distinction between public constructions of a Jamaican lady and a woman: "A lady is educated and refined. She exudes femininity in all her attributes, from her diminutive size and unobtrusive manner, to her high heels and exquisite grooming, to her soft voice and careful diction. . . . She does not use vulgar language or even patois" (1992, 75). Higglers do not fit into a middle-class construction of ladies. Higglering occurs in the public sphere, particularly in the streets, a space traditionally imagined and often practiced as masculine. According to Douglass, the street is the domain not only of men but also of lower-class women. An uptown lady would not venture out into the streets without her car or unaccompanied. The work site of higglers, then, always already frames how these women are perceived. Ladies don't higgle in the streets.

Another important characteristic in the construction of a Jamaican lady, Douglass notes, is its association with race/color and class. Ladies are generally understood as middle- and upper-class brown and white women. Higglers do not conform to this ideal of femininity. These predominantly working-class and poor dark-skinned women are stereotyped in the public discourse as loud, aggressive black women who are vulgar, unruly. and essentially unfeminine, a stark contrast to the construction of the Jamaican lady.

An example of this figuring of higglers as women rather than ladies is evidenced in Morris Cargill's 1986 editorial suggesting that modern higglers were the result of "selective breeding" (see Chapter 5). His construction of higglers violates middle-class definitions of a lady, which include her diminutive size. His claim that higglers use their "huge" breasts as "battering rams" speaks to the higgler's perceived obtrusive manner, which also makes her unfeminine, for ladies are socialized to take up as little space with their bodies as possible. Higglers, then, in their practice and presence make space as much as they take up space. In addition to disrupting the commercial and social-urban order, their racialized, out-of-place bodies also disrupt classed gender arrangements and assumptions. The image of the higgler as a woman as opposed to a lady justifies Cargill's suggesting their removal from public view, and this justification trades on a host of racist associations that inform Jamaica's more general public discourse.

All the articles reviewed suggest that the activities of higglering and their conflicts with the state, uptown residents, and formal businesses reveal how the social imaginary (as evidenced in the public discourse) is translated into spatial hierarchies that polarize and fragment the city of Kingston. The physical presence of higglers is conceptualized as polluting middle- and upper-class areas because, among many things, their black bodies make poverty visible. Moreover, their bodies are mobile, and so test established social and spatial boundaries and make them vulnerable simply by these working class/poor black women's moving into previously restricted areas. The conflicts between higglers, the state, city residents, and formal businesses, then, reveal challenges to those long-established social and spatial boundaries, and attempts to fortify them. At the heart of these conflicts is the question of order: who is out of order, and who wants to and is able to maintain order?

The case of Afro-Jamaican higglers suggests that to understand markets as lived experiences, we must not limit our investigations solely to economic factors but also examine social-ideological ones, particularly the ways in which constructions of race/color and gender are indicative of disorder and pollution. Embodied intersectionality helps tease out these multiple dimensions of power by focusing on the multitextured bodies of actors and the broader social and economic contexts within which they work. This approach offers an in-depth assessment of the lived experiences of markets by exposing complex and sometimes subtle obstacles that may shape and constrain those experiences.

In contracting urban economies, particularly in developing countries, competition for "scarce benefits and spoils" intensifies as local elites vie to maintain their privileged positions, and the poor struggle to earn a living. Managing this competition involves magnifying differences among groups and developing mechanisms of inclusion and exclusion. In these processes of inclusion and exclusion, categories of race/color and gender are given greater meaning; they work with notions of class (and other categories of inequality) to organize bodies and structure contexts in which market (including informal marketing) activities occur.

In Jamaica, the elite and traditional middle class have managed to hold firm despite a contracting economy (Clarke and Howard 2006, 114). Of course, multiple factors can account for their success, including quality educational opportunities and greater access to high-income jobs and housing. But to what extent is success the result of these groups' ability to secure (with support from the government) privileged positions in the economy by containing informal workers? To what extent are uptown residents able to secure access to privileged residential areas by excluding those deemed less desirable? In short, are the economic successes of the elite and traditional middle classes in Jamaica intertwined with the reproduction and reinforcement of racial/color hierarchies that are used to legitimize and protect their privileged positions in the economy and society? The case of Afro-Jamaican higglers suggests that a singular focus on economic factors only scratches the surface of our understanding of their lived experiences. Indeed, their lived experiences raise much larger questions around the complex ways in which societies are stratified, the varied positions of groups within that stratification system, and its effects on their life worlds.

In his elaboration of the history of struggles between higglers and formal businesses over city space, Espeut asserts in his 2003 editorial on Christmas vending:

> This script has played out—with a few variations—over many decades. A comedy or tragedy? It is almost the archetype of class struggle—between the rich and the poor, between the poor and the powerless, between the merchants and the higglers, between the formal and the informal sector. It demonstrates how the powerful can amass the forces of the state to act in their interests;

and it shows the ability of the Jamaican underclass to struggle and survive in the face of great adversity."

Espeut describes this drama as a class struggle. However, as I have demonstrated, more is at work here. The lived experiences of higglering reveal a complex web of power that goes beyond informal/formal divisions. Tragic, comic, or even epic, I am not sure—but I am convinced that these lived experiences illuminate racialized/colored, classed, and gendered contexts of inclusion and exclusion that lower-class, black women in Jamaica grapple with as they struggle "fi mek a sale" and thereby dis-ease the everyday order.

CONCLUSION

Understanding the Nuances of Informality

> "Economically conditioned" power is not, of course, identical with "power" as such. On the contrary, the emergence of economic power may be the consequence of power existing on other grounds.
> **MAX WEBER**, "Class, Status, and Party"

> A *butu* in a Benz is still a *butu*!
> **REX NETTLEFORD**

Most scholars understand that to gain a better grasp of the nuances of informality we must not focus on the economic practices or material conditions of individual actors while ignoring structural and cultural factors that help shape those conditions.[1] Max Weber clarifies this point in his description of the multidimensionality of power. Indeed, power wielded in certain spaces by, and over, certain bodies is often the product of a combination of structural and cultural factors. Weber elaborates on this idea in his description of the "status order": "The way in which social honor is distributed in a community between typical groups participating in this distribution we call the 'status order.' The social order and economic order are related in a similar manner to the legal order. However, the economic order merely defines the way in which economic goods and services are distributed and used. Of course, the status order is strongly influenced by it, and in turn reacts upon it" (1993, 126). Weber's explanation suggests that the social and economic order are mutually reinforcing. Feminist scholarship convincingly demonstrates this point by explicating how structures and cultural ideologies around gender influence women's participation in the economy, both formal and informal, and in many ways create barriers to women's success in these economic spaces. Most agree that gender ideologies influence where and how women participate in the economy, and that the manner in which women participate in the economy helps reinforce those ideologies.

But if we resist treating gender as an abstract category and instead interrogate how gender is racialized and classed, we discover a more complicated story. The experiences of Afro-Jamaican higglers reveal that economically conditioned power is by no means a recognized basis of social honor in Jamaica, and that gender is not the only factor that determines this. We see, for example, that despite the economic power they may have, wealthy ICIs are still considered socially unacceptable and are stigmatized among the Jamaican middle and upper classes.

The late Rex Nettleford, Jamaican scholar and vice chancellor emeritus of the University of the West Indies, reveals this viewpoint in his famous quip: "A *butu* in a Benz is still a *butu*." In Jamaican parlance, a *butu* is a person who exhibits behaviors that violate middle-class norms of respectability and decency. The image of the *butu* is usually embodied by a lower-class black person and is associated with stereotypes of the black poor. Nettleford's statement suggests that despite a *butu*'s economic power (ability to own a Mercedes-Benz), that person is still unable to penetrate the upper social strata because despite economic gains, a *butu* continues to embody social deviance. These conceptualizations of deviance are not limited to ideas around gender but include race/color and class.

Nettleford's remark is confirmed by an ICI in my study, who said that "in Jamaica, people divide themselves. If you are a higgler and own a house in Norbrook they run us [chase us away]. They are racist over their own colors" (#34). Norbrook is an upper-class residential area in uptown Kingston occupied primarily by Jamaica's brown and white elite. This ICI explained that, despite their economic power, higglers are not perceived as socially acceptable among the brown and white residents there. She attributed higglers' social unacceptability to racism and revealed that the distribution of social honor is not determined solely by one's economic power but also by social factors, including race.[2]

What does all this suggest? What can the experiences of Afro-Jamaican higglers teach us about the informal economy and women's work experiences? I opened this book by arguing that as we attempt to understand the whole of informality, scholars must examine the ways in which gender as well as race and class combine to thwart the life chances of so many women in the informal economy. This study demonstrates that as we try to understand the experiences of women in the informal economy, in addition to examining economic factors, we must expand our understanding to include multiple social factors that affect these outcomes as well. We must avoid collapsing women's experiences under the rubric of gender inequality and instead take into account how women's experiences vary by their race/color as well as their social class. Indeed, race/color, class, and gender coalesce and influence how bodies and spaces—and bodies *in* particular spaces—are imagined, lived, and disciplined in the informal economy.

Embodied Intersectionality and Women's Informal Work

In a report published in 2008 that examined the vast research undertaken by the International Labour Office (ILO) on women and the informal economy, the authors highlighted the study's many strengths but identified some key analytical concerns. One concern related to "the need to develop and apply a more 'intersectional' approach to gender analysis, which pays more careful attention to the differences and relationships between women (as well as women and men and men and men) within particular social and geo-political contexts." Noting that only a few ILO publications engage in intersectional gender analyses, the authors worried that "the majority of studies continue to treat 'women' (or in some cases 'poor' or 'third-world' women) as a self-evident and homogenous group" (Chant and Pedwell 2008, 8). The authors call for more studies that not only examine the constitutive articulation of gender, race, and class, but also include other categories of inequality such as sexuality and age. They assert that "intersectional relations of power which position different groups of women (and men) in differing relations of privilege and marginality to one another in the labour market . . . [remain] important" (18).

Embodied intersectionality responds to this concern by examining how the combined effects of race, class, and gender impinge upon the lifeworlds of women in the informal economy. But embodied intersectionality does not limit its analysis to social structures. Instead the concept acknowledges that structures of race, class, and gender are also embodied. That is to say, we experience structures of race, class, and gender through our bodies. A critical assumption, then, is that bodies and societies are intricately connected; our bodies are embedded in multiple, intersecting structures of power, especially race/color, class, and gender, which contributes to their multitextured quality.

As we examine the body-society relationship in our analysis of women in the informal economy, we note that spaces are also intersectional. That is to say, public (and private) spaces are not blank slates; they are often infused with meanings shaped by ideas around race/color, class, gender, or all of these. The economy, for instance, is not to be conceptualized in abstraction; it is a set of relations located within particular spaces. For example, the global economy is based on a set of relations between economic actors (i.e., multinational corporations and global workers) that are located in certain spaces. Multinational corporations are frequently headed by white elite men located in the global North and employ, among others, poor women of color—conceptualized as cheap and exploitable labor—located in peripheral nations, or the global South, such as those in the Caribbean, India, and Latin America. The economic relationships between the global North and South, then, reinforce not only economic or class differences between these two spaces, but also racial and gender differences and inequalities.

Racialized, classed, and gendered differences are also spatially reproduced within particular geographical contexts. As we have seen, the formal economy is often associated with the public sphere, which is imagined and experienced as masculine. But in Jamaica, the public economic sphere is not only gendered but also racialized. This is one of the legacies of colonialism that privileged white elite males as the legitimate actors in the formal economy. By attributing legitimacy to this group and representing black female economic actors as illegitimate, the formal economy is imagined and experienced as a white and masculine space. In other words, formal public economic spaces are not simply masculine. Instead, a particular kind of masculinity is at work in this imaginary—one racialized as white. At the time of Jamaica's independence in 1962, economic power was transferred from British elites to brown/white elites; today, the legitimate economic actor in the formal economy is brown/white and male. The formal economy is thus imagined as masculine, brown/white, and thereby legitimate, whereas the informal economy is predominantly black, female, and illegitimate.

However, intersectional gender analyses never offer the complete picture. Indeed, more research is needed that examines the impact of sexuality, disability, and age along with gender, race, and class on women's experiences in the informal economy. In fact, this is a common critique of intersectionality. Many scholars have called attention to the tendency of intersectional analyses to focus primarily on race, class, and gender, and their failure to be more inclusive of other differences. But instead of viewing this as a failure, I view this as a challenge. The incompleteness of intersectionality—and in my case, of embodied intersectionality—makes room for scholars (including myself) to continue thinking of ways in which to develop intersectionality and push it in new directions. My hope is that the focus of embodied intersectionality on bodies and/in space contributes to this new direction and, at the very least, brings us closer to a more nuanced approach to informality.

Women, Informality, and Microcredit

To echo U.S. pragmatist William James (1907), what is the "cash value" of all this? The phenomenon of women's informal work has sparked considerable discussion among researchers, academics, and policy makers on how to understand women's experiences in the informal economy and how to assist these microentrepreneurs. One strategy that has grown out of this discussion is the development of microcredit agencies, influenced in large part by the pioneering work of Bangladeshi economist and Nobel Peace Prize winner Mohammad Younus. In the 1980s, bilateral and multilateral agencies such as the ILO (International Labor Organization), USAID (United States Agency for International Development), and the World Bank developed and promoted several credit institutions in Jamaica whose primary goal was to provide credit to microentrepreneurs.[3] Two institutions in Kingston that offer microloans to microentrepreneurs, including higglers, are the Credit Union of Kingston (COK) and the Jamaica National Heritage Trust.[4]

A major concern over recent years has been higglers' underutilization of microcredit programs (Brown 1995; Honig 1993; Macfarlane-Gregory and Ruddock-Kelly 1993). Scholars and practitioners attribute women's underutilization of these programs to the fact that higglers were simply poorly informed of the resources available to them. Others claim that perhaps women as opposed to men were more "naturally hesitant" to borrow money from lending institutions (Brown 1995, 22–23).

I reject these views. The women in my study were well aware of the existence of microcredit programs. In fact, several ICIs reported that microloan officers frequently visited their arcades. They handed out literature about microloans and discussed lending options with the women. What I discovered, however, is that while most of the higglers were aware of the loan and credit programs available to them, they consciously chose not to take advantage of these opportunities.

Microcredit institutions rely on collateral based on liquid assets such as land, homes, vehicles, and household appliances to secure their microloans. Collateral, however, is the source of these women's fears: many women in the study were concerned that if they borrowed money and could not repay it, the bank would take their stove, car, refrigerator, or other pieces of furniture away from them. Economists may view these kinds of collateral as low-risk ventures, but for these higglers, losing such items would have a negative impact on their families. Losing a refrigerator or a stove, for instance, would hamper their ability to feed their children. Losing their car would hamper their ability to take their children to school and to go to work. For these women, then, the risks were simply too high.

The state of these higglers' businesses, where sales have been depressingly low, placed them at greater risk of going into default on their microloans. One ICI at the Constant Spring Arcade explained that business has been so slow that she sometimes puts her "house money" into her business; another said that sometimes her husband gives her money to purchase supplies for her business. This suggests that the low rate of borrowing among these higglers is not the result of natural hesitance but of rational choice based on their economic circumstances and family obligations. Indeed, these higglers' decisions were not based solely on economic factors but also on their social responsibilities as women and (for many) as mothers.

They chose not to take financial risks that could negatively impact their families' well-being. Only three women in my study used or would even consider using banks or microcredit agencies; almost all instead chose to use informal sources of credit that would not place their families at risk.

But I am particularly interested in another potential barrier to higglers' access to microcredit. I am reminded of an interview I conducted with a credit manager at the Credit Union of Kingston (COK) in July 2001, who told me that along with financial statements—reports of the size and productivity of higglers' businesses—higglers have to submit "character references" indicating their "trustworthiness." "Sometimes first impression is all that is needed," the credit manager said. "Just talking to that person, you can know their character." Although he suggested that character references played a secondary role in the decision-making process, the issue of character raises important questions regarding the stigma of higglering: If higglers are publicly imagined as deviants or undesirables in Jamaican society, what impact do these stigmas have on the ways in which microloans are distributed? What does this credit manager see on higglers' bodies that would allow him to determine their character? How might questions of character influence the ways in which microloans are distributed?

In my conversations with higglers, many mentioned with disdain that microloan applications required at least four letters of reference, despite the small size of the loans. One ICI declared: "They [credit officers] tell me that I must get four references. Four! All of this, plus collateral, for [US]$100?" (#34). This higgler had no problem providing references, but she was offended that the number of references she would be required to provide sent a clear message that she and women like her were not to be trusted. The requirement of microcredit institutions of four references plus collateral for small loans reinforced a larger public discourse around higglering as illegitimate, and higglers as a devalued and untrustworthy group of entrepreneurs.

Most of the higglers in my study chose informal sources of credit, including "partners." "Partners" (also called *susus*) are rotating savings and credit associations (ROSCA) in which a group of individuals get together, and every participant contributes the same agreed-upon amount of money weekly. All contributions are collected by one individual in the group (this is sometimes referred to as a "draw"). This process is repeated each week until every person in the group has had a draw. Weekly draws can range from US$200 to $2,000 or more, depending on the amount of the contributions and the size of the group. The partner system is overseen by one individual who is responsible for collecting the weekly contributions and ensuring that each member of the group collects their draw.

What is significant is that partners are based on a system of "enforceable trust" among participants, as Alejandro Portes explains: "Trust in informal exchanges is generated both by shared identities and feelings and by the expectation that fraudulent actions will be penalized by the exclusion of the violator from key social networks" (1994, 430). Trust, then, is enforced among members of the partner system, who value not only this social network for its economic gains but also their own good reputations. Good reputations and social networks are important components of social capital that many workers rely on in the informal economy. The idea of trust binds the group together in the partner system and is also an important component of members' identities.[5]

Trust is critical among higglers, who rely on their reputations and social networks in order to thrive in the informal economy. Many higglers extend credit—or, as they say, "trus"—among themselves when they need products to sell. One market woman explained: "If I am running low on red peas, I can trus a cup from Ms. [T], sell it, and then pay her back" (#20). This system operated primarily among the market women; almost half would obtain certain produce on credit from other higglers or farmers, sell it, and at the end of the day, pay the farmers or higglers for the items while keeping the profits. A slightly different system is enforced among the ICIs, in which those who are unable to travel gave their money to an ICI traveling abroad and entrusted her with the responsibility of purchasing items on their behalf and bringing them back to Jamaica for the women to sell.

Both market women and ICIs utilize their system of trust in other ways. I observed in the market and arcades that higglers looked out for each other by referring customers seeking a particular item and by keeping a close eye on each other's stalls. If a higgler had to step away for a moment, leaving her stall unattended, her coworkers sold items for her if a customer approached while she was away. Some higglers also sold for coworkers unable to come to work. When asked what would happen if they were unable to come to work because of illness, four market women and two ICIs reported that they would ask another higgler in the market to open their stall and sell for them. One ICI at the Constant Spring Arcade described being able to leave her stall in the middle of the day to take her son to the passport office or go to the hairdresser without worry, because other ICIs in the arcade would watch over her stall and sell for her. Another ICI similarly described being able to go to the doctor and not having to worry or close down her stall.

Trust, then, is a critical feature of higglering. In order to thrive in the informal economy, higglers have to establish a sense of trustworthiness among themselves. Many have successfully established good reputations they have relished for years. But when confronted with microcredit procedures that call their trustworthiness into question (partly influenced, I suggest, by a public image of higglers as deviants), many are offended and choose instead to continue relying on their informal networks, which in many ways help maintain their dignity. As one women declared in response to my asking whether she would seek a microloan: "I would trus from a farmer, not a bank, or I would throw [contribute to] my partner" (#6). Intervention strategies have to address the stigma of higglering so that microcredit agencies can create procedures that do not compromise the dignity of these workers. In fact, intervention strategies that pay close attention to the specificity of women's experiences (especially the constitutive relations of gender, race, class, etc.) are likely to prove the most effective.

It is also critical to consider the stigmas around women's informal work that impact their physical work spaces. My observations of public markets and arcades reveal that these economic spaces are not built with a business sensibility. The physical structures of these sites, particularly the arcades, do not attract customers and promote selling. The arcades are not properly roofed, and each stall is like a small and confining storage room where passersby can see only one quarter of the ICI's products.

Arcades and markets are constructed by the Metropolitan Parks and Market (MPM) and the Kingston and St. Andrew Corporation (KSAC), organizations that are responsible for the beautification and cleanliness of the city. The relationship between these organizations and higglers is always contentious. The KSAC and MPM often discipline higglers by removing them from city streets. Because higglers are perceived as a devalued group of workers, or simply as nuisances, the primary goal of the MPM and KSAC appears simply to be policing their public presence, not enhancing or promoting their businesses. The markets and arcades thus become warehouses, not shopping centers. Studying this issue more closely may allow us to understand why many higglers refuse to remain in these sites and to suggest better ways to address their business needs.

The general insight here is that our analysis of the relationships between higglers and state organizations (MPM, KSAC, or microcredit institutions) must include the discursive setting within which those relationships take place: how higglers are publicly imagined, and the way those constructions reproduce race, class, and gender inequalities. This approach enables us to keep in view the overdetermined complexity of the problems that higglers confront as they negotiate the ways the state attempts to contain them.

The complex realities of women informal workers resist reductionist accounts. Those realities reflect the historical legacies of colonialism, as well as the contemporary constraints of contracting economies and persistent gender, class, and racial inequalities. No single causal explanation will suffice. This book has attempted to demonstrate that, in the context of Jamaica, the constitutive articulation of race, class, and gender must be kept in view if we are to understand, at a significant level of detail, the multifaceted problems women face in the informal economy and the complex identities they perform. Third-world women in general and Jamaican women in particular must be situated within the complex histories of Western domination and the effects of that domination on their lifeworlds. This effort requires, as this book has reflected, a historical sensibility in which contextualization is absolutely critical if we are to grasp the simultaneous impact of race, class, and gender on the labor patterns of women. In short, attention must be given to the setting (the discourse and the material conditions) in which these women work.

Failure to keep this overdetermined complexity in view keeps us from understanding, to paraphrase Max Weber, that economic powerlessness may be the consequence of power that exists on other grounds.

Perhaps this is a bit too strong. The women in my study were far from powerless. They demonstrated throughout an amazing capacity to understand and negotiate their marginal position in contemporary Jamaican life. From informal networks to stigma management, higglers showed a knack for intervening in the micro- and macrostructures of power that shaped their lifeworlds. The women in this study are caught in webs of power and domination that define contemporary Jamaica. Their efforts do not result in a subversion of race and class hierarchies. Nor do they fundamentally challenge gender inequality. But the women's activities reveal that their situations are not simply ones of constraint. The women act, contest, and create in their lifeworlds. Theirs is a reality experienced as a natural weave of both constraint and possibility.

To return to one of the basic motivations driving this study: there is something particular about these women and their work that warrants attention to the specific history and present context of Jamaica that shapes their choices and informs their efforts to provide for themselves and their children. If we are to understand these experiences, we must resist the temptation to reduce the complexity of their lives to those of what Chandra Talpade Mohanty (1991) calls "average third-world women." Instead, we must think of ways to include the myriad factors that influence their subordination, and recognize that, all along, these women, these women of color on the periphery, are thinking, speaking—and acting.

APPENDIX

List of Higglers Interviewed

Unless otherwise noted, these are in-person interviews. All information was collected in 2001.

MARKET WOMEN
#1 Papine Market, February 19
#2 Papine Market, June 27
#3 Papine Market, July 2
#4 Papine Market, July 5
#5 Papine Market, July 7
#6 Papine Market, July 7
#7 Papine Market, July 14
#8 Papine Market, July 14
#9 Papine Market, July 10
#10 Survey, July 10
#11 Survey, July 10
#12 Papine Market, July 7
#13 Papine Market, July 7
#14 Papine Market, July 14
#15 Papine Market, July 14
#16 Papine Market, July 14
#17 Papine Market, July 14
#18 Papine Market, July 14
#19 Papine Market, July 14
#20 Papine Market, July 16
#21 Papine Market, July 16
#22 Papine Market, July 18
#23 Papine Market, July 18

INFORMAL COMMERCIAL IMPORTERS (ICIS)
#24 Constant Spring Arcade, February 12
#25 Constant Spring Arcade, February 16

#26 Constant Spring Arcade, June 13
#27 Constant Spring Arcade, June 13
#28 Constant Spring Arcade, June 13
#29 Constant Spring Arcade, June 14
#30 Constant Spring Arcade, June 18
#31 Constant Spring Arcade, June 19
#32 Constant Spring Arcade, June 25
#33 Constant Spring Arcade, June 26
#34 Constant Spring Arcade, June 26
#35 People's Arcade, June 19
#36 People's Arcade, June 19
#37 People's Arcade, June 22
#38 People's Arcade, June 28
#39 People's Arcade, June 28
#40 People's Arcade, July 3
#41 Survey, July 23
#42 Telephone interview, July 15
#43 Survey, July 23
#44 Survey, July 23
#45 Telephone interview, July 17

Notes

INTRODUCTION

1. The term "Afro-Jamaican" refers to Jamaican people who are descendants of the Africans and Europeans who peopled the West Indies during the periods of slavery and colonialism. I use this category to distinguish this group from post-emancipation immigrants such as the Chinese and East Indians.
2. One Friday evening, December 19, 2008, a truck transporting higglers and their produce from Portland (on the northeast coast of the island) to Coronation market in downtown Kingston overturned into a precipice. Fourteen people, including a ten-year-old boy, perished. This tragedy, which occurred days before Christmas, shook the nation. See "14 Killed in Truck Crash" 2008.
3. In this study, "microentrepreneurs" refers to individuals who own very small businesses that employ no more than five workers. These microbusinesses are informal in the sense that they are usually not registered with government agencies and are frequently excluded or undercounted by official statistics. Many of these businesses do not comply with regulations governing labor practices, taxes, and licensing (Berger and Buvinic 1989); they rely on family labor and local resources, low capital endowments, and labor-intensive technology. Barriers to entry into these informal businesses are few, and the skills needed to operate them are acquired outside the formal educational system. The microenterprises of ICIs and market women usually involve one worker, who is also the owner, since many rarely hire help (Le Franc 1989; Witter 1989).
4. The category "higgler" includes country higglers, town higglers, farmers cum higglers, fish vendors, farmer vendors, and many others. See, e.g., LeFranc 1989.
5. See, e.g., "Higglers' Paradise" 2009.
6. I borrow the term "re/producing" from Cecilia Green (1995) to connote the simultaneous production and reproduction of categories of difference.
7. Kiran Mirchandani (1999, 228–29) makes a similar argument; although her focus was female self-employment in small businesses in Canada (not

female microentrepreneurship in developing countries), Mirchandani's critique of the essentialism implicit in the category "woman/female entrepreneur" in the development literature is similar to my own. Mirchandani discusses ways in which the category "woman/female entrepreneur" highlights certain forms of difference at the expense of others and insists that scholars should instead focus on ways in which entrepreneurship is embedded in a society that is not only classed but also racialized and gendered.
8. The exception here is Gina Ulysse's 2007 work *Downtown Ladies*, in which Ulysse skillfully investigates how informal commercial importers redefine local constructions of femininity that historically excluded them, and embody an alternate construction of racialized femininity in their daily lives.
9. In previous studies, the term "higgler" is used or replaced with "vendor" without close attention to the stigma of this work and how relevant it is in shaping women's experiences in the informal economy. I use the term as a rhetorical device to not lose sight of the stigma associated with this type of informal labor.
10. See, e.g., "Spectre of Violence" 2001.
11. Many argued that the police used unnecessary force on the West Kingston residents, leaving many innocent people dead or injured. See "War Downtown" 2001; "Day of Terror" 2001.
12. Also see Kitzinger and Wilkinson 1996; Visweswaran 1994.
13. This notion of expatriates as the lucky ones who escape the hardships of Jamaica is evident in the treatment of deportees, who often face hostilities and at times violence from Jamaicans who believe that these individuals are lucky to live in the United States (as opposed to thousands who are desperately trying to leave Jamaica), yet they have ruined or wasted that opportunity.
14. For instance, in Jamaica the members of the elite are primarily whites or light-skinned people; the middle classes are primarily fair—browns and a few blacks (or dark skinned)—and the masses of the poor are predominantly black.
15. Ross argued that "skin colour can be the difference between success and failure in Jamaican society" (1993, 7).
16. It is significant that it's the Jamaican *men* who identify me as a browning, because many Jamaican men believe the ideal Jamaican woman or partner is a browning. This has been a sore point for many dark-skinned Jamaican women.

CHAPTER 1
1. The epigraph quote is from Beneria and Roldan 1987, 11.
2. Throughout this study I use the term "racial/color" in my discussion of Afro-Jamaican higglers to keep in focus the specific historical and social

contexts of Jamaica. In Jamaica race is often discussed, if discussed at all, in terms of variations of "color." As opposed to the U.S. context, where race is generally understood in binary categories of black versus white, race is generally understood in Jamaica and the greater Caribbean as consisting of a three-tiered system—black, brown, and white (Braithwaite 1953, 1960; Girvan 1981; Greene 1993; Hall, 1977; Hoetink 1971; Mintz 1974, 1987; Mintz and Price 1985; Patterson 1972; Smith 1974, 1984; Stinchcombe 1995).

3. Matthew McKeever (1998) discovered that the informal economy in South Africa was stratified in similar ways to the formal economy: whites, males, and the well educated did better than nonwhites, women, and the poorly educated in both sectors. His study demonstrated that social categories of race, gender, and class carry similar meanings and shape social relations in similar ways in both the informal and formal economies.

4. In her description of approaches to the body in current sociology, Alexandra Howson explains that "an embodied approach views the self and society as constituted through the practical work done with and through the body in interaction with others and with the physical environment" (2004, 15). Following this line of thinking, my use of the terms "embodied" and "embodiment" places the body and its interaction with society at the center of my analysis and rejects a Cartesian dualist model of the mind-body relationship that subordinates the body. Here the body, like the mind, plays a crucial role in human experiences.

5. For a helpful overview of this field of study see Howson's, description of several features of the body on which sociologists agree: (1) the body in sociology is more than a physical and material phenomenon and inseparable from society and culture; (2) the body has increasingly become the target of political control, rationalization, and discipline; and (3) the body forms the basis of social experience and action and is therefore more than a material object (2004, 11).

6. This is not to elevate experience as the only source of truth. What is suggested is that our bodily experience of social structures and cultures shapes, and is shaped by, meanings. They influence our orientations to our surroundings, which in turn influence our choices and behaviors.

7. This point is somewhat implied but not explicitly developed in Shilling's work. See, e.g., Shilling 2005, chapters 4 and 5.

8. See also Krane, Oxman-Martinez, and Ducey 2000; Meyers 2004; Sokoloff and Dupont 2005.

9. For this reason, scholars, myself included, use the category "race/color" in their discussion of race in the Caribbean.

10. Crenshaw discusses the use of a framework of intersectionality to understand the experiences of abused women of color, arguing that "the intersection of racism and sexism factors into Black women's lives in

ways that cannot be captured wholly by looking at the race or gender dimensions of those experiences separately," noting that in addition to race and gender, the concept of intersectionality should be expanded to include issues such as class, sexual orientation, age, and color (1991, 1242).

11. By "formations," I mean structural configurations (Omi and Winant 1994).
12. It is important to note that in Jamaica's system of stratification there is a high correlation of race/color and class: those racialized as browns and whites dominate the middle- and upper-class structures. One's identification as a brown man or woman, for example, reveals his/her presumed color and middle-class status. See Hall 1977.
13. This concept also avoids a simplistic binary analysis of race, class, and gender as either intersecting or interlocking.
14. For a thoughtful essay that attempts to study intersectionality quantitatively, see McCall 2005.
15. As Gary Bridge and Sophie Watson tell us: "Cities are not simply material or lived spaces, they are also spaces of the imagination and spaces of representation. How cities are envisioned has effects" (2001, 350).
16. Stuart Hall (1980, 341) maintains that in the Caribbean race/color is "the modality in which class is 'lived,' the medium through which class relations are experienced, the form in which it is appropriated and 'fought through.'" When one examines the impact of the multiracial nationalist ideology on the ways in which race is understood in the Jamaican public imagination and lived in this society, however, one can argue that class has become the modality through which race is lived.
17. A UNICEF study reports that close to 45 percent of Jamaican households are headed by women and that these households are more vulnerable to poverty, arguing that this is one reason for the rise in child labor in Jamaica. See "Children Selling to Survive" 2001.
18. The debt crisis has also triggered, in part, the expansion of the drug trade in Jamaica, which has brought with it unprecedented levels of violence. In recent years Jamaica has had one of the world's highest per capita murder rates. See, e.g., "Priests Gunned Down in Jamaica" 2005.
19. These are October 2009 estimates (see STATIN 2008b). For an in-depth analysis of the plight of poor Jamaicans, see Wyss and White 2004.

CHAPTER 2

1. The epigraph quote is from Browne and Misra 2003, 506.
2. A few women in this study reported that they inherited their businesses from their mothers and grandmothers. Others chose higglering because

owning their own business gave them a sense of independence and also allowed them the flexibility they needed to take care of their children.
3. The remaining few higglers responded that they did not know. It is important to note that I did not originally intend to pursue this issue in my research. This line of inquiry emerged in my discussions with higglers, who often compared themselves to Chinese shopkeepers and commented on the success of the Chinese in the Jamaican economy in comparison to black Jamaicans. Their comments shifted my research focus and enriched my study. I am in their debt. In my interviews I specifically focused on Chinese, light-skin/brown, and white women because these racialized/ethnic groups dominate the formal business sector on the island and tend to be concentrated in the middle and upper socioeconomic strata. The light skin/brown group refers to mixed race (black and nonblack) individuals and includes Lebanese/Syrians. The questions I asked were: "How many Chinese women do you see doing the same kind of vending/higglering in the market/arcade where you work?" and "How many light-skin/white women do you see doing the same kind of vending/higglering in the market/arcade where you work?" I asked the women to respond in one of three ways: (a) I've seen a lot; (b) I've seen some; or (c) I haven't seen any. A follow-up open-ended question was "Why do you think that is the case?"
4. The Jamaican economy underwent a significant transformation between emancipation and World War II; the balance of power between planters and merchants shifted in the post-emancipation era with the drastic decline of the sugar industry. Eventually, banana replaced sugar as a source of wealth and thus created new opportunities for white planters devastated by the fall of sugar to reassert their dominance in the economy, becoming part of a new agro-elite that included urban Jewish merchants (see Chapter 3).
5. Slaves—both men and women—continued to resist in various ways on plantations in spite of their investments in their plots of land (Beckles 1989, 1999; Bush 1990; Higman 1995).
6. The British often complained about the "dear" prices of the provisions sold in the markets, yet there is little evidence that they dictated prices to the slaves (Mintz 1989, 197).
7. This division of domestic versus field slave does not imply that domestic slaves did not experience hardships. Indeed, numerous historians have identified various kinds of cruelty endured by domestics, ranging from the unpredictable ire of white slave mistresses to rape by their male owners (Beckles 1999; Bush 1990).
8. Lynette Brown (1995, 12) argues that survey findings show women outnumbering men in the category of petty trade 78 percent to 21 percent.

9. Dance-hall culture is a modern version of reggae culture that emerges out of poor, urban, black ghettoes. Batty riders are shorts worn by dance-hall women. The shorts are usually very short and tight, exposing some of their wearer's buttocks.
10. In her study of the Jamaican elite families, Lisa Douglass explains that "language is a clear marker of class." Standard Jamaican English, she tells us, not only marks one's educational background and class, but also reflects who one's associates are (1992, 81).
11. Most poor and working-class Jamaicans do not buy olive oil, despite its health benefits, because it is very expensive. They usually buy the more affordable vegetable or coconut oil.
12. I am not suggesting that a brown customer would never buy from an ICI in the flea market, but local middle-class norms (which are also racialized) are likely to preclude a brown middle-class woman from buying a pair of batty riders or imitation designer clothing from the ICI, limiting the interaction between the two. Because the products of the brown sellers are consistent with middle-class norms, the level of interaction between them and brown customers is likely to be higher.
13. A soda vendor at this site reported that the stall fees ranged from JA$800 to $1,000 per day, roughly US$20 to $25 at that time, while the stall fees for the market women in the public markets ranged from JA$50 (outside the market) to $250 per week. One market woman reported paying JA$600 per week for her large stall inside the market. The stall fees among ICIs ranged from JA$600 to $1,200 per week in the Constant Spring Arcade and $150 to $1,500 *per week* in People's Arcade.
14. Douglass tells us that "uptowners" (members of the middle and upper classes who live in uptown Kingston) listened to Soca, U.S. funk, love songs, reggae, classical music, and jazz, and that the predominant music "downtowners" (the lower classes who live in downtown Kingston) listened to is dance hall (1992, 85).
15. Sometimes one encounters the smell of marijuana at these sites as well. This was common at the People's Arcade in downtown. The use of marijuana is often associated with the black poor, particularly black ghetto youths, and is perceived by the middle classes as another indicator of their indecency.
16. More than half the market women (twelve) and ICIs (thirteen) reported serving a working-class/poor clientele. The remainder reported that their customers were mixed in terms of class. Only five market women and seven ICIs reported serving a predominantly black clientele. Others reported serving "anybody" or declared, "Don't matter." In short, most of the women evaded the question.
17. Although the brown and middle classes are more comfortable buying from the women at Papine, this is not the case at Coronation Market. This had much to do with the public perception of the women at Papine

18. The ackee is the national fruit of Jamaica and is a main ingredient in Jamaica's national dish—ackee and saltfish. Callaloo is similar to spinach.
19. For instance, the newspapers often portrayed the market women at the Papine Market as respectful, in comparison to those at Coronation Market.
20. This situation was especially the case on Saturday mornings, when I observed large numbers of brown, middle-class customers shopping at Papine Market, something I did not observe at the arcades on Saturday mornings or on other days of the week.
21. As mentioned earlier, Jamaica portrays itself as a (harmoniously) multiracial society in its national motto, "Out of many, one people." In an interesting way, the national foods of Jamaica symbolize that ideal of racial unity. The consumption of ackee and banana by members of the brown elite, for instance, marks their connection to other Jamaicans in ways that are not determined by such factors as race/color or class.
22. Racial, class, and gender constraints limit women's options in the labor market by relegating them to the lowest-paying sex-segregated jobs in the education, domestic, and health sectors, for instance, which are usually the first to be curtailed in the country's debt-servicing efforts (Robotham 2000).
23. The question was "Why did you go into this sort of business?" Responses fell into five areas: family business; family responsibility (which includes supporting the family and paying bills, paying school fees, and having time for other domestic responsibilities such as preparing children for school in the morning or taking them to the doctor); no other options; being unemployed/laid off; and first choice.
24. All the women described taking care of the household as their primary responsibility, although more than half explicitly reported that was the *reason* they went into higglering. More than half the women in the entire sample were the primary wage earners of their homes, and almost half (nineteen) reported being the head of their household.
25. Three market women described their business as a "family business." In explaining this family business, they described a gendered division of labor: fathers and brothers farmed, and mothers and daughters sold their produce. As adults, these women inherited the selling component of the family business and used it to support their own families as well as their parents.

CHAPTER 3

1. The epigraph is from Puwar 2004, 8.
2. As the sugar industry expanded in the Caribbean and the slave population grew, there were great concerns over the small size of the

white community in comparison to an increasing number of slaves. Various deficiency laws were created, including liberal immigration laws, that aimed to help grow the white population and keep slaves in subjection (see, e.g., Beckels 2000, 228–35).
3. Slave provisions not only made their way to urban markets in the hands of slaves who frequented the markets every week, but also were purchased by local merchants and resold in the formal economy. Local entrepreneurs also exported slave provisions (Clarke 1975, 16). Local white residents, including planters, also relied on slave provisions.
4. Ann Norton and Richard Symanski report that regular markets were held early in the British colonies and that by the 1670s a number of markets had been established under government supervision. They add that the first legal market was established in Spanish town in 1662, a quarterly market dealing mainly with livestock supplied by European small farmers. With the rise of the sugar plantation economy, however, small European farming was unable to compete, and this sector of the economy eventually failed. The markets later were supplied by slaves from their provision grounds (1975, 463). Slaves were allowed to sell in the markets as long as they had tickets signed by a white person allowing them to do so. See, for instance, Edwards 1793, 165.
5. In fact, Bickell is appealing to these purportedly respectable people to fulfill their obligation to teach slaves proper moral and religious values by doing away with the Sunday market and forbidding slaves to work on their grounds on Sundays. Bickell suggests, instead, that slaves be given another day on which they can work and sell, but plantation demands meant that his appeals fell on deaf ears.
6. May Fair is the name of an infamous fifteen-day spring fair that took place on the site of today's Shepherd Market in London. It was established in the 1680s, ran from the first of May to the middle of the month, and was intended to be a simple cattle market but quickly grew to include various kinds of entertainment, including puppet shows, and to attract thousands of visitors. By the early eighteenth century, efforts were made to suppress the May Fair because of its reputation for attracting the "loose, idle and disorderly." By 1764 the May Fair had ended and the fashionable district, Mayfair, was born, catering primarily to the well to do with its grand architecture and luxurious landscapes, a high-end market, and a theater. Today, it is mainly a commercial district that continues to cater to the wealthy. See "Reviving the Mayfair May Fair," BBC News, April 30, 2002, *news.bbc.co.uk/2/hi/uk_news/1959418.stm*. Pyle did not specify whether he was referring to the annual fair suppressed more than a century earlier, or to the fashionable district, Mayfair, flourishing at the time of his writing. It is reasonable to believe, however, that he was comparing the fashionable district to the market

in Kingston to exaggerate differences in the development of modern England and the underdevelopment of Jamaica.
7. Pyle notes: "Within a radius of twenty miles of Kingston one may see perhaps all, or nearly all, that most is characteristic of the island of Jamaica. For Kingston is the heart of the island, and to and from it the quaint life comes and goes along the smooth, white level highways" (1889–1890, 177).
8. One can often tell how well the peasant economy is doing by looking at what is being sold in the market, and at the vibrancy of the market itself. If severe drought hits peasant farmers, for example, it will be evidenced in the market by the scarcity of produce.
9. In 1866, after the famous Morant Bay rebellion, Jamaica became a Crown Colony. Under the Crown Colony system, the Jamaican assembly gave up its power of self-government and subjected itself to direct rule from Britain.
10. Led by Paul Bogle, a black Baptist deacon, and George William Gordon, a brown member of the House of Assembly, the Morant Bay rebellion consisted of 1,500 to 2,000 Jamaicans, mostly poor blacks, who marched into the town of Morant Bay to protest their lack of political participation since they could not vote, an unfair justice system that typically favored white interests, economic hardships compounded by oppressively high taxes on the poor as opposed to the wealthy, and the imposition of high rents on land where peasants lived and grew their provisions. The hardship of the poor was further intensified by irregular employment and low wages. The government's response to the rebellion, swift and brutal, was followed by the implementation of a Crown Colony government (Heuman 2006; Holt 1992; Sherlock and Bennett 1998).
11. Jamaican planters originally dismissed the cultivation of bananas, viewing it as "backwoods nigger business" (Holt 1992, 353; Thompson 2006, 49).
12. The legacies of the Garvey movement, the formation of Rastafarianism, and the Rodney riots of the 1960s all attest to the active resistance of black Jamaicans to persistent racial and class inequalities.

CHAPTER 4
1. According to Barbara Bush (1990, 49), slave markets were dominated by enslaved and free black and colored women because it was difficult for male slaves to obtain passes.
2. That is, they presented an alternate identity or image that countered the usually demeaning dominant images of higglers and black women in general.
3. Bryan Edwards, an eighteenth-century Jamaican planter and politician, noted that "of clothing, the allowance of the master is not always so liberal as might be wished, but much more so of late years than formerly.

Few of the Negroes, however on Sundays and holydays, appear deficient in this point, or shew any want of raiment, not only decent but gaudy" (1793, 135).

4. For a wonderful essay on how black women today use dance-hall fashion to contest dominant middle-class constructions of femininity that tend to exclude them, see Bakare-Yusuf 2006.
5. For a discussion of the association of black women with evil, see Mohammed 2000, 26, and Cooper 1994.
6. In the census of 1844, the first official census of Jamaica, 4.2 percent of the population of 377,433 was white, 18.1 percent was brown, and 77.7 percent was black (Mohammed 2000, 28).
7. Higglers were not an economic threat to plantation owners. In fact, higglering aided plantation owners by providing slaves a means by which they could sustain themselves, thus saving planters the additional expense.
8. As Toni Morrison suggests, black slavery enriched the country's creative possibilities, for in that construction of blackness and enslavement could be found not only the not-free but also, with the dramatic polarity created by skin color, the projection of the not-me. The result was a playground for the imagination (see Morrison 1990, 38). Although Morrison's primary focus is U.S. slavery and the construction of an American Africanism, she argues that there exists a similar European Africanism with a counterpart in colonial literature.
9. Veront M. Satchell (1995) notes that in contrast to the significant decline of the sugar industry between the 1840s and the 1880s, the peasantry experienced significant growth. Peasants provided food for local consumption and also for export. Indeed, production of ground provisions increased from 27 percent of total agricultural output in 1832 to 55 percent in 1890. Although by 1900 this total output fell to 50 percent, this is still a significant percentage.
10. This sketch accompanied Hawthorne's article "A Tropic Climb," in which Hawthorne offers a detailed description of the island of Jamaica and its inhabitants to the potential U.S. tourist (Hawthorne 1896–1897b).
11. According to Thompson: "The most factious component of the island's image world, its representational fault line, ran through representations of black labor and split for the most part along British and American lines. In contrast to 'American scribblers' who denounced blacks as lazy, lecturers for the British Elder, Dempster and Company and those 'who live[d] in Jamaica' stressed the industriousness of the island's black population" (2006, 76–77).
12. Of course, these national pageants and their privileging of brownness have been vehemently challenged by black Jamaicans, from Marcus Garvey to higglers. In fact, Ulysse (2007) describes the emergence of

tertiary beauty contests in Jamaica in opposition to the national pageant, among them the Miss UVA contest organized in honor of the hard work of vendors.
13. For examples from the Bahamas, see Thompson 2006, chapter 2. Also see Strachan 2002.

CHAPTER 5

1. The epigraph is from Min-ha 1997, 415.
2. Nelson 1999, 336. See also the works of Judith Butler on gender and sexuality.
3. What is interesting to me is that many Jamaicans (across class) praise the higgler for her entrepreneurial spirit. Traditional higglers (market women) are also loved as folk figures. This affection, however, is often lost in the public discourse.
4. In a country that is predominantly black, these cultural distinctions are of greater significance for the brown middle classes, who are positioned much closer in the hierarchical structure to the black masses than to whites.
5. For a great example, see Blinde and Taub 1992, a study of female athletes who attempt to manage stigmas associated with their athleticism, particularly those that accuse them of lesbianism.
6. Examining how higglers performed their identities was not among the original goals of this study. During our interviews in the markets and arcades, the women themselves often raised the issue of the behaviors of higglers and ICIs. This topic always emerged in our conversations, revealing the issue as important to these women in my study; I pursued this further to learn why.
7. Three market women did not see themselves fitting into the categories I had created; two identified themselves as "sellers" and one identified herself as a "housewife trying to do a little selling." One woman who stated that she preferred to identify herself as a vendor instead of a market woman said: "I don't like 'market woman' because it reminds me of [being] old" (#17).
8. In the informal economy, education is the most reliable indicator of class status because in this sector occupation and income tend to be unstable. In this study, the market women were associated with the peasant class not only because of their education but also because almost half (ten) grew their own produce (as well as purchased produce from other higglers and farmers) or were from farming communities (their husbands or families farmed), and the produce they sold connected them to the agricultural sector. This was not the case among the ICIs.
9. These principles are being contested by Jamaicans today, especially by the black urban poor. In fact, Deborah Thomas (2004) describes an emerging

"modern blackness" among Jamaica's poor urban youth that rejects a multiracial nationalist ideology, challenges the persistence of structural inequality, and proudly invokes blackness in the public sphere.
10. I asked the women in the sample if they thought their color can affect their social advancement in Jamaican society. Most were reluctant to answer the question. Only twelve women answered the question directly, and all twelve said that color did not affect their ability to advance, only money, education, and "ambition."
11. The embrace of a meritocracy can also explain why many higglers, and Jamaicans in general, are reluctant to talk about color and gender as factors impacting a person's life chances.
12. This status, of course, depends greatly on the size of an ICI's business. An ICI with multiple stalls and a staff would enjoy greater status than the ones in my sample. Her move from a factory job to her business would certainly be a vertical one.
13. See "Cheap Thrills" 2001; "Independent Woman" 2001; "Coming Up through the Cracks" 2001; "Service with a Smile" 2001; "At Home in the Market" 2001.

CHAPTER 6

1. The epigraph is from Douglas 2002, 2.
2. The *Jamaica Gleaner* (the oldest extant newspaper in Jamaica) and the *Jamaica Observer* (launched in 1993) are widely circulated on the island. For this chapter I analyzed 57 articles from both newspapers over a twenty-year period from the features section, editorial section, or letters to the editor; if the topic was vendor protests, these were cover stories. I accessed articles registered with "higgler" or "vendor" as a topic, those published from 1998 on electronically, and those published before 1998 at the University of the West Indies (Mona campus, Jamaica) library. Of the 57 articles, 9 were feature articles that highlighted a particular higgler or market; the remaining 48 articles discussed higglering as a "problem." Of these 48, 38 articles discussed efforts to remove higglers/vendors from the Kingston metropolitan area; the remaining 10 articles discussed such efforts in other cities on the island.
3. I turn to these newspaper sources to gain insight into the ways in which higglering and higglers are publicly imagined today, because these representations serve as a backdrop to the lived experiences of informal economic activities. Using an interpretive content analysis, I identify a series of themes and theoretical insights that illuminate popular conceptions of higglers as illegitimate, undisciplined, indecent, and threats to the well-being of Jamaican society. My reading of these articles also generates insights into the social organization of public space in the city of Kingston. I include in this chapter the voices of some higglers,

market women, and ICIs to offer a glimpse of ways in which these women view their experiences in this context.
4. See Cook 2008, in which this idea of markets as lived experience is discussed fully, using several case studies inside and outside the United States.
5. One can be identified as belonging downtown without actually living there, so those who live in poor communities uptown are often not associated with uptown living; their behaviors and lifestyles are more likely associated with downtown. Here, then, "downtown" is associated with social standing.
6. On April 1, 2004, Dr. Omar Davies, finance minister of Jamaica, announced the 2004–2005 national budget: debt servicing amounted to approximately seventy cents of every dollar. See, e.g., "330B Budget" 2004; "Budgeting for Debt" 2004.
7. The MPM and KSAC are government agencies responsible for the beautification and maintenance of parks and city streets, the operation of markets, and public cleaning and sanitation. The KSAC is also responsible for the redevelopment of downtown Kingston in the effort to transform it from its current deteriorating state into a modern financial sector.
8. In the news articles, I found the terms "higglering"/"higgler," and "street vending"/"vendor" used interchangeably, mainly the result of attempts by higglers to rename themselves to avoid the stigma associated with this type of work. I use the term "higgler," however, to draw attention to the stigma associated with this work and its continued effects on the lived experiences of these workers. The literature on higglering in Jamaica fails to adequately address this issue.
9. Over the last several decades, efforts have been made to redevelop downtown Kingston and transform it into the financial capital of Jamaica and the wider Caribbean. These efforts have met obstacles, and although some development has occurred, downtown Kingston has a long way to go to reach its full potential.
10. Dons were local drug dealers and gang leaders whom, it is assumed, the government used to assist in the removal of the vendors.
11. These residents are not chastised in the public discourse, a differentiation that exemplifies the ambivalence that Jamaicans feel toward higglers, as Burton (1997) notes. Higglers, particularly market women, are recognized for their important role in distributing local produce from rural to urban areas and making it available to Kingstonians at affordable prices.
12. Barbican is a middle-class area in uptown Kingston. To emphasize the unfair treatment the writer believes she is getting from the government, she suggested half in jest that since these vendors are not paying taxes, maybe she should open up her own stall and not pay taxes as well. By calling this woman a "black gal," the male vendor disrespected her,

assigning her to the lowest social status of black and "gal" (as opposed to "lady," which is often associated with browns).

CONCLUSION

1. The epigraphs are from Weber 1993, 126, and Cooke 2001, where the Nettleford quote appears on page 1.
2. Also see Douglass's (1992, 11) discussion of class in Jamaica, where she draws from Max Weber as well and argues the need to examine the impact of color and gender on the class status and experiences of members of the Jamaican elite.
3. For an extensive discussion of such credit institutions, see Honig 1993, 2000.
4. The credit manager of COK said the source of credit for his institution is the Government of Jamaica/European Union (GOJEU). The European Union provides funds to Trafalgar Development Bank in Jamaica, which identifies banks, credit unions, and other institutions that Trafalgar can do business with. COK receives funds from Trafalgar at an interest, identifies potential borrowers, and extends the loans; then COK repays Trafalgar. The money, then, is a loan, not a grant. COK distributes loans to microentrepreneurs, putting strategies in place to ensure that COK will be able to collect on the loans in order to repay Trafalgar. Collateral is thus a major factor in this loan-distribution process.

    The credit manager at Jamaican National Micro-Credit institution explained that the Financial Sector Adjustment Company (FINSAC), which was organized by the Jamaica government, developed this institution. Jamaica National adopted the partner system, except that the lump sum (or draw, as it is referred to in the partner system) is received first and paid for last. Loans vary from JA$5000 (US$111) to JA$120,000 (US$2,666). The first loan is usually $5,000 to $7,000 ($111 to $155), which is repaid weekly for forty weeks at 1 percent interest per week. A forty-week loan thus generates 40 percent interest. This institution uses household appliances as collateral.
5. If one is considered untrustworthy, not only is one's access to informal credit and savings impeded, but also one's business is negatively affected, because this reputation quickly spreads to others.

Bibliography

"14 Killed in Truck Crash—Major Catastrophe, Says PM." 2008. *Jamaica Gleaner*, December 21. *jamaica-gleaner.com/gleaner/20081221/lead/lead1.html.* Accessed May 25, 2010.

"330B Budget: Most of Increase to Finance Debt." 2004. *Jamaica Gleaner*, April 1.

Abbensetts, Joanne M. E. 1990. "International Higglering in Jamaica: An Informal Sector Study." PhD diss., University of Toronto.

Acker, Joan. 1990. "Hierarchy, Jobs, Bodies: A Theory of Gendered Organizations." *Gender and Society* 4, no. 2: 139–58.

———. 2004. "Gender, Capitalism and Globalization." *Critical Sociology* 30, no. 1: 17–41.

———. 2006. "Inequality Regimes: Gender, Class, and Race in Organizations." *Gender and Society* 20, no. 4 (August): 441–64.

Acosta-Belén, Edna, and Christine Bose. 1990. "From Structural Subordination to Employment: Women and Development in Third World Contexts." *Gender and Society* 4, no. 3 (September): 299–320.

Allen, D., J. Allen, and Geoffrey Wall. 1997. "Selling to Tourists: Indonesian Street Vendors." *Annals of Tourism Research* 24, no. 2 (April): 322–40.

Andersen, Margaret L., and Patricia Hill Collins, eds. 1998. *Race, Class, and Gender: An Anthology*. 3rd ed. Belmont, CA: Wadsworth.

Anderson, Wanni W., and Robert G. Lee, eds. 2005. *Displacements and Diasporas: Asians in the Americas*. Piscataway, NJ: Rutgers University Press.

Anthias, Floya. 1991. "Parameters of Difference and Identity and the Problem of Connections: Gender, Ethnicity, and Class." *Revue Internationale de Sociologie* 2 (April): 29–51.

———. 1998. "Rethinking Social Divisions: Some Notes towards a Theoretical Framework." *Sociological Review* 50, no. 3 (August): 405–36.

Anthias, Floya, and Nira Yuval-Davis. 1983. "Contextualizing Feminism: Gender, Ethnic, and Class Divisions." *Feminist Review* 15 (November): 62–75.

Aspaas, Helen Ruth. 1988. "Heading Households and Heading Businesses: Rural Kenyan Women in the Informal Sector." *Professional Geographer* 50, no. 2 (May): 192–207.

"At Home in the Market." 2001. *Jamaica Gleaner*, March 1. go.jamaica.com/gleaner/20010301/star/star2.html.

Austin-Broos, Diane. 1994. "Race/Class: Jamaica's Discourse of Heritable Identity." *New West Indian Guide* 68, nos. 3–4: 213–33.

———. 1998. "Falling through the 'Savage Slot': Postcolonial Critique and the Ethnographic Task." *Australian Journal of Anthropology* 9, no. 3: 295–309.

Baca Zinn, Maxine, and Bonnie Thorton Dill, eds. 1994. *Women of Color in U.S. Society*. Philadelphia: Temple University Press.

Bakare-Yusuf, Bibi. 2006. "Fabricating Identities: Survival and the Imagination in Jamaican Dancehall Culture." *Fashion Theory* 10, no. 3: 1–24.

Barnes, Natasha. 1994. "Face of the Nation: Race, Nationalism, and Identities in Jamaican Beauty Pageants." *Massachusetts Review* 53, nos. 3–4 (Fall/Winter): 471–97.

Barriteau, V. Eudine. 2003. "Confronting Power and Politics: A Feminist Theorizing of Gender in Commonwealth Societies." *Meridians: Feminism, Race, Transnationalism* 3, no. 2: 57–92.

———. 2006. "The Relevance of Black Feminist Scholarship: A Caribbean Perspective." *Feminist Africa* 7 (December): 9–31.

Barrow, Christine, ed. 1998. *Caribbean Portraits: Essays on Gender Ideologies and Identities*. Kingston: Ian Randle.

Barrow, Christine, and Rhoda Reddock, eds. 2001. *Caribbean Sociology: Introductory Readings*. Kingston: Ian Randle.

Beckles, Hilary. 1989. *Natural Rebels: A Social History of Enslaved Black Women in Barbados*. New Brunswick, NJ: Rutgers University Press.

———. 1995. "Sex and Gender in the Historiography of Caribbean Slavery." In *Engendering History: Caribbean Women in Historical Perspective*, ed. V. Shepherd, B. Brereton, and B. Bailey. New York: St. Martin's Press, 125–40.

———. 1999. *Centering Woman: Gender Discourses in Caribbean Slave Society*. Princeton, NJ: Markus Weiner.

———. 2000a "A Riotous and Unruly Lot: Irish Indentured Servants and Freemen in the English West Indies, 1644–1713." In *Caribbean Slavery in the Atlantic World: A Student Reader*, ed. Verene Shepherd and Hilary Beckles. Princeton, NJ: Marcus Weiner, 226–38.

———. 2000b. "White Women and Slavery in the Caribbean." In *Caribbean Slavery in the Atlantic World: A Student Reader*, ed. Verene Shepherd and Hilary Beckles. Princeton, NJ: Marcus Weiner, 659–69.

———. 2000c. "An Economic Life of Their Own: Slaves as Community Producers and Distributors in Barbados." In *Caribbean Slavery in the Atlantic World: A Student Reader*, ed. Verene Shepherd and Hilary Beckles. Princeton, NJ: Marcus Weiner, 732–42.

Beneria, Lourdes, and Shelley Feldman, eds. 1992. *Unequal Burden: Economic Crises, Persistent Poverty, and Women's Work*. Boulder, CO: Westview Press.

Beneria, Lourdes, and Martha Roldan. 1987. *The Crossroads of Class and Gender: Industrial Homework, Subcontracting, and Household Dynamics in Mexico City.* Chicago: University of Chicago Press.

Beneria, Lourdes, and Gita Sen. 1981. "Accumulation, Reproduction, and Women's Role in Economic Development: Boserup Revisited." *Signs* 7, no. 2 (Winter): 279–98.

———. 1982. "Class and Gender Inequalities and Women's Role in Economic Development: Theoretical and Practical Implications." *Feminist Studies* 8, no. 1 (Spring): 157–76.

Berger, Iris. 1992. "Categories and Contexts: Reflections on the Politics of Identity in South Africa." *Feminist Studies* 18, no. 2 (Summer): 283–94.

Berger, Marguerite. 1995. "Key Issues on Women's Access to and Use of Credit in the Micro- and Small-Scale Enterprise Sector." In *Women in Micro- and Small-Scale Enterprise Development*, ed. Louise Dignard and Jose Havet. Boulder, CO: Westview Press, 189–216.

Berger, M., and M. Buvinic. 1989. *Women's Ventures: Assistance to the Informal Sector in Latin America.* Boulder, CO: Kumarian Press.

Berlin, Ira, and Philip Morgan, eds. 1993. *Cultivation and Culture: Labour and the Shaping of Slave Life in the Americas.* Charlottesville: University Press of Virginia.

Bernstein, Henry. 1971. "Modernization Theory and the Sociological Study of Development." *Journal of Development Studies* 7, no. 2: 141–61.

———. 1979. "Sociology of Underdevelopment vs. Sociology of Development." In *Development Theory: Four Critical Essays*, ed. D. Lehman. London: Frank Cass, 71–106.

Lloyd-Evans, Sally, and Robert Potter. 1993. "Government Response to Informal Sector Retail Trading: The People's Mall, Port of Spain, Trinidad." *Geography* 78, no. 3 (July): 315–18.

Bickell, Rev. Richard. 1825. *The West Indies as they are; or, a real picture of Slavery: but more particularly as it exists in the island of Jamaica in three parts.* London: J. Hatchard and Sons.

Blinde, Elaine M., and Diane E. Taub. 1992. "Women Athletes as Falsely Accused Deviants: Managing the Lesbian Stigma." *Sociological Quarterly* 33, no. 4: 521–33.

Bolles, Lynn. 1996. *Sister Jamaica: A Study of Women, Work, and Households in Kingston.* Lanham, MD: University Press of America.

Boserup, Ester. 1970. *Women's Role in Economic Development.* New York: St. Martin's Press.

Bouknight-Davis, Gail. 2004. "Chinese Economic Development and Ethnic Identity Formation in Jamaica." In *The Chinese in the Caribbean*, ed. Andrew Wilson. Princeton, NJ: Markus Weiner, 69–90.

Braithwaite, Lloyd. 1953. "Social Stratification in Trinidad." *Social and Economic Studies* 2, nos. 2–3: 5–175.

———. 1960. "Social Stratification and Cultural Pluralism." In *Social and*

Cultural Pluralism in the Caribbean, ed. Vera Rubin. Annals of the New York Academy of Sciences 83 (1960): 816–31.
Bridge, Gary, and Sophie Watson. 2001. "Retext(ur)ing the City." City 5, no. 3 (November): 350–62.
———. 2002. "Lest Power Be Forgotten: Networks, Division, and Difference in the City." Sociological Review 50, no. 4 (November): 505–24.
Brodber, Erna. 1989. "Socio-Cultural Change in Jamaica." In Jamaica in Independence: Essays on the Early Years, ed. Rex Nettleford. Kingston: Heinemann Caribbean, 55–74.
Broom, Leonard. 1954. "The Social Differentiation of Jamaica." American Sociological Review 19, no. 2: 115–25.
Brown, Elaine Barkley. 1992. "'What Has Happened Here': The Politics of Difference in Women's History and Feminist Politics." Feminist Studies 18, no. 2 (Summer): 295–312.
Browne, Irene, and Joya Misra. 2003. "The Intersection of Gender and Race in the Labor Market." Annual Review of Sociology 29: 487–517.
Brown, Lynette. 1994. "Women and Micro-enterprise Development in Jamaica: Examination of the Potential for Micro-Enterprise Development among Women Engaged in Projects Initially Established for the Purpose of Training or Income Generation, Final Report." Mona, Jamaica: Center for Gender and Development Studies, University of the West Indies.
———. 1995. "State of the Art Review: Women and Micro-Enterprise Development in Jamaica, Final Report." Mona, Jamaica: Center for Gender and Development Studies, University of the West Indies.
Brown, Vivienne. "Higglering: The Language of Markets in Economic Discourse." In Higgling: Transactors and Their Markets in the History of Economics, ed. Neil de Marchi and Mary S. Morgan. Durham, NC: Duke University Press, 1994, 66–93.
Brown-Glaude, Winnifred. 2006. "Size Matters: Figuring Gender in the Black Jamaican Nation." Meridians: Feminism, Race, Transnationalism 7, no. 1: 38–68.
———. 2007. "Fact of Blackness? The Problem of the Bleached Body in Contemporary Jamaica." Small Axe: A Caribbean Platform for Criticism 24: 34–51.
Bryan, Patrick. 1998. "The White Minority in Jamaica at the end of the Nineteenth Century." In The White Minority in the Caribbean, ed. Howard Johnson and Karl Watson. Kingston: Ian Randle, 116–32.
"Budgeting for Debt." 2004. Jamaica Gleaner, April 2.
Buckridge, Steeve O. 2004. Language of Dress: Resistance and Accommodation in Jamaica, 1750–1890. Kingston: University of the West Indies Press.
Burton, Richard D. E. 1997. Afro-Creole: Power, Opposition, and Play in the Caribbean. Ithaca, NY: Cornell University Press.
Bush, Barbara. 1985. "Towards Emancipation: Slave Women and Resistance to Coercive Labour Regimes in the British West Indian Colonies, 1790–

1838." In *Abolition and Its Aftermath: The Historical Context, 1790–1916*, ed. David Richardson. London: Frank Cass, 27–54.

———. 1990. *Slave Women in Caribbean Society: 1650–1838*. Bloomington: Indiana University Press.

Butler, Judith. 1990. *Gender Trouble: Feminism and the Subversion of Identity.* New York: Routledge.

Cardoso, Fernando Henrique, and Enzo Faletto. 1979. *Dependency and Development in Latin America.* Berkeley: University of California Press.

Carmichael, A. C. 1834. *Domestic Manners and Social Condition of the White, Coloured, and Negro Population of the West Indies.* Vol 1. 2nd ed. London: Whittaker.

Carty, Linda. 1987. "Women and Labour Force Participation in the Caribbean." *Fireweed* no. 24 (Winter): 39–53.

Chant, Sylvia, and Carolyn Pedwell. 2008. "Women, Gender, and the Informal Economy: An Assessment of ILO Research and Suggested Ways Forward." Geneva: International Labour Office.

"The Cheap Thrills of Coronation Market." 2001. *Jamaica Gleaner,* April 2, go.jamaica.com/gleaner/20010421/life/life1.html.

Chen, Martha Alter. 2003. "Rethinking the Informal Economy." *Seminar* 531 (November). www.india-seminar.com/2003/531.htm. Accessed September 20, 2010.

———. 2007. "Rethinking the Informal Economy: Linkages with the Formal Economy and the Formal Regulatory Environment." DESA Working Paper No. 46. *un.org/esa/desa/papers/2007/wp46_2007.pdf.* Accessed September 16, 2008.

"Children Selling to Survive." 2001. *Jamaica Gleaner,* June 2.

CIA [Central Intelligence Agency]. 2005. *CIA: The World Factbook 2005.* cia.gov/library/publications/the-world-factbook. Accessed October 31, 2005.

———. 2010. *CIA: The World Factbook 2010.* cia.gov/library/publications/the-world-factbook/geos/jm.html. Accessed May 21, 2010.

Clarke, Colin. 1975. *Kingston, Jamaica: Urban Development and Social Change, 1692 to 1962.* Berkeley: University of California Press.

Clarke, Colin, and David Howard. 1999. "Colour, Race and Space: Residential Segregation in Kingston, Jamaica, in the Late Colonial Period." *Caribbean Geography Testing* 10, no. 1: 4–18.

———. 2006. "Contradictory Socio-Economic Consequences of Structural Adjustment in Kingston, Jamaica." *Geographical Journal* 172, no. 2: 106–29.

Clarke, Colin, and Trevor Pinch. 1994. "The Interactional Study of Exchange Relationships: An Analysis of Patter Merchants at Work in Street Markets." In *Higgling: Transactors and Their Markets in the History of Economics,* ed. Neil de Marchi and Mary S. Morgan. Durham, NC: Duke University Press, 370–400.

Cliff, Michelle. 1985. *The Land of Look Behind: Prose and Poetry*. New York: Fire Brand Books.

Collins, Patricia Hill. 1990. *Black Feminist Thought: Knowledge, Consciousness, and the Politics of Empowerment*. New York: Routledge.

———. 1998. "It's All in the Family: Intersections of Gender, Race, and Nation." *Hypatia* 13, no. 3 (Summer): 73–75.

"Coming Up through the Cracks." 2001. *Jamaica Gleaner*, October 2. go.jamaica.com/gleaner/20011002/star/star1.html. Accessed March 12, 2002

Connell, R. W. 1993. *Gender and Power: Society, the Person, and Sexual Politics*. Stanford, CA: Stanford University Press.

Cook, Daniel, ed. 2008. *Lived Experiences of Public Consumption: Encounters with Value in Marketplaces on Five Continents*. New York: Palgrave Macmillan.

Cooke, Melville. "Man of the Year—Born to Be Rex." 2001. *Jamaica Gleaner*, December 30. jamaica-gleaner.com/gleaner/20011230/lead/lead1.html. Accessed July 1, 2002.

Cooper, Carolyn. 1994. *Noises in the Blood: Orality, Gender, and the "Vulgar" Body of Jamaican Popular Culture*. London: Macmillan Education.

Cowell, Lynda. 1999. "The Lighter They Come." *Weekly Journal*, January 30, 16.

Crenshaw, Kimberle. 1991. "Mapping the Margins: Intersectionality, Identity Politics, and Violence against Women of Color." *Stanford Law Review* 43, no. 3: 1249–99.

Davies, Omar, and Patricia Anderson. 1989. "The Impact of Recession and Structural Adjustment Policies on Poor Urban Women in Jamaica." Paper presented at the Fourteenth Meeting of the Caribbean Studies Association, Barbados, May 23–27.

Davies, Omar, and Michael Witter. 1989. "The Development of the Jamaican Economy since Independence." In *Jamaica in Independence: Essays on the Early Years*, ed. Rex Nettleford. Kingston: Heinemann Caribbean, 75–104.

Davis, F. James. 1991. *Who Is Black: One Nation's Definition*. University Park: Pennsylvania State University Press.

"Day of Terror." 2001. *Sunday Observer*, July 18.

De Certeau, Michel. 1984. *The Practice of Everyday Life*. Trans. Steven Randall. Berkeley: University of California Press.

De Marchi, Neil, and Mary S. Morgan, eds. 1994. *Higglering: Transactors and Their Markets in the History of Economics*. Durham, NC: Duke University Press.

De Soto, Hernando. 1989. *The Other Path: The Invisible Revolution in the Third World*. New York: Harper and Row.

De Soto, Hernando, and Deborah Orsini. 1991. "Overcoming Underdevelopment." *Journal of Democracy* 2, no. 2 (Spring): 105–13.

Dignard, Louise, and Jose Havet, eds. 1995. *Women in Micro- and Small-Scale Enterprise Development*. Boulder, CO: Westview Press.
Douglas, Mary. 2002. *Purity and Danger: An Analysis of Concepts of Pollution and Taboo*. New York: Routledge.
Douglass, Lisa. 1992. *The Power of Sentiment: Love, Hierarchy, and the Jamaican Family Elite*. Boulder, CO: Westview Press.
Durant-Gonzalez, Victoria. 1983. "The Occupation of Higglering." *Jamaica Journal* 16, no. 3 (Winter): 2–12.
———. 1985. "Higglering: Rural Women and the Internal Market System in Jamaica." In *Rural Development in the Caribbean*, ed. P. I. Gomes. New York: St. Martin's Press, 103–22.
Durkheim, Emile. 1982. *The Rules of the Sociological Method*. Ed. Steven Lukes. Trans. W. D. Halls. New York: Free Press.
Edwards, Bryan. 1793. *The History, Civil and Commercial, of the British Colonies in the West Indies. In Two Volumes*. Dublin: Luke White. galenet.galegroup.com/servlet/ecco?C=1&Stp=Author&Ste=11&=. Accessed March 4, 2007.
Edwards, Melvin R. 1980. *Jamaican Higglers: Their Significance and Potential*. Swansea, UK: University College of Swansea, Center for Development Studies.
Ehlers, Tracy, and Karen Main. 1998. "Women and the False Promise of Micro-enterprise." *Gender and Society* 12, no. 4: 424–40.
Espinal, Rosario, and Sherri Grasmuck. 1997. "Gender, Households, and Informal Entrepreneurship in the Dominican Republic." *Journal of Comparative Family Studies* 28, no. 1 (Spring): 103–28.
Evans, Peter. 1979. *Dependent Development: The Alliance of Multinational, State, and Local Capital in Brazil*. Princeton, NJ: Princeton University Press.
Eversole, Robyn. 2004. "Change Makers? Women's Microenterprises in a Bolivian City." *Gender, Work, and Organization* 11, no. 2 (March): 123–42.
Featherstone, Mike, Mike Hepworth, and Bryan Turner, eds. 2001. *The Body: Social Process and Cultural Theory*. London: Sage.
Fincher Ruth, and Jane A Jacobs, eds. 1998. *Cities of Difference*. New York: Guilford Press.
Foucault, Michel. 1995. *Discipline and Punish: The Birth of the Prison*. Trans. Alan Sheridan. New York: Vintage.
Frank, Andre Gunder. 1986. "The Development of Underdevelopment." In *Promise of Development: Theories of Change in Latin America*, ed. Peter F. Klaren and Thomas J. Bossert. Boulder, CO: Westview Press, 111–23.
Freeman, Carla. 1988. "From Higglering to High-Tech and Home Again: Barbadian Women Workers in a Transnational Arena." *Folk* 36, no. 1: 5–24.
———. 1997. "Reinventing Higglering across Transnational Zones: Barbadian

Women Juggle the Triple Shift." In *Daughters of Caliban: Caribbean Women in the Twentieth Century*, ed. C. Lopez Springfield. Bloomington: Indiana University Press, 68–95.

———. 2000. *High Tech and High Heels in the Global Economy: Women, Work, and Pink-Collar Identities in the Caribbean*. Durham, NC: Duke University Press.

Girvan, Norman. 1981. "Aspects of the Political Economy of Race in the Caribbean and in the Americas." Working Paper No. 7. Mona, Jamaica: Institute of Social and Economic Research, University of the West Indies.

Girvan, Norman, and Richard Bernal. 1982. "The IMF and the Foreclosure of Development Options: The Case of Jamaica." *Monthly Review* 33, no. 9 (February): 34–48.

Gordon, Colin, ed. 1980. *Power/Knowledge: Selected Interviews and Other Writings by Michel Foucault, 1972–1977*. New York: Pantheon.

Gordon, Derek. 1991. "Race, Class, and Social Mobility in Jamaica." In *Garvey: His Work and Impact*, ed. R. Lewis and P. Bryan. Trenton, NJ: Africa World Press: 265–82.

"Government Slashes Debt Cost in Budget." 2010. *Jamaica Observer*, March 26. jamaicaobserver.com/news/Budget2010_7506003. Accessed May 24, 2010.

Grasmuck, Sherri, and Rosario Espinal. 2000. "Market Success or Female Autonomy? Income, Ideology, and Empowerment among Microentrepreneurs in the Dominican Republic." *Gender and Society* 14, no. 2: 231–55.

Gray, Obika. 1991. *Radicalism and Social Change in Jamaica: 1960–1972*. Knoxville: University of Tennessee Press.

Green, Cecilia. 1986. "Marxist Feminism and Third World Liberation." In *Fireworks: The Best of Fireweed*, ed. M. Silvera. Toronto: Women's Press, 210–24.

———. "Gender, Race, and Class in the Social Economy of the English-speaking Caribbean." *Social and Economic Studies* 44, nos. 2–3: 65–102.

Greene, J. Edward, ed. 1993. *Race, Class, and Gender in the Future of the Caribbean*. Mona, Jamaica: Institute of Social and Economic Research, University of the West Indies.

Green-Powell, Patricia. 1997. "Methodological Considerations in Field Research: Six Case Studies." In *Oral Narrative Research with Black Women*, ed. Kim Marie Vaz. London: Sage, 197–222.

Grosz, Elizabeth. 1994. *Volatile Bodies: Towards a Corporeal Feminism*. Bloomington: Indiana University Press.

Hall, Douglass. 1971. "Closing the Alexander Era: Grace, Kennedy and Company Limited—A Story of Jamaican Enterprise, 1922–1992." gracekennedy.com/history/Alexander/template.html. Accessed April 17, 2000.

Hall, Stuart. 1977. "Pluralism, Race, and Class in Caribbean Society." In *Race* and *Class in Post-Colonial Society: A Study of Ethnic Group Relations in the English-Speaking Caribbean, Bolivia, Chile, and Mexico.* Paris: UNESCO, 150–82.

———. 1980. "Race, Articulation, and Societies Structured in Dominance." Poole, UK: UNESCO.

Handbook of Jamaica for 1898 published by authority, comprising Historical, Statistical and General Information Concerning the Island. Eighteenth Year of Publication. Compiled from official and other reliable records by T. L. Roxburg and Jos C. Ford (of the Jamaica Civil Service). 1898. Kingston: Government Printing Office. books.google.com. Accessed October 4, 2009.

Harding, Sandra. 1986. "The Instability of the Analytical Categories of Feminist Theory." *Signs* 11, 4: 645–64.

———. 1992. "Subjectivity, Experience, and Knowledge: An Epistemology from/for Rainbow Coalition Politics." *Development and Change* 23, no. 3: 175–93.

Harrison, Faye V. 1988. "Women in Jamaica's Urban Informal Economy: Insights from a Kingston Slum." *Nieuwe West-Indische Gids* 62, nos. 3–4: 103–28.

Hart, Keith. 1973. "Informal Income Opportunities and Urban Employment in Ghana." *Journal of Modern African Studies* 2, no. 1: 61–89.

Hawthorne, Julian. 1896–1897a. "Summer at Christmas-Tide." *Century Illustrated Monthly Magazine,* November 1896–April 1897, 428–34.

———. 1896–1897b. "A Tropic Climb" *Century Illustrated Monthly Magazine,* November 1896–April 1897, 593–600.

Hays-Mitchell, M. 1999. "From Survivor to Entrepreneur: Gendered Dimensions of Micro-enterprise Development in Peru." *Environment and Planning A* 31, no. 2 (February): 251–71.

Heuman, Gad. 2006. *The Caribbean (Brief Histories).* London: Hodder Arnold.

Hewitt, Nancy A. 1992. "Compounding Differences." *Feminist Studies* 18, no. 2 (Summer): 313–26.

"Higglers' Paradise, Jamaican ICIs Take Advantage of Low Prices in China." 2009. *Jamaica Gleaner,* December 13. jamaica-gleaner.com/gleaner/20091213/lead/lead7.html. Accessed February 16, 2010.

Higman, B. W. 1984. *Slave Population of the British Caribbean, 1807–1834.* Baltimore: Johns Hopkins University Press.

———. 1995. *Slave Population and Economy in Jamaica, 1807–1834.* Kingston: University of the West Indies Press.

Hill, Donald R. 1993. *Calypso Calaloo: Early Carnival Music in Trinidad.* Gainesville: University Press of Florida, 1993.

Hoetink, H. 1971. *Caribbean Race Relations: A Study of Two Variants.* New York: Oxford University Press.

Holland, Jeremy. 1995. "Female Labour Force Integration and the Alleviation of Urban Poverty: A Case Study of Kingston, Jamaica." *Habitat International* 19, no. 4: 473–84.

Holt, Thomas. 1992. *The Problem of Freedom: Race, Labor, and Politics in Jamaica and Britain, 1832–1938*. Baltimore: Johns Hopkins University Press.

Honig, Benson. 1993. "Organizational Structure and Characteristics of Demand in the Jamaican Microenterprise Credit Market." Paper presented at the Jamaica Macro Policy Conference, Kingston, June.

———. 2000. "Small Business Promotion and Microlending: A Comparative Assessment of Jamaican and Israeli NGOs." *Journal of Microfinance* 2, no. 1: 92–111.

Horowitz, Donald L. 1973. "Color Differentiation in the American Systems of Slavery." *Journal of Interdisciplinary History* 3, no. 3 (Winter): 509–41.

Howson, Alexandra. 2004. *The Body in Society: An Introduction*. Cambridge: Polity Press.

Huber, Evelyn, and John Stephens. 1992. "Changing Development Models in Small Economies: The Case of Jamaica from the 1950's to the 1990's." *Studies in Comparative International Development* 27, no. 2 (Fall): 57–92.

"Independent Woman." 2001. *Jamaica Gleaner*, August 29. go.jamaica.com/gleaner/20010829/star/star1.html. Accessed February 3, 2003.

International Labour Office. 2002. "Women and Men in the Informal Economy: A Statistical Picture." Geneva: International Labour Organization. *wiego.org/publications/women20and20men20in20the20informal20economy.pdf*. Accessed September 17, 2008.

Joseph, Gloria I. 1980. "Caribbean Women: The Impact of Race, Sex, and Class." In *Comparative Perspectives of Third World Women: The Impact of Race, Sex, and Class*, ed. Beverly Lindsay. New York: Praeger, 143–61.

Kantor, Paula. 2005. "Determinants of Women's Microenterprise Success in Ahmedabad, India: Empowerment and Economics." *Feminist Economics* 11, no. 2: 63–83.

Kasinitz, Philip. 1992. *Caribbean New York: Black Immigrants and the Politics of Race*. Ithaca, NY: Cornell University Press.

Katzin, Margaret Fisher. 1959. "The Jamaican Country Higgler." *Social and Economic Studies* 8, no. 4: 421–40.

———. 1960. "The Business of Higglering in Jamaica." *Social and Economic Studies* 9, 3: 297–331.

Kay, Cristobal. 1993. "For a Renewal of Development Studies: Latin American Theories and Neoliberalism in the Era of Structural Adjustment." *Third World Quarterly* 14, no. 4: 691–702.

Kitzinger, Celia, and Sue Wilkinson. 1996. "Theorizing Representing the Other." In *Representing the Other: A Feminism and Psychology Reader*, ed. Sue Wilkinson and Celia Kitzinger. London: Sage, 1–32.

Knight, Franklin W., and Colin A. Palmer, eds. 1989. *The Modern Caribbean*. Chapel Hill: University of North Carolina Press.

Knowles, Caroline. 1999. "Race, Identities, and Lives." *Sociological Review* 47, no. 1 (February): 110–35.

Krane, Julia, Jacqueline Oxman-Martinez, and Kimberley Ducey. 2000. "Violence against Women and Ethnoracial Minority Women: Examining Assumptions about Ethnicity and Race." *Canadian Ethnic Studies* 32, no. 3: 1–18.

Kurlansky, Mark. 1992. *A Content of Islands: Searching for the Caribbean Destiny.* Reading, MA: Addison-Wesley.

Landes, Joan. 2003. "Further Thoughts on the Public/Private Distinction" *Journal of Women's History*, 15, no. 2: 28–39.

LeFranc, Elsie. 1989. "Petty Trading and Labour Mobility: Higglers in the Kingston Metropolitan Area." In *Women and the Sexual Division of Labour in the Caribbean*, ed. Keith Hart. Kingston: Consortium Graduate School of Social Sciences, 105–38. Reprinted in Barrow, Christine, and Rhoda Reddock, eds. 2001. *Caribbean Sociology: Introductory Readings.* Kingston: Ian Randle, 801–24.

Lengel, Laura B. 1998. "Researching the "Other," Transforming Ourselves: Methodological Considerations of Feminist Ethnography." *Journal of Communication Inquiry* 22, no. 3 (July): 229–50.

Lewis, Rupert, and Patrick Bryan, eds. 1991. *Garvey: His Work and Impact.* Trenton, NJ: Africa World Press.

Look Lai, Walton. 2005. "Images of the Chinese in West Indian History." In *Displacements and Diasporas: Asians in the Americas*, ed. Wanni W. Anderson and Robert G. Lee. Piscataway, NJ: Rutgers University Press, 54–77.

Lorde, Audre. 1984. "Age, Race, Class, and Sex: Women Redefining Difference." In *Sister Outsider*. Trumansburg, NY: Crossing Press, 114–23.

Low, Setha M. 1996. "Spatializing Culture: The Social Production and Social Construction of Public Space in Costa Rica." *American Ethnologist* 23, no. 4: 861–79.

Luckock, Benjamin. 1846. *Jamaica: Enslaved and Free.* London: Religious Tract Society.

Lummis, Douglas C. 1991. "Development against Democracy." *Alternatives* 16: 31–66.

MacFarlane-Gregory, Donna, and Thalia Ruddock-Kelly. 1993. "The Informal Commercial Importers of Jamaica: Research Project on Jamaican Micro-Enterprises." Kingston: Institute of Social and Economic Research, University of the West Indies.

Mair, Lucille Mathurin. 2006. *A Historical Study of Women in Jamaica, 1655–1844.* Ed. Hilary McD. Beckles and Verene A. Shepherd. Kingston: University of the West Indies Press.

Maldonado, Carlos. 1995. "The Informal Sector: Legalization or Laissez-faire?" *International Labour Review* 134, no. 6 (November–December): 705–24.

Manzo, D. 1991. "Modernist Discourse and the Crisis of Development

Theory." *Studies in Comparative International Development* 26, no. 2: 3–36.

Marques, M. Margarida, Rui Santos, and Fernanda Araujo. 2001. "Ariadne's Thread: Cape Verdean Women in Transnational Webs." *Global Network* 1, no. 3: 283–306.

Mason, Beverly J. 1985–1986. "Jamaican Working-Class Women: Producers and Reproducers." *Review of Black Political Economy* 14, nos. 2–3 (Fall–Winter): 259–75.

Massiah, Joycelin. 1986. "Work in the Lives of Caribbean Women." *Social and Economic Studies* 35, no. 2: 177–239.

Mayoux, Linda. 1993. "A Development Success Story? Low-Caste Entrepreneurship and Inequality: An Indian Case Study." *Development and Change* 24: 541–68.

———. 2001. "Tackling the Down Side: Social Capital, Women's Empowerment, and Micro-Finance in Cameroon." *Development and Change* 32, no. 3 (June): 421–50.

Mayur, Rashmi, and Bennett Daviss. 1998. "How Not to Develop an Emerging Nation." *Futurist*, January–February, 27–32.

McCall, Leslie. 2005. "The Complexity of Intersectionality." *Signs* 30, no. 3: 1771–1800.

McClaurin, Irma, ed. 2001. *Black Feminist Anthropology: Theory, Politics, Praxis, and Poetics*. New Brunswick, NJ: Rutgers University Press.

McKeever, Matthew. 1998. "Reproduced Inequality: Participation and Success in the South African Informal Economy." *Social Forces* 76, no. 4 (June): 1209–42.

McKittrick, Katherine. 2000. "'Black and 'Cause I'm Black I'm Blue': Transverse Racial Geographies in Toni Morrison's *The Bluest Eye*." *Gender, Place, and Culture: A Journal of Feminist Geography* 7, no. 2 (June): 125–42.

Mediatore, Shari Stone. 1998. "Chandra Mohanty and the Revaluing of 'Experience.'" *Hypatia* 13, no. 2 (Spring): 116–34.

Meyers, Maria. 2004. "African American Women and Violence: Gender, Race, and Class in the News." *Critical Studies in Media Communication* 21, no. 2 (June): 95–118.

Mies, Maria. 1986. *Patriarchy and Accumulation on a World Scale: Women and the International Division of Labour*. London: Zed Press.

Milgram, Lynne B. 2005. "From Margin to Mainstream: Microfinance, Women's Work, and Social Change in the Philippines." *Urban Anthropology and Studies of Cultural Systems and World Economic Development* 34, no. 4: 341–83.

Minh-ha, Trinh T. 1997. "Not You/Like You: Post-Colonial Women and the Interlocking Questions of Identity and Difference." In *Dangerous Liaisons: Gender, Nation, and Postcolonial Perspectives*, ed. Anne McClintock,

Aamir Mufti, and Ella Shohat. Minneapolis: University of Minnesota Press, 415–19.

Mintz, Sidney W. 1954. "The Jamaican Internal Marketing Pattern: Some Notes and Hypotheses." *Social and Economic Studies* 4: 95–103.

———. 1987. "Labour and Ethnicity: The Caribbean Conjuncture." In *Crisis in the Caribbean Basin*, ed. Richard Tardinco. New York: Sage, 47–57.

———. 1989. *Caribbean Transformations*. New York: Columbia University Press.

Mintz, Sidney W., and Douglas Hall. 1960. "The Origins of the Jamaican Marketing System," *Yale University Publications in Anthropology* 57. 1–26.

Mintz, Sidney W., and Sally Price, eds. 1985. *Caribbean Contours*. Baltimore: Johns Hopkins University Press.

Mirchandani, Kiran. 1999. "Feminist Insight on Gendered Work: New Directions in Research on Women and Entrepreneurship." *Gender, Work, and Organization* 6, no. 4: 224–35.

Moghadam, Valentine. 1999. "Gender and Globalization: Female Labor and Women's Mobilization." *Journal of World Systems Research* 5, no. 2 (summer): 367–88.

Mohammed, Patricia. 1994. "Nuancing the Feminist Discourse in the Caribbean." *Social and Economic Studies* 43, no. 3: 135–67.

———. 1998. "Towards Indigenous Feminist Theorizing in the Caribbean." *Feminist Review* 59 (Summer): 6–33.

———. 2000. "'But Most of All Mi Love Me Browning': The Emergence in Eighteenth- and Nineteenth-Century Jamaica of the Mulatto Woman as the Desired." *Feminist Review* 65 (Summer): 22–48.

———. 2007. "Gendering the Caribbean Picturesque." *Caribbean Review of Gender Studies* 1 (July 4). sta.uwi.edu/crgs/currentissue.asp. Accessed November 23, 2009.

Mohanty, Chandra Talpade. 1991. "Under Western Eyes: Feminist Scholarship and Colonial Discourses." In *Third World Women and the Politics of Feminism*, ed. Chandra Mohanty, Ann Russo, and Lourdes Torres. Bloomington: Indiana University Press, 333–60.

———. 2003. *Feminism without Borders: Decolonizing Theory, Practicing Solidarity*. Durham, NC: Duke University Press.

Morrison, Toni. 1990. *Playing in the Dark: Whiteness and the Literary Imagination*. Cambridge, MA: Harvard University Press.

Mosley, Paul, and David Hulme. 1998 "Microenterprise Finance: Is There a Conflict between Growth and Poverty Alleviation?" *World Development* 26, no. 5: 783–90.

Mouzelis, Nicos. 1980. "Modernization, Underdevelopment, and Uneven Development: Prospects for a Theory of Third World Formation." *Journal of Peasant Studies* 7, no. 3: 353–74.

Nakano Glenn, Evelyn. 1985. "Racial Ethnic Women's Labor: The Intersection of Race, Gender, and Class Oppression." *Review of Radical Political Economics* 17, no. 3: 86–108.

———. 2002. *Unequal Freedom: How Race and Gender Shaped American Citizenship and Labor.* Cambridge, MA: Harvard University Press.

Nash, Heidi, and Steve Pile, eds. 1998. *Places through the Body.* London and New York: Routledge.

Natrajan, Balmuri, and Radhika Parameswaran. 1997. "Contesting the Politics of Ethnography: Towards an Alternative Knowledge Production." *Journal of Communication Inquiry* 21, no. 1: 27–59.

Nelson, Lise. 1999. "Bodies (and Spaces) Do Matter: The Limits of Performativity." *Gender, Place, and Culture: A Journal of Feminist Geography* 6, no. 4 (December): 331–53.

New York Times. 1859. "Emancipation in Jamaica: Its Results upon the Present and Future Welfare of the Island." *New York Times,* November 18. ProQuest Historical Newspapers, *New York Times* (1851–2003). www.nytimes.com. Accessed March 5, 2007.

Norton, Ann, and Richard Symanski. 1975. "The Internal Marketing Systems of Jamaica." *Geographical Review* 65, no. 4 (October): 463–75.

Omi, Michael, and Howard Winant. 1994. *Racial Formation in the United States: From the 1960s to the 1990s.* New York: Routledge.

Osirim, Mary J. 1992. "The State of Women in the Third World: The Informal Sector and Development in Africa and the Caribbean." *Social Development Issues* 14, nos. 2–3: 74–87.

Pader, Ellen J. 1993. "Spatiality and Social Change: Domestic Space Use in Mexico and the United States." *American Ethnologist* 20, no. 1 (February): 114–37.

Paravisini-Gebert, Lizabeth. 1997. "Decolonizing Feminism: The Home-Grown Roots of Caribbean Women's Movements." In *Daughters of Caliban: Caribbean Women in the Twentieth Century,* ed. Consuelo Lopez Springfield. Bloomington: Indiana University Press, 3–17.

Patterson, Orlando. 1972. "Toward a Future That Has No Past: Reflections on the Fate of Blacks in the Americas." *Public Interest* 27 (Spring): 60–61.

Peattie, Lisa. 1987. "An Idea in Good Currency and How It Grew: The Informal Sector." *World Development* 15, no. 7: 851–60.

Pennigroth, Dylan. 1997. "Slavery, Freedom, and Social Claims to Property among African Americans in Liberty County, Georgia, 1850–1880." *Journal of American History* 84 (September): 405–35.

Petley, Christer. 2005. "Legitimacy and Social Boundaries: Free People of Colour and the Social Order in Jamaican Slave Society." *Social History* 30, no. 4: 481–98.

Pettman, Jan Jindy. 2006. "On the Backs of Women and Children." In *Beyond Borders: Thinking Critically about Global Issues,* ed. Paula Rothenberg. New York: Worth, 437–40.

Pfuhl, Edwin H., and Stuart Henry. 1993. *The Deviance Process.* 3d ed. New York: Aldine De Gruyter.

Phillips, Peter. 1977. "Jamaican Elites: 1938 to Present." In *Essays on Power and Change in Jamaica,* ed. Carl Stone and Aggrey Brown. Kingston: Jamaica Publishing House, 1–14.

Portes, Alejandro. 1976. "On the Sociology of National Development: Theories and Issues." *American Journal of Sociology* 82, no. 1: 55–85.

———. 1994. "The Informal Economy and Its Paradoxes." In *The Handbook of Economic Sociology,* ed. N. Smelser and R. Swedberg. Princeton, NJ: Princeton University Press, 426–52.

Portes, Alejandro, and Lauren Benton. 1984. "Industrial Development and Labor Absorption: A Reinterpretation." *Population and Development Review* 10, no. 4: 589–611.

Portes, Alejandro, Manuel Castells, and Lauren Benton, eds. 1989. *The Informal Economy: Studies in Advanced and Less Developed Countries.* Baltimore: Johns Hopkins University Press.

Portes, Alejandro, and Saskia Sassen-Koob. 1987. "Making It Underground: Comparative Material on the Informal Sector in Western Market Economies." *American Journal of Sociology* 93, no. 1 (July): 30–61.

Portes, Alejandro, and Richard Schauffler. 1993. "Competing Perspectives on the Latin American Informal Sector." *Population and Development Review* 19, no. 1 (March): 33–60.

Portes, Alejandro, Jose Itzigsohn, Carlos Dore-Cabral. 1994. "Urbanization in the Caribbean Basin: Social Change During the Years of Crisis." *Latin American Research Review* 29, no. 2: 3–37.

Portes, Alejandro, Luis Eduardo Guarnizo, and William J. Haller. 2002. "Transnational Entrepreneurs: An Alternative Form of Immigrant Economic Adaptation." *American Sociological Review* 67: 278–98.

Powell, Patricia Green. 1997. "Methodological Considerations in Field Research: Six Case Studies." In *Oral Narrative Research with Black Women,* ed. Kim Marie Vaz. London: Sage, 197–22.

Powers, Lindsay. 2006. "Empowering Haiti's Ti Machann through Business, Literacy, and Life-Skills Training: An Evaluation of Fonkoze's Educational Programs." *www.fonkoze.org/docs/Fonkozeevaluation_final.pdf.* Accessed November 13, 2009.

Pragg, Sam. 1997. "A Lighter Shade of Sale: Thousands Are Using Skin-Lightening Creams Hoping to Move Up in Society." *The Voice,* February 10, 16.

"Priests Gunned Down in Jamaica." 2005. CNN.com/International, October 28. *edition.cnn.com/2005/WORLD/americas/10/28/jamaica.priests.reut/.* Accessed November 22, 2005.

Puwar, Nirmal. 2004. Space *Invaders: Race, Gender, and Bodies out of Place.* Oxford: Berg.

Pyle, Howard. 1889–1890. "Jamaica, Old and New." *Harper's New Monthly Magazine*, December–May, 175.

Raynolds, Laura T. 1998. "Harnessing Women's Work: Restructuring Agricultural and Industrial Labor Forces in the Dominican Republic." *Economic Geography* 74, no. 2 (April): 149–69.

Reddock, Rhoda. 2000. "Why Gender, Why Development?" In *Theoretical Perspectives on Gender and Development*, ed. Jane I. Parpart, M. Patricia Connelly, and V. Eudine Barriteau. Ottawa: International Development Research Center, 23–50.

———. 2001. "Conceptualizing 'Difference' in Caribbean Feminist Theory." In *New Caribbean Thought: A Reader*, ed. Brian Meeks and Folke Lindahl. Kingston: University of the West Indies Press, 196–209.

Reid, Stanley. 1977. "An Introductory Approach to the Concentration of Power in the Jamaican Corporate Economy and Notes on Its Origin." In *Essays on Power and Change in Jamaica*, ed. Carl Stone and Aggrey Brown. Kingston: Jamaica Publishing House, 15–44.

Reinharz, Shulamit. 1992. *Feminist Methods in Social Research*. New York: Oxford University Press.

Ritch, Dawn. 1999. "Colour Coding in Jamaica." *Jamaica Gleaner*, June 28.

Robotham, Don. 2000. "Blackening the Jamaican Nation: The Travails of a Black Bourgeoisie in a Globalized World." *Identities* 7, no. 1 (March): 11–37.

Ross, Leone. 1993. "Boy Browning Girl Think She Nice!" *Weekly Journal*, August 5, 7.

Safa, Helen I. 1981. "Runaway Shops and Female Employment: The Search for Cheap Labor." *Signs* 7, no. 2 (Winter): 418–33.

Satchell, Veront M. 1995. "Women, Land Transactions, and Peasant Development in Jamaica, 1866–1900." In *Engendering History: Caribbean Women in Historical Perspective*, ed. Verene Shepherd, Bridget Brereton, and Hilary Beckles. New York: St. Martin's Press, 213–32.

Schiller, Riva Berleant. 1999. "Women, Work, and Gender in the Caribbean: Recent Research." *Latin American Research Review* 34, no. 1 (Winter): 201–9.

Sen, Gita, and Caren Grown. 1987. *Development Crisis and Alternative Visions: Third World Women's Perspectives*. New York: Monthly Review Press.

"Service with a Smile." 2001. *Jamaica Gleaner*, January 3. go.jamaica.com/gleaner/20010103/star/star3.html.

Servon, Lisa, and Timothy Bates. 1998. "Microenterprise as an Exit Route from Poverty: Recommendations for Programs and Policy Makers." *Journal of Urban Affairs* 20, no. 4: 419–41.

Sheller, Mimi. 2002. "Quasheba, Mother, Queen: Black Women's Public Leadership and Political Protest in Postemancipation Jamaica." comp.lancs.ac.uk/sociology/papers/Sheller-Quasheba-Mother-Queen.pdf. Accessed July 17, 2006.

Shepherd, Verene, Bridget Brereton, and Hilary Beckles, eds. 1995. *Engendering History: Caribbean Women in Historical Perspective*. New York: St. Martin's Press.

Shepherd, Verene. 2002. "Land, Labour, and Social Status: Non-sugar Producers in Jamaica in Slavery and Freedom." In *Working Slavery, Pricing Freedom: Perspectives from the Caribbean, Africa, and African Diaspora*, ed. Verene Shepherd. New York: Palgrave Macmillan, 153–80.

Sherlock, Phillip, and Hazel Bennett. 1998. *The Story of the Jamaican People*. Kingston: Ian Randle.

Shilling, Chris. 2004. *The Body and Social Theory*. 2d ed. London: Sage.

———. 2005. *The Body in Culture, Technology, and Society*. London: Sage.

Simmonds, Lorna. 1987. "Slave Higglering in Jamaica, 1780–1834." *Jamaica Journal* 20, no. 1 (February–April): 31–38.

Slocum, Karla. 2001. "Negotiating Identity and Black Feminist Politics in Caribbean Research." In *Black Feminist Anthropology: Theory, Politics, Praxis, and Poetics*, ed. Irma McClaurin. New Brunswick, NJ: Rutgers University Press, 126–49.

Small, Stephen. 1994. "Racial Group Boundaries and Identities: People of 'Mixed Race' in Slavery across the Americas." *Slavery and Abolition* 13, no. 3 (December): 17–37.

Smith, M. G. 1974. *The Plural Society in the British West Indies*. Berkeley: University of California Press.

———. 1984. *Culture, Race, and Class in the Commonwealth Caribbean*. Mona, Jamaica: University of the West Indies.

Soja, Edward, and B. Hooper. 1993. "The Spaces That Difference Makes: Some Notes on the Geographical Margins of the New Cultural Politics." In *Place and the Politics of Identity*, ed. M. Keith and S. Pile. London: Routledge, 183–205.

Sokoloff, Natalie J., and Ida Dupont. 2005. "Domestic Violence at the Intersection of Race, Class, and Gender." *Violence against Women* 11, no. 1: 36–64.

"Spectre of Violence," 2001. *Jamaica Gleaner*, June 6.

Springfield, Consuelo Lopez, ed. 1997. *Daughters of Caliban: Caribbean Women in the Twentieth Century*. Bloomington: Indiana University Press.

Stacey, Judith. 1988. "Can There Be a Feminist Ethnography?" *Women's Studies International Forum* 11, no. 1: 21–27.

STATIN [Statistical Institute of Jamaica]. 2008a. "Interesting Facts and figures." *statinja.com*. Accessed December 13, 2009.

———. 2008b. "Main Labour Force Indicators, 2008–2009." *statinja.gov/LabourForceMainIndicators/aspx*. Accessed November 24, 2008.

Stinchcombe, Arthur L. 1995. *Sugar Island Slavery in the Age of Enlightenment: The Political Economy of the Caribbean World*. Princeton, NJ: Princeton University Press.

Strachan, Ian Gregory. 2002. *Paradise and Plantation: Tourism and Culture in the Anglophone Caribbean.* Charlottesville: University of Virginia Press.

Sundstrom, Ronald R. 2003. "Race and Place: Social Space in the Production of Human Kinds." *Philosophy and Geography* 16, no. 1 (February): 83–96.

Taylor, Alicia. 1988. "Women Traders in Jamaica: The Informal Commercial Importers." Trinidad and Tobago: UNECLAC.

Telles, Edward E. 2004. *Race in Another America: The Significance of Skin Color in Brazil.* Princeton, NJ: Princeton University Press.

Thomas, Deborah. 2004. *Modern Blackness: Nationalism, Globalization, and the Politics of Culture in Jamaica.* Durham, NC: Duke University Press.

———. "The Emergence of Modern Blackness in Jamaica" *NACLA Report on the Americas: Report on Race, Part 3*, 39, no. 3 (November–December 2005): 30–35.

Thompson, Krista. 2004. "Black Skin, Blue Eyes: Visualizing Blackness in Jamaican Art, 1922–1944." *Small Axe* 16 (September): 1–31.

———. 2006. *An Eye for the Tropics: Tourism, Photography, and Framing the Caribbean Picturesque.* Durham, NC: Duke University Press.

Timothy, Dallen, and Geoffrey Wall. 1997. "Selling to Tourists: Indonesian Street Vendors." *Annals of Tourism Research: A Social Science Journal* 24, no. 2: 322–40.

Tinker, Irene. 1987. "Street Foods." *Current Sociology* 35, no. 3 (Winter): 51–68.

———. 1995. "The Human Economy of Micro-entrepreneurs." In *Women in Micro- and Small-Scale Enterprise Development*, ed. Louise Dignard and Jose Havet. Boulder, CO: Westview Press, 25–40.

———. 2000. "Alleviating Poverty, Investing in Women's Work." *Journal of the American Planning Association* 66, no. 3: 229–42.

———. 2003. "Street Foods: Traditional Microenterprise in a Modernizing World." *International Journal of Politics, Culture, and Society* 16, no. 3 (Spring): 331–49.

Tipps, Dean. 1973. "Modernization Theory and the Comparative Study of Societies: A Critical Perspective." *Comparative Studies in Society and History* 15, no. 2: 199–26.

Ulysse, Gina. 1999. "Uptown Ladies and Downtown Women: Female Representations of Color and Class in Jamaica." In *Representations of Blackness and the Performance of Identities*, ed. Jean Muteba Rahier. Westport, CT: Bergin and Garvey, 147–72.

———. 2007. *Downtown Ladies: Informal Commercial Importers, a Haitian Anthropologist, and Self-Making in Jamaica.* Chicago: University of Chicago Press.

Van Der Wees, Catherine, and Henny Romijn. 1995. "Entrepreneurship and Small- and Microenterprise Development for Women: A Problematique in Search of Answers, a Policy in Search of Programs." In *Women in*

Micro- and Small-Scale Enterprise Development, ed. Louise Dignard and Jose Havet. Boulder, CO: Westview Press, 41–84.

Visweswaran, Kamala. 1988. "Defining Feminist Ethnography." *Inscriptions* 3, no. 4: 27–44.

———. 1994. *Fictions of Feminist Ethnography*. Minneapolis: University of Minnesota Press.

Wade, Peter. 1997. *Race and Ethnicity in Latin America*. London: Pluto Press.

Wallerstein, Immanuel. 1979. *The Capitalist World Economy*. Cambridge: Cambridge University Press.

———. 1993. "The Modern World System." In *Social Theory: The Multicultural and Classic Readings*, ed. Charles Lemert. Boulder, CO: Westview Press, 391–96.

"War Downtown." 2001. *Sunday Gleaner*, July 18.

Watson, Sophie. 2000. "Bodies, Gender, Cities." *City* 4, no. 1: 101–5.

Weber, Max. 1993. "Class, Status, and Party." In *Social Theory: The Multicultural and Classic Readings*, ed. Charles Lemert. Boulder, CO: Westview Press, 115–16.

Weis, Tony. 2004. "A Precarious Balance: Neoliberalism, Crisis Management, and the Social Implosion in Jamaica." *Capital and Class* 85: 115–47.

Welch, Pedro L. V. 2003. *Slave Society in the City: Bridgetown, Barbados, 1680–1834*. Kingston: Ian Randle.

Williams, Eric. 1984. *From Columbus to Castro: The History of the Caribbean, 1492–1969*. New York: Vintage Books.

Wilson, Andrew, ed. 2004. *The Chinese in the Caribbean*. Princeton, NJ: Markus Weiner.

Wint, Eleanor. 1993. "Micro-Enterprise Support and the Double Bind of Gender in Jamaica." *Labour, Capital, and Society* 26, no. 2 (November): 182–202.

Witter, Michael, ed. 1989. *Higglering/Sidewalk Vending/Informal Commercial Trading in the Jamaican Economy: Proceedings of a Symposium*. Mona, Jamaica: Department of Economics, University of the West Indies.

Witter, Michael, and Claremont Kirton. 1990. "The Informal Economy in Jamaica: Some Empirical Exercises." Working Paper No. 36. Mona, Jamaica: Institute of Social and Economic Research, University of the West Indies.

Wong, David C. 1996. "A Theory of Petty Trading: The Jamaican Higgler." *Economic Journal* 106, no. 435 (March): 507–18.

Wyss, Brenda, and Marceline White. 2004. "The Effects of Trade Liberalization on Jamaica's Poor: An Analysis of Agriculture and Services." Report by the Women's Edge Coalition and CAFRA, June. *eldis.org/static/DOC16084.htm*. Accessed April 16, 2006.

Index

Page numbers in bold refer to illustrations.

absentee owners, 67
Acker, Joan, 6, 66
Afro-Jamaicans, 1–2, 34, 54, 62–63, 161–62, 177n1
agism, 167–68
Agricultural Development Corporation, 45
agro-elites, 83, 181n4
Ammar, Michael, Jr., 147
Ammar, Michael, Sr., 153
Anthias, Floya, 28–29
arcades, 2, 37, 57–58, 153, 156–57, 172–73, 182n15
artisans, 51, 68, 92
autonomy, 135, 141
Azan, Milade, 149

Babylon system, 14
Baker, Captain Lorenzo, 83
Banana Board, 45
banana industry, 43–44, 83–84, 86–87, 118, 181n4
banking, 42
Barbados Mulatto Girl, The, 102, **103**
Barrow, Christine, 28
bartering, 92
batty riders, 55, 60, 182n9
bauxite, 88
beauty pageants, 116–17, 186–87n12
Beckles, Hilary, 47, 91
begging, 125
Beneria, Lourdes, 21, 23
Bennett, Hazel, 85
Berger, Iris, 31–32
Bickell, Rev. Richard, 73–75, 184n5
black females
    aggressive behaviors and, 133, 161
    Barbados Mulatto Girl, The, 102, **103**
    city spaces and, 152
    during colonialism, 108
    as contaminants, 157–58
    as deviants, 121, 131
    Domestic Scene—Two Mulatto Women and Child and Seated Negro Woman, 107
    femininity of, 52
    as field laborers, 92
    illegitimate economy and, 168
    informal economies and, 148, 166–67
    manual labor of, 141–42
    marginalized, 112
    as microentrepreneurs, 169
    post-emancipation economy and, 117–18
    poverty of, 131
    public spaces and, 117
    stereotyping of, 161
    Sunday markets and, 91–95, 185n1
    unfeminine, 141–42, 161
    as work horses, 114
    See also higglers
blacks
    aggressive behaviors and, 132
    banana growing and, 83
    beauty pageants and, 116
    as "butus," 166
    class (social) of, 43
    as concubines, 53
    customers of, 58–62
    dance-hall culture and, 182n9
    depression era poverty and, 86
    as deviants, 101, 166
    downtown shopping and, 133
    excluded by economic elites, 46
    as field laborers, 51–52, 102–3
    formal economy and, 54
    gender role inversion of, 115
    hierarchy of shades and, 101
    as higglers, 32, 39–40, 63–64

211

blacks, *continued*
  as ICIs (informal commercial importers), 129
  as immigrants, post-emancipation, 85
  independence and, 87
  industriousness of, 116–17
  in Jamaica, 34
  at Lady Musgrave Flea Market, 55
  males, as lazy, 113–14
  as mammy figures, 119–20
  marijuana and, 182n15
  market women, 53–54
  modern blackness and, 187–88n9
  Morant Bay rebellion and, 83, 185n10
  Moyne Commission and, 87
  Patterson as first black prime minister, 145
  as percentage of Jamaican population, 55, 88, 186n6
  poverty and, 161
  public domain and, 69, 87
  Rodney riots and, 185n12
  social mobility of, 166
  social status of, 27, 69, 166
  stereotyping of, 166
  upside down ice cream cone and, 143–44
  uptown/downtown division and, 144
  urban culture and, 59
  as wage laborers, 78, 83
  See also black females
Bogle, Paul, 185n10
Bolles, Lynn, 17
Boston Fruit Company, 83
"Bras with Cement," 119
Britain, 76
Brodber, Erna, 35
Broom, Leonard, 52
Browne, Irene, 39
Browne-Glaude, Winnifred, 7–18
brownings
  banana industry and, 83–84, 87
  beauty pageants and, 116–17, 186–87n12
  class (social), 17–18, 33, 43
  class status, 33
  clothing sold by, 55–57
  customers of, 56–58
  Domestic Scene—Two Mulatto Women and Child and Seated Negro Woman, 107
  as elites, 46, 84, 127–28, 145
  formal economy and, 168
  higglers and, 54–56
  as ICIs (informal commercial importers), 36–37, 129
  lady vs. woman, 30, 160–61
  and market women, 98
  as skilled labor, 84
  skin color, 43, 128–29
  social mobility, 18
  social status, 139, 157
  social stratification, 180n12
  as unfit for field labor, 52–53
  uptown shopping and, 133
Brunias, Agostino, 102, **103**, 104–5, 117
Buckridge, Steeve O., 93–95, 104
Buck Town vendors arcade, 153
Burton, Richard, 141
Bush, Barbara, 51, 69, 95, 185n1
"Businessmen Renew Call for Vendor Removal," 149
businesswomen, 124, 127, 132, 134–35
Bustamante, Alexander, 86

Cape Verde, 6
capitalism, 66–67, 78, 96–97, 142, 153
Cargill, Morris, 119–21, 139, 161
Caribbean nations, 6, 27–28, 41–42, 70, 73–74, 101–2, 108, 178–79n2
Carmichael, Mrs. A. C., 71–72, 74
census, 186n6
Central Board of Health, 78
Century Illustrated Monthly Magazine, **109**, 112, **113**
Chamber of Commerce, 147, 149, 156
character references, 170–71
children's gangs, 51
China, 1, 2
Chinese, 42–45, 54–56, 86, 88, 129, 132, 145
Christianity, 73–75
Christmas shopping, 146–47, 150, 153, 162–63
city spaces, 24, 143–44, 146–48, 151–52, 157, 161
civilizing effect, 104, 113, 115–17
Clarendon Parish Council, 149
Clarke, Colin, 74
Clarke, Petulia, 155
class (social)
  antipathy among, 16–17
  Barbados Mulatto Girl, The, 103
  blacks and, 43
  brownings and, 17–18, 33, 43
  in Caribbean nations, 27

city spaces and, 143, 147–48
"Class, Status, and Party," 165
clothing and, 55–57, 59
colonialism and, 46, 67, 108
Crossroads of Class and Gender, The
  (Beneria and Roldan), 21
division of labor and, 53–54
economic power and, 166
and education, 124–25
embodied intersectionality and, 5–6,
  29, 167
femininity and, 122
hierarchies of power and, 26–27
higglers and, 32
ICIs (informal commercial importers)
  and, 129
identity formation and, 122–23
imaginaries and, 142
inclusion/exclusion and, 162
independence and, 86
informal economies and, 3, 31–32, 148
and Jamaican "lady" vs. Jamaican
  "woman," 30–32, 148
and lady vs. woman, 160–61
music tastes and, 182n14
North/South economic relationships
  and, 168
post-emancipation economy and, 118
and privacy, 15–16
and race, 34
research impact and, 16–17
and respectability, 130
shopping patterns and, 56–57, 182n12
sisterhood and, 11–12
social stratification and, 18, 58, 180n12
uptown/downtown division and, 143–
  44, 159
women's work and, 173–74
See also social mobility
class status, 32–33, 68–69, 139
Clement, Eric, 9, 12–13, 17
clerks, 54
clothing, 55–59, 92–93, **94**, 102, 104, 107,
  122, 185–86n3
coffee farmers, 67
coinage, 92
COK (Credit Union of Kingston), 169–70,
  190n4
collateral, 169–70, 190n4
colonialism
  absentee owners and, 67
  Afro-Jamaicans and, 177n1
  Barbados Mulatto Girl, The, 104–5

black females and, 108
capitalism and, 66–67
civilizing effect of, 113
class stratification, 46
concubines and, 108
Crown Colony rule and, 82–84, 87,
  111, 113–17, 185n9
females and, 69, 93–94
formal economy and, 147
gender and, 67, 108
hierarchies of power and, 44, 87–88,
  108
hierarchy of shades and, 27, 43–44, 102
higglers and, 4, 120
informal economies and, 48–49, 173
Jamaica and, 34–35
labor rebellions and, 83, 86
Lebanese immigrants and, 44
and males as first in economic order,
  98, 168
motherhood and, 107–8
plantations and, 75, 77–78
public spaces and, 91
race/color and, 67
slavery and, 35
social spaces and, 67
social status and, 67
Sunday markets and, 184n4
three-tiered economy and, 48
tourism and, 108
colored, 51–54, 69, 70, 185n1. *See also* skin
  color
Columbian Magazine, 81, 100
Columbus, Christopher, 35
commodity production, 66
concubines, 53, 107–8
"Congested Streets of Downtown
  Kingston," 148
Constant Spring Arcade, 1, 8–9, 12–13, 15,
  55, 58, 129–30, 132–33, 136, 139, 159,
  182n13
consumers, 93, 104–5
contaminants, 157–58
content analysis, 188–89n3
Coronation Market, 8–10, 55, 61, 135
Credit Union of Kingston (COK), 169–70
Crenshaw, Kimberle, 26–27, 179–80n10
Creole, 68, 74–75, 83
criminality, 101, 149–50
Crossroads of Class and Gender, The
  (Beneria and Roldan), 21
Crown Colony rule. *See* colonialism
Cuba, 77, 86

customers, 56–62, 98, 147, 153, 155, 157, 172
customs duties, 126–27, 154

Daily Gleaner, 120–21, 135, 142, 146, 148–50, 152, 155–59, 188n2
dance-hall culture, 55–57, 60, 182n9
debt-to-GDP ratio, 35–36, 40, 145–46, 180n18, 183n22
deficiency laws, 68, 183–84n2
depression, 85
destigmatization, 123–24
developing economies, 141, 162
deviants
    black females as, 121, 131
    blacks as, 101, 166
    Deviance Process, The (Pfuhl and Henry), 123
    higglers as, 32, 60, 95, 97, 107, 110, 117–18, 120, 130–31, 133, 141, 170
    Sunday markets and, 73, 75, 89, 184n5
disability, 168
disease/dirt, 144–45, 157
division of labor, 42, 50–54, 69, 76, 181n7, 183n25
Domestic Scene—Two Mulatto Women and Child and Seated Negro Woman, 105, **106**, 107
domestic servants, 51–52, 54, 68–70, 85, 134, 181n7
Dominican Republic, 6
"'Dons' Set the Stage, The," 152
Dore-Cabral, José Carlos, 143
Douglas, Mary, 141, 144
Douglass, Lisa, 15, 32, 56, 83–84, 160–61, 182n10
"Drama of Christmas Vending, The," 146
drug dealers, 129, 152, 189n10
drugs, 58, 155, 180n18, 182n15

economic development policy, 145
"Economic Life of Their Own, An," 91
economic power, 165, 168, 174
education, 124–26, 137–38, 162, 187n8
Edwards, Bryan, 72
Edwards, Melvin R., 40–42, 185–86n3
egalitarianism, 126, 131
elections, 7–8, 145, 155
elites
    agro-elites as, 83, 181n4
    Barbados Mulatto Girl, The, 105
    brownings as, 46, 84, 127–28, 145
    Chinese as, 45, 88, 145
    clothing and, 93
    developing economies and, 162
    economic development policy and, 145
    economic elites, 148
    economy post-WWII and, 44–45
    endogamy and, 45–46
    formal economy and, 152
    hierarchy of shades and, 162
    vs. higglers, 65
    hip-hop culture and, 59–60
    in Jamaica, 15–16, 88
    Jews as, 45, 88, 145, 181n4
    Lebanese as, 145
    multinational corporations and, 168
    Norbrook residential area and, 166
    plantations and, 43, 53
    political, 45
    post-emancipation economy and, 88
    Power of Sentiment, The: Love, Hierarchy, and the Jamaican Family Elite (Douglass), 15
    power relations and, 16
    privacy and, 15–16
    public domain and, 67
    public spaces and, 112
    shopping patterns and, 59
    slavery and, 51
    speech patterns and, 182n10
    Syrians as, 45
    twenty-one families as, 88
    uptown/downtown division and, 144
emancipation, 50, 53–54, 68, 76–77, 82, 88, 94–95, 97–98, 109–12, 114. *See also* post-emancipation economy
embodied intersectionality
    Afro-Jamaicans and, 161–62
    city spaces and, 24
    and hierarchies of power, 5, 26, 161–62
    higglers and, 5–6, 23–24, 32–33, 37
    identity formation and, 30–31
    informality and, 169
    market research and, 23
    market sites and, 142
    research and, 11–16, 18–19
    sisterhood and, 11–12
    social change and, 25
    social construction theory and, 25
    social spaces and, 65
    social stratification and, 26
    sociological research and, 179n4
    women's work and, 167–69
    See also class (social); gender; race/color

endogamy, 45–46
entrepreneurs, 96, 117, 124, 133, 135
Espeut, Peter, 146, 162–63
European club, 74
European Union, 190n4
expatriates, 16, 178n13

Falmouth, 99
fees, 2, 49, 57, 182n13
female-headed households, 1–2, 34, 36, 62–63, 85, 114, 136–38, 141–42, 146, 170, 183n22, 183n24
Female Negro Peasant in Her Sunday and Working Dress, **94**
femininity
    Barbados Mulatto Girl, The, 105
    among black females, 52
    class (social) and, 122
    class status and, 139
    clothing and, 93–94, 122
    Domestic Scene—Two Mulatto Women and Child and Seated Negro Woman, 105, **106**, 107–8
    Fruit Vendor, A, 109–10
    human reproduction and, 66
    ICIs (informal commercial importers) and, 178n8
    identity formation and, 30
    in Jamaica, 31–32
    lady vs. woman, 123, 160–61
    mulattos and, 115
    race/color and, 116, 122
    racialized gender norms and, 116
    self-identification and, 122
    among whites, 53
feminist research, 12, 24, 26–29
field laborers, 51–53, 67–68, 76, 92, 102–3, 181n7
Financial Sector Adjustment Company (FINSAC), 190n4
flea markets, 10, 37, 55, 57, 182n13
flirtation, 110
foreign investment, 97–98, 110–11, 115–16, 118, 141–42
formal economy
    banana industry and, 83, 85
    blacks and, 54
    brownings and, 168
    Chinese and, 42
    Christmas shopping and, 146–47
    depression era and, 86
    East Kingston and, 151
    elites and, 152
    emancipation and, 76
    gender and, 118, 168
    higglers and, 89, 98–101, 117–18, 147–56
    IMF (International Monetary Fund) and, 120–21
    vs. informal economy, 95–101, 120
    legitimacy and, 141, 151, 168
    neoliberal policies and, 120–21, 151
    plantations and, 48
    post-emancipation, 78, 111–12, 186n9
    post-WWII, 44–45, 181n4
    preferential treatment and, 154
    race/color and, 42
    skin color and, 118, 181n3
    unemployment in, 146
    whites and, 112
    See also informal economies
free trade, 77
Frenchmen, 73–74
Frome Estate, 86
Fruit Vendor, A, **109**, 110

gang warfare, 8
Garvey, Marcus, 87, 185n12, 186–87n12
Gaul, Gilbert, **109**, 110, 112
gender
    Afro-Jamaicans and, 62
    Barbados Mulatto Girl, The, 104–5
    in Caribbean nations, 27
    city spaces and, 143, 147
    clothing and, 93
    colonialism and, 67, 108
    Crossroads of Class and Gender, The (Beneria and Roldan), 21
    and division of labor, 53–54, 183n25
    Domestic Scene—Two Mulatto Women and Child and Seated Negro Woman, 107
    economic power and, 165
    embodied intersectionality and, 5, 29, 161, 167
    female-headed households and, 64, 137–38
    female-on-female slavery and, 52
    formal economy and, 118, 168
    hierarchies, 34, 118
    of higglers, 114
    imaginaries and, 142
    inclusion/exclusion, 162
    independence and, 86
    inequality and, 6, 22, 29, 31, 66–67, 174, 177–78n7

gender, *continued*
  informal economies and, 3, 6
  intersectional gender analyses, 167–69
  inversion of roles among blacks, 115
  "Making of a Slum, The," 160
  microentrepreneurs and, 22, 177–78n7
  neutrality and, 66
  plantations and, 50
  sisterhood and, 11–12
  social mobility and, 131
  Space Invaders: Race, Gender, and Bodies out of Place (Puwar), 65
  stereotyping, 22
  subordination, 28–29
  of vendors, 114
  violence against women, 26–27, 179–80n10
  and women's work, 173–74
  See also class (social); femininity; race/color
global economy, 21–23, 34–37, 88, 145, 168
Golding, Bruce, 145
Gordon, George William, 185n10
Government of Jamaica/European Union (GOJEU), 190n4
Grant, Sir John Peter, 82
Gray, Obika, 16–17
Grosz, Elizabeth, 30–31

Haitian, 6
Hall, Stuart, 159
Handbook of Jamaica, 81
Harper's Monthly Magazine, 79–80, 114
Hawthorne, Julian, **109**, 110–11, **113**
hegemonic discourse, 122, 131–32
Henry, Stuart, 123
hierarchies of power
  after independence, 86
  city spaces and, 143
  class (social) and, 26–27
  colonialism and, 44, 87–88, 108
  embodied intersectionality and, 5, 26, 161–62
  higglers and, 3, 33, 139
  independence and, 145
  informal economies and, 23
  intersectional gender analyses, 167–68
  intersectionality and, 23, 26
  market sites and, 142

  plantation division of labor and, 50
  post-emancipation economy and, 82, 108
hierarchy of shades, 27, 43–44, 84, 86, 101–3, 109, 162
higglers
  aggressive behaviors of, 60–61, 97, 129–30
  arcades and, 2, 37, 156–57
  asexuality, 119
  assertiveness, 141
  Barbados Mulatto Girl, The, 105
  and begging vs. vending, 125
  black females as, 152
  blackness, 32, 39–40, 63–64
  "Bras with Cement," 119
  brownings and, 54–56
  "Businessmen Renew Call for Vendor Removal," 149
  as capitalists, 96–97
  Central Board of Health report on, 78–79
  Christmas shopping and, 146–47, 162–63
  city spaces and, 146
  as criminals, 101, 149–50
  customers of, 58–62, 155
  defined, 2
  destigmatization of, 123–24
  disease/dirt associated with, 144–45, 157
  as disruptive force in society, 3–4
  Domestic Scene—Two Mulatto Women and Child and Seated Negro Woman, 105, **106**, 107–8
  "'Dons' Set the Stage, The," 152
  as drug dealers, 129
  economic factors affecting, 40
  embodied intersectionality and, 5–6, 23–24, 32–33, 37
  female-headed households and, 36, 141–42, 183n24
  flirtation and, 110
  vs. formal economies, 98–101, 117–18, 147–56
  Fruit Vendor, A, **109**
  government vs. higglers, 152–55, 160, 162–63, 173, 189n10
  hierarchies of power and, 3, 33, 139
  "On Higglers," 119
  Higglers Association, 120–21
  "Higglers Blast Cargill Article As 'an Insult to All Women,'" 120–21

vs. ICIs, 127, 132
as icons, 115
identity formation, 138–39
illegitimate economy and, 139
indecency, 150
indiscipline, 150, 156–57
as infestation, 98–99
informal labor and, 4–7
and intergenerational transmission of property, 63–64, 183n25
Lady Musgrave Flea Market and, 60
lady vs. woman, 160–61
legitimacy, 98, 114, 139
"Making of a Slum, The," 159
males and, 64
marginalization, 153–55
market sites and, 8–9, 142
microcredit loans and, 169–74
microentrepreneurs, 2–3, 6, 32, 54, 55
monopoly during scarcity, 97
as natural rebels, 91
negative views of, 3–4, 6–7, 60
"No Such Thing as a Happy Higgler," 156–57
as nuisances, 147, 158, 173
as objects of production, 117
"On the Way to Market," 112, **113**
out of order, 4, 156
peasant production and, 77–78
plantation owners and, 186n7
pollution and, 144–45
post-emancipation economy and, 85
post-emancipation representations, 109–10
power relations with government, 139
as public nuisances, 147
public spaces and, 26
rebellions by, 155–56
removal of, from market sites, 189n7
renaming, 189n8
reputation, 171
respectability, 126
rise of, 88
ROSCA (rotating savings and credit associations) and, 171
selective breeding, 161
self-identifications, 19–20, 32, 119, 124–39, 187n6
self-sufficiency, 125–26, 131–32
"Slave Higglering in Jamaica, 1780–1834," 95
slavery and, 2, 32, 46–50, 63–64
social status, 123

status order, 32, 65, 134
stereotyping of, 57–58, 119, 139
stigma of, 7, 121, 135, 170, 174, 178n9, 189n8
as trespassers, 4
as unfeminine, 116
vs. uptown, 156–63
urban/rural distinction among, 97–98
Victoria Market and, 82
as wage laborers, 112, 118
women's work and, 32, 65
See also deviants; informal economies; market women; microentrepreneurs; Sunday markets
Higman, Barry, 50–51, 53
Hill Collins, Patricia, 28–29, 63–64
hip-hop culture, 59–60
Holt, Thomas, 76–78
House of Assembly, 76, 99
Howson, Alexandra, 179nn4–5
hucksters, 91
human reproduction, 66
hypersexuality, 108

ICIs (informal commercial importers)
blacks as, 129
brownings as, 36–37, 129
China as supplier to, 1–2
class (social), 129
clothing sales by, 58–59
Constant Spring Arcade and, 1, 12–13, 129–30, 132–33, 136, 139
customers of, 58–62, 172
customs duties and, 126–27, 154
defined, 2
economic power, 166
education, 137–38
emergence of, 88
as entrepreneurs, 124
fees paid by, 2, 182n13
female-headed households and, 136–37, 170
femininity and, 178n8
vs. higglers, 127, 132
identity formation, 135
import duties and, 131
and intergenerational transmission of property, 64, 137–38
market sites and, 9
microcredit loans and, 169–70
as microentrepreneurs, 177n3

ICIs, *continued*
   People's Arcade and, 133–34
   race/color, 36–37
   respectability, 126, 135–36
   self-identifications, 124–25, 128, 132–34
   social mobility, 137–38
   stigmas, 135, 166
   trustworthiness, 172
   as ultimate rude gal, 98
   unemployment, 134
   and unsanitary conditions of market sites, 154–55
   uptown/downtown division, 133–34, 139
   working conditions, 173
identity formation, 30–31, 122–23, 135, 138–39, 180n12
illegal vending, 147
illegitimate economy, 120, 139, 141, 151, 158, 168
illiteracy, 88
ILO (International Labour Office), 167, 169
imaginaries, 142–45, 151, 153, 157–58, 160–61, 168, 173
IMF (International Monetary Fund), 120–21, 151
immigrants, 41–44, 85–86, 183–84n2
import duties, 131
inaccessibility, 16
inclusion/exclusion, 162
indecency, 150
indentured servants, 35, 42, 53–54, 67–68, 83, 86
independence, 33, 86, 116–17, 145–46, 168
India, 83, 86
Indian women, 53–55
indiscipline, 150–51, 156–58
individual initiative, 126
industriousness, 98, 113, 116–17
infertility, 99
informal commercial importers (ICIs). *See* ICIs (informal commercial importers)
informal economies
   black females and, 148, 166–67
   blackness and, 62
   in Caribbean nations, 6
   Christmas shopping and, 146–47
   city spaces and, 151
   class (social) and, 3, 31–32, 148
   colonialism and, 48–49, 173
   in depression era, 86
   education and, 187n8
   expansion of, 36, 157–58
   female-headed households and, 2, 36, 63, 137–38, 146
   femininity and, 178n8
   vs. formal economies, 95–101, 120
   gender inequality and, 3, 6
   hierarchies of power in, 23
   higglers and, 2, 91
   illegitimate economy in, 141
   independence and, 146
   in Jamaica, 2, 10, 142
   males and, 146
   market sites and, 142
   microcredit institutions and, 169–74
   microentrepreneurs and, 21–23
   plantations and, 48–50
   pollution and, 151
   race/color and, 3, 22, 32
   reputation and, 172
   in South Africa, 179n3
   Sunday markets and, 69–71
   susus (partners) and, 171
   trustworthiness of, 172
   unemployment in, 54, 121
   in West Africa, 39
   women's work and, 2, 19, 39
   See also formal economy; higglers
informality, 2–3, 5, 165, 169
informal labor, 4–7
intergenerational transmission of property, 63–64, 137–38, 183n25
International Labour Office (ILO), 167, 169
International Monetary Fund (IMF), 120–21
intersectionality, 23, 26, 28–29, 31, 167–68, 179–80n10. *See also* embodied intersectionality
interviews (research), 7, 10–14, 42, 63, 181n3, 183n23, 187n6
Issas, 44
Itzigsohn, Jose, 143

Jamaica
   Agricultural Development Corporation, 45
   Banana Board, 45
   beauty pageants in, 116–17
   census, 186n6
   Chamber of Commerce, 147, 149, 156

under colonialism, 34–35
debt-to-GDP ratio, 35–36, 40, 145–46, 180n18
drug trade in, 180n18
economic development policy, 145
elections, 7–8
elites in, 15–16
expatriates, 178n13
foreign investment in, 110–11
Handbook of Jamaica, 81
hip-hop culture, 59–60
House of Assembly, 76, 99
ICIs' custom duties, 127
illiteracy, 88
independence, 33, 35, 86
informal economies, 2, 10, 142
Jamaica: Its Past and Present State (Phillippo), **94**
Jamaica Labor Party (JLP), 8, 86, 145
Jamaica National Heritage Trust, 169
Jamaican National Micro-Credit, 190n4
"Jamaica: Summer at Christmas-Tide," **109**, 110–11
lady vs. woman in, 30–32
matrilineal society, 63
meritocracy, 33
microcredit institutions, 169, 190n4
microentrepreneurs, 32
Morant Bay rebellion, 185nn9–10
motto, 126, 183n21
murders per capita, 180n18
national debt, 120–21
nationalist movement, 86
national motto, 33
peasant production, 112
People's National party (PNP), 8, 86
plantations, 77–78
population density, 35
poverty, 36
race/color in, 178–79n2
Revenue Board, 2
self-sufficiency, 131
social mobility, 18, 35–36
social stratification, 26, 180n12
speech patterns, 182n10
as tropical paradise, 112
twenty-one families, 88
unemployment, 10, 36, 121
World War I effects, 85
during World War II, 44–45
See also emancipation; Kingston
Jamaica Gleaner, 119, 149–50

Jamaica Observer, 142, 153, 155, 188n2
James, William, 169
Jews, 44–45, 67, 73–74, 83, 88, 145, 181n4
JLP (Jamaica Labor Party), 8, 86, 145

Kingston
arcades, 173
Barbican round-a-bout, 158
"Cat-and-Mouse Game Downtown Kingston," 155
class antipathy, 16–17
"Congested Streets of Downtown Kingston," 148
East Kingston, 151
European club, 74
Fruit Vendor, A, 110
Harper's Monthly Magazine, 79–80
higglers and, 100, 146, 155–56, 189n7
informal economies, 142
"Jamaica: Summer at Christmas-Tide," 111
Kingston and St. Andrew Corporation (KSAC), 146, 150, 155–56, 173, 189n7
"Kingston Vendors Stay off the Streets," 155
market women and, **40, 41**
microcredit institutions, 169–70, 190n4
"Monday Is D-Day for Vendors," 149–50
Norbrook, 166
political violence, 8–9
population density, 143–44
public spaces, 188–89n3
slave trade, 80–81
uptown/downtown division, 9, 33–34, 87, 133, 143–44, 151
Victoria Market, 81–82
white elite males in, 67
See also Sunday markets
kinship ties, 45
KSAC (Kingston and St. Andrew Corporation), 146, 150, 155–56, 173, 189n7

labor patterns, 42, 54, 69–70, 87
labor rebellions, 85
Lady Musgrave Flea Market, 55–58, 60, 129
lady vs. woman, 30–32, 123, 160–61. *See also* femininity
land barons, 84

Language of Dress, The: Resistance and Accommodation in Jamaica, 1750–1890 (Buckridge), 93
Latin America, 27
lawlessness, 159
Lebanese, 41–43, 45, 88, 127, 145, 181n3
legitimacy, 98, 114, 139, 141, 151, 168
Lengel, Stacey, 16
letters of reference, 171
Liguanea, 56
living wages, 66
Look Lai, Walton, 43
Low, Setha, 143
Luckock, Rev. Benjamin, 72–75

Mair, Lucille Mathurin, 53, 92–93
"Making of a Slum, The," 159
males
    blacks as lazy, 113–14
    colonialism and, 98, 168
    division of labor, 183n25
    higglering and, 64
    "Illegal Street Vendors," 158
    imaginaries and, 168
    immigrants, post-emancipation, 85
    informal economies and, 146
    "Police Arrest 48 Montego Bay Vendors," 149
    public domain and, 66–67, 89
    public spaces and, 32, 112, 118, 160
    as slave labor, 51
    slaves as artisans, 92
    social spaces and, 65
    sugar plantations and, 67
    Sunday markets and, 75, 185n1
    unemployment, 34, 62, 185n1
    urban slavery and, 68
malnutrition, 85
mammy figures, 119–20
Mandeville, 148–49
Manley, Norman Washington, 86
Manor Park, 159–60
manual labor, 68, 107, 115–16, 141–42
manufacturing, 44–45, 88
marchantas, 6
marginalization, 112, 153–56, 173
marijuana, 58, 182n15
market sites, 142, 146, 153–54
market women
    blacks as, 53–54
    brownings as, 98
    as businesswomen, 134
    female-headed households and, 138
    industriousness, 113
    in Kingston, **40**, **41**
    meritocracy among, 131
    Papine Market and, 60, 98, 134–35
    peasant economy and, 125
    respectability, 130
    ROSCA (rotating savings and credit associations) and, 171–72
    self-identifications, 124, 187n7
    social status, 124–25, 187n8
    tourism and, 112–13, 115–17
    uptown/downtown division, 157
    See also higglers
masculinity, 168
matrilineal society, 63
May Fair, 79, 184–85n6
McKeever, Matthew, 179n3
merchants, 67, 84
meritocracy, 33, 126, 131–32, 188n11
Metropolitan Parks and Markets (MPM), 146, 149–50, 152, 173, 189n7
microbusinesses, 157
microcredit institutions, 169–74, 190n4
microentrepreneurs, 2, 5–6, 21–23, 54–55, 142, 169, 177n3, 177–78n7.
    See also higglers
Middle East, 86
migration, 143–44, 146
Min-ha, Trinh T., 119
minorities, 41, 45, 73–74
Mirchandani, Kiran, 177–78n7
miscegenation, 27, 51, 53, 101
Misra, Joya, 39
missionaries, 48
Miss Jamaica contests, 116
Mohammed, Patricia, 104
Mohanty, Chandra Talpade, 11, 174
"Monday Is D-Day for Vendors," 149
monopoly, 84–85, 97
Morant Bay rebellion, 82–83, 185nn9–10
Morrison, Toni, 122, 186n8
motherhood, 107–8, 137
motto, 126, 183n21
Moyne Commission, 87
MPM (Metropolitan Parks and Markets), 146, 149–50, 152, 173, 189n7
Mr. Ammar, 128
Mr. Issa, 127–28, 132, 135
mulattos, 102, **103**, 105, **106**, 107–8, 115.
    See also race/color
multidimensional power, 165
multinational corporations, 66, 168
murder rate, 180n18

music tastes, 182n14

Nakano Glenn, Evelyn, 10–11
nationalist movement, 86
Negro markets. *See* Sunday markets
Nelson, Lise, 122
neoliberal policies, 120–21, 151
Nettleford, Rex, 165–66
New Kingston, 56
newspaper articles, 142, 188n2, 188–89n3
New York Times, 114
Norbrook, 166
Norton, Ann, 75, 184n4
nuisances, 147, 158, 173

objectivity, 11
objects of production, 117
"On the Way to Market," 112, **113**
osnaburg, 93
otherness, 122
out of order, 4, 156

panopticism, 82
Papine Market, 1, 8–9, 14, 55, 58–60, 98, 134–35, 157
Paravisini-Gebert, Lizabeth, 28
partners (susus), 171
patois, 30–32, 57, 136
Patterson, P. J., 8, 145
peasant economy, 125
peasant production, 71, 76–78, 80, 83–87, 96, 111–12, 135, 186n9
pedestrians, 100, 148–49, 158–59
penkeepers, 67–68
People's Arcade, 8–9, 13–14, 55, 58, 130, 133–34, 182n13
People's National Party (PNP), 8, 86
Pfuhl, Edwin H., 123
phenomenologists, 25
Phillippo, James M., **94**
photography, 108
pirating, 80
plantations
  banana industry, 84
  colonialism and, 75, 77–78
  division of labor, 42, 50–54, 69, 181n7
  elites and, 43, 53
  emancipation, 76–77
  formal economy and, 48
  hierarchy of shades, 84
  higglers and, 46–50, 186n7
  indentured servants and, 35, 42, 67–68
  informal economies and, 48–50

Sunday markets and, 75, 184n5
whites and, 43, 51
See also slavery; sugar plantations
PNP (People's National Party), 8, 86
polarization, 151, 161
"Police Arrest 48 Montego Bay Vendors," 149
politics, 7, 8–10, 45, 76, 86, 139, 155
pollution, 144–45, 151, 161
population density, 143–44
Portes, Alejandro, 143, 171
post-emancipation economy, 78, 82, 84–85, 88, 108–12, **109**, 117–18, 125–26, 186n9
poverty, 21, 36, 40, 60–62, 84–86, 131, 133–34, 145, 151, 161–62, 187–88n9
Power of Sentiment, The: Love, Hierarchy, and the Jamaican Family Elite (Douglass), 15
power relations, 16
primary wage earners, 136
privacy, 15–16
private domain, 65, 107, 115, 117
Problem of Freedom, The: Race, Labor, and Politics in Jamaica and Britain, 1832–1938 (Holt), 76
proletarians, 77
public domain, 66–67, 69, 75, 87, 89
public spaces, 26, 32, 34, 74, 91, 96, 112, 117–18, 120, 160, 167–68, 188–89n3
Purity and Danger (Douglas), 141, 144
Puwar, Nirmal, 4, 65
Pyle, Howard, 79–81, 114, 184–85n6

race/color
  in beauty pageants, 116–17
  in Caribbean nations, 27
  city spaces and, 143, 147, 157
  class and, 34
  colonialism and, 67
  Constant Spring Arcade and, 58
  and division of labor, 50, 53–54
  economic power and, 166
  embodied intersectionality and, 5–6, 29, 161, 167
  femininity and, 116, 122
  formal economy and, 42
  and hierarchies of power, 44
  of ICIs (informal commercial importers), 36–37
  imaginaries and, 142
  impact on research, 17–18
race/color, *continued*

inclusion/exclusion based on, 162
independence and, 86
informal economies and, 3, 22, 32
in Jamaica, 178–79n2
of Jamaican lady, 31–32
labor patterns and, 42, 69
Lady Musgrave Flea Market and, 55–58
lady vs. woman, 160–61
in Latin America, 27
lawlessness and, 159
and North/South economic relationships, 168
Papine Market and, 58–59
and plantation division of labor, 50
post-emancipation economy and, 118
Problem of Freedom, The: Race, Labor, and Politics in Jamaica and Britain, 1832–1938 (Holt), 76
retail sales and, 42
sisterhood and, 11–12
social stratification and, 58, 180n12
vendors and, 55–58
women's work and, 173–74
See also blacks; brownings; gender; mulattos; skin color
racism, 166
rape, 77, 181n7
Ras Historian. *See* Clement, Eric
Rastafarian, 185n12
rebellions, 83, 111, 155–56, 185n10, 185n12
rebidantes, 6
reggae, 182n9, 182n14
Reid, Stanley, 45
relationships of power, 142–43, 167–68
reputation, 171, 172
research methodology, 7–11, 13, 16–19, 42, 63, 124, 125, 181n3, 187n6, 188n2, 188–89n3
respectability, 30, 126, 130, 135–36
retail sales, 42–43, 54
Rhone, Jean, 14–15
Ritch, Dawn, 156–57
Robotham, Don, 84
Rodney riots, 185n12
Roldan, Martha, 21, 23
Romijn, Henny, 22
Ross, Leone, 17–18
rotating savings and credit associations (ROSCA), 171
Royal Gazette, 96
rural economy, 70, 87, 125

sanitation, 78–79
Satchell, Veront M., 186n9

scarcity, 162
Seaga, Edward, 8
segregation, 157
self-identifications, 19–20, 32, 92–94, 119, 121–22, 124–39, 186n8, 187nn6–7
self-reflexivity, 19
self-sufficiency, 112, 125–26, 131–32, 135
"Sellers Squabble over Space," 147
seminudity, 104
sensuality, 105, **106**, 107
sexuality, 122
sexual orientation, 167–68
Sheller, Mimi, 78–79
Shepherd, Verene, 67, 84
Sherlock, Phillip, 85
Shilling, Chris, 24–26
silk, 93–94
Simmonds, Lorna, 47–48, 95
sisterhood, 11–12, 16
skilled labor, 84
skin color, 18, 27, 33, 43, 116–18, 128–29, 148, 181n3, 186n8, 188nn10–11. *See also* race/color
slavery
    artisans and, 51
    in Caribbean nations, 70
    census and, 186n6
    under colonialism, 35
    Cuba and, 77
    and division of labor, 69
    Domestic Scene—Two Mulatto Women and Child and Seated Negro Woman, 107
    domestic servants and, 51, 70, 181n7
    elites and, 51
    emancipation and, 50, 76
    female-on-female, 52, 70
    field laborers and, 51, 181n7
    freemen ownership and, 68
    and hierarchy of shades, 27, 102–3, 109
    higglers and, 2, 32, 46–50, 63–64
    Kingston's role in, 80–81
    miscegenation and, 99
    osnaburg cloth and, 93
    rape and, 77, 181n7
    self-identifications and, 186n8
    skin color and, 186n8
    social mobility and, 52
    stereotyping and, 52
    sugar plantations and, 35
    taxation and, 49
    urban slavery, 68
    vendors and, 98

women's work and, 70
   See also Sunday markets
Slocum, Karla, 18–19
slums, 159–60
Small Business Association of Jamaica Family Market. *See* Lady Musgrave Flea Market
snowball effect, 13
social capital, 171
social construction theory, 25, 143–44
social mobility, 18, 35–36, 41–44, 52, 54, 131–32, 137–38, 166, 188nn10–11.
   See also social status
social networks, 171
social production of space, 143–44
social relationships, 122
social spaces, 65, 67, 157
social status
   of blacks, 27, 69, 166
   of brownings, 139, 157
   class status and, 131
   colonialism and, 67
   Creole, 68, 74
   education and, 162, 187n8
   of freemen, 68
   of higglers, 123
   of indentured servants, 67–68
   inequality and, 131
   of Jews, 73–74
   lady vs. woman, 123
   of market women, 124–25, 187n8
   of merchants, 67
   of minorities, 73–74
   of penkeepers, 67–68
   stratification and, 162
   uptown/downtown division and, 157, 189n5
   of whites, 68–69
   See also social mobility
social stratification, 51, 58, 162, 180n12
sociology of the body, 24–26, 179n5
South Africa, 31, 179n3
Space Invaders: Race, Gender, and Bodies out of Place (Puwar), 65
Spaniards, 73–74
Spanish Town, 75, 95, 184n4
speech patterns, 56–57, 182n10
squatting, 150
stall fees, 127–28
St. Ann's Bay, 35
status order, 134, 144, 165
stereotyping, 22, 52, 57–58, 119, 139, 161, 166

stigmas, 7, 56, 121–23, 135, 166, 170, 172, 174, 178n9, 189n8
St. Jago Gazette, 95, 99
storekeepers, 148
street vendors. *See* vendors
structuration theory, 25
St. Vincent, 71
subordination, 28–29
Sugar Duties Act, 77
sugar plantations, 35, 46, 67, 70, 75, 77–78, 81, 85–86, 110, 181n4, 183–84n2, 184n4, 186n9
Sunday markets
   as bait of Satan, 73
   bartering in, 92
   black females and, 91–95, 185n1
   Christianity and, 73–75
   clothing at, 92–94, 185–86n3
   coinage and, 92
   colonialism and, 184n4
   Columbian Magazine and, 81
   deviants and, 73, 75, 89, 184n5
   freemen and, 68
   informal economies and, 69–71
   Jews and, 73–74
   Lady Musgrave Flea Market, 55
   males and, 75, 185n1
   miscegenation and, 101
   missionaries and, 48
   Morant Bay rebellion and, 83
   as necessary evil, 72, 88–89
   newspaper articles on, 95–101
   peasant production and, 71, 80, 96
   plantations and, 75, 184n5
   as public domain, 75
   as public spaces, 74
   rise of, 47–49, 71, 75, 184n4
   self-identifications and, 92–94
   Spanish Town, 75, 95, 184n4
   urban culture in, 69–71, 75
   Victoria Market, 81–82
   whites and, 71–75, 92, 95, 184n4
   See also Kingston
Sundstrom, Ronald, 157
susus (partners), 171
Symanski, Richard, 75, 184n4
Syrians, 45, 127, 181n3

taxation, 49, 82, 150, 158, 185n10, 189n12
Ten Types, One People, 116
Thomas, Deborah, 187–88n9
Thompson, Krista, 108, 112, 115
ti machan, 6

tolls, 82
tourism, 43, 54, 88, 97–98, 108, 110–13, 115–17
traders, 41–43, 77, 84, 98–99
trade unionism, 86
Trafalgar Development Bank, 190n4
Trinidad, 71
tropical paradise, 112
"Tropic Climb, A," **113**
trustworthiness, 7, 170–72
twenty-one families, 88

Ulysse, Gina, 116, 178n8, 186–87n12
unemployment
    debt-to-GDP ratio and, 40, 146, 183n22
    female-headed households and, 34, 62, 183n22
    formal economy and, 146
    ICI vendors and, 134
    informal economies and, 54, 121
    in Jamaica, 10, 36, 121
    among males, 34, 62, 185n1
    post-emancipation economy and, 85, 88
    rural economy and, 87
    uptown/downtown division and, 151
unfeminine, 122, 141–42, 161
United Fruit Company, 83–84, 115
United States, 59–60, 83, 86, 113–14
United States Agency for International Development (USAID), 169
United Vendors Association (UVA), 9, 12
uptown/downtown division, 34, 133–34, 139, 143–44, 151, 153, 156–63, 189n5. *See also* Kingston
urban culture, 59, 67–71, 75, 78, 84, 187–88n9
urban decay, 151
urban economy, 92, 96, 109–10
USAID (United States Agency for International Development), 169

Van der Wees, Catherine, 22
vegetables, 58–59
vendors
    as alternative name for higglers, 121, 123–24
    at Constant Spring Arcade, 1
    gender of, 114
    "Illegal Street Vendors," 158
    "Kingston Vendors Stay off the Streets," 155
    marginalization of, 153–55, 173
    "Monday Is D-Day for Vendors," 149–50
    "MPM Smashes Vendors' Stalls," 150
    negative views of, 17
    "Police Arrest 48 Montego Bay Vendors," 149
    race/color of, 55–58
    self-identifications, 124, 187n7
    slavery and, 98
    stigmas and, 56
    "Street Vending Wrecking Mandeville," 148–49
    "Uptown Businesses Outdoing Downtown," 153
    UVA (United Vendors Association) and, 9, 12
    "Vending: The Bigger Picture," 147
    "Vendors' Claims Settled," 150
    "Vendors Evicted Permanently," 149
    "Vendors Must Obey the Rules," 150
    "Vendors Protest . . . but KSAC Vows Not to Back Down," 155
    "Vendors to Sue Government for Smashed Stalls," 150
    See also higglers; ICIs (informal commercial importers); market women
Victoria Market, 81–82
vulgarity, 57–58

wage laborers, 76, 78, 83, 85, 112, 118
warehouses, 173
washer women, 51
Watchman and Jamaica Free Press, 97
Watson, Sophie, 143
Weber, Max, 144, 165, 174
Welch, Pedro L. V., 70
welfare state, 66
West Africa, 39
West Indies, 93
whites
    banana industry and, 83
    census and, 186n6
    as clerks, 67
    in colonial socioeconomic system, 67
    Creole, 74
    Crown Colony rule and, 87
    deficiency laws and, 68

female-on-female slavery and, 52, 70
and females under colonialism, 69
femininity and, 53
formal economy and, 112
infertility fears among, 99
lower-class status, 68–69
migration to Jamaica by, 110–11
miscegenation and, 53
multinational corporations and, 168
plantations and, 43, 51
public domain dominance by, 67
social status, 68–69
social stratification and, 180n12
Sunday markets and, 71–75, 92, 95, 184n4
Williams, John H., 159–60
Williams-Edwards, Mrs., 120–21
women's work, 150
in Caribbean nations, 36
class (social) and, 173–74
emancipation and, 76–77
embodied intersectionality and, 167–69
female-on-female slavery and, 70
field laborers and, 51, 76
gender and, 173–74
higglers and, 32, 65
indentured servants and, 68
informal economies and, 2, 19, 39
microcredit institutions and, 169–74
in the private domain, 65, 115, 117
race/color and, 173–74
slavery and, 70
stigmas and, 172
See also female-headed households
World Bank, 21, 169
World War I, 85
World War II, 44–45, 181n4

Younus, Mohammad, 169

www.ingramcontent.com/pod-product-compliance
Lightning Source LLC
Chambersburg PA
CBHW030647230426
43665CB00011B/996